Dualities, Dialectics, and Paradoxes in Organizational Life

Perspectives on Process Organization Studies
Series Editors: Ann Langley and Haridimos Tsoukas

Perspectives on Process Organization Studies is an annual series, linked to the International Symposium on Process Organization Studies, and is dedicated to the development of an understanding of organizations and organizing at large as processes in the making. This series brings together contributions from leading scholars, which focus on seeing dynamically evolving activities, inter-actions, and events as important aspects of organized action, rather than static structures and fixed templates.

Volume 1: Process, Sensemaking, and Organizing
Editors: Tor Hernes and Sally Maitlis

Volume 2: Constructing Identity in and around Organizations
Editors: Majken Schultz, Steve Maguire, Ann Langley, and Haridimos Tsoukas

Volume 3: How Matter Matters: Objects, Artifacts, and Materiality in Organization Studies
Editors: Paul R. Carlile, Davide Nicolini, Ann Langley, and Haridimos Tsoukas

Volume 4: Language and Communication at Work: Discourse, Narrativity, and Organizing
Editors: François Cooren, Eero Vaara, Ann Langley, and Haridimos Tsoukas

Volume 5: The Emergence of Novelty in Organizations
Editors: Raghu Garud, Barbara Simpson, Ann Langley, and Haridimos Tsoukas

Volume 6: Organizational Routines: How They Are Created, Maintained, and Changed
Editors: Jennifer Howard-Grenville, Claus Rerup, Ann Langley, and Haridimos Tsoukas

Volume 7: Skillful Performance: Enacting Capabilities, Knowledge, Competence, and Expertise in Organizations
Editors: Jörgen Sandberg, Linda Rouleau, Ann Langley, and Haridimos Tsoukas

Volume 8: Dualities, Dialectics, and Paradoxes in Organizational Life
Editors: Moshe Farjoun, Wendy Smith, Ann Langley, and Haridimos Tsoukas

Dualities, Dialectics, and Paradoxes in Organizational Life

Edited by
Moshe Farjoun, Wendy Smith, Ann Langley,
and Haridimos Tsoukas

OXFORD
UNIVERSITY PRESS

Great Clarendon Street, Oxford, OX2 6DP,
United Kingdom

Oxford University Press is a department of the University of Oxford.
It furthers the University's objective of excellence in research, scholarship,
and education by publishing worldwide. Oxford is a registered trade mark of
Oxford University Press in the UK and in certain other countries

© Oxford University Press 2018

The moral rights of the authors have been asserted

First Edition published in 2018
Impression: 1

Published in the United States of America by Oxford University Press
198 Madison Avenue, New York, NY 10016, United States of America

British Library Cataloguing in Publication Data
Data available

Library of Congress Control Number: 2018937430

ISBN 978–0–19–882743–6

Printed and bound by
CPI Group (UK) Ltd, Croydon, CR0 4YY

Contents

Contents

List of Figures

List of Tables

List of Contributors

Jean-Luc Bédard is Associate Professor, Department of Education, TÉLUQ University. His research focus examines interactions between professions, access to regulated professions, and mobility of foreign-trained professionals. His work has been published in various journals, including *International Journal of Migration and Border Studies*, *Revue européenne des migrations internationales*, and *Recherches sociographiques*.

Rebecca Bednarek is Senior Lecturer of Management at Birkbeck, University of London. Her research on strategizing within complex organizational settings, the global reinsurance industry, and organizational ethnography has been published in *Human Relations, Long Range Planning, Organizational Studies, Strategic Management Journal*, and *Strategic Organization*. She also co-authored *Making Markets for Acts of God: Risk Trading Practices in the Global Reinsurance Industry*.

Kathleen Bentein is Professor of Organizational Behaviour at École des sciences de la gestion, University of Quebec at Montreal. Her main research areas include attitude change over time, commitment towards different foci at work, identification and disidentification processes, and socialization of newcomers. Her work has been published in a variety of journals, including *Journal of Management, Journal of Applied Psychology, Leadership Quarterly, Journal of Organizational Behavior, Journal of Occupational and Organizational Psychology*, and *Journal of Vocational Behavior*.

Stewart Clegg is Research Professor at the University of Technology Sydney, Director of the Centre for Management and Organization Studies Research, and Visiting Professor at the Nova School of Business and Economics and at Newcastle University Business School. His research is driven by a fascination with power and theorizing. Stewart is a prolific writer and is the author or editor of a number of books, including *Frameworks of Power, The Sage Handbook of Organization Studies*, and *The Sage Handbook of Power*.

Carl-Ardy Dubois has a multidisciplinary background with initial qualifications in medicine, advanced degrees in administration of health services, and a PhD in Public Health. He is currently Professor and Head of the Department of Management, Evaluation and Health Policy (School of Public Health of the University of Montreal) and Researcher at the Institute of Public Health Research, University of Montreal. His research programme focuses on the management of health human resources, analysis of work in the healthcare sector, and analysis of the organization of health services. His work has been published in various journals, including *International Journal for Quality in Health Care, BMC Health Services Research, Human Resources for Health*, and *International Journal of Nursing Studies*.

John D. Dunne is Distinguished Professor of Contemplative Humanities at the Center for Healthy Minds of the University of Wisconsin-Madison, where he is also Professor in the Department of Asian Languages and Cultures. His work focuses on Buddhist philosophy and contemplative practice, especially in dialogue with cognitive science and psychology. His publications include a monograph on the Buddhist epistemologist Dharmakīrti, various translations from Tibetan and Sanskrit, and scientific studies—both theoretical and empirical—on the effects and mechanisms of contemplative practices in collaboration with colleagues from several institutions. His current research focuses especially on the varieties of mindfulness and the contemplative theories that inquire into its nature.

Moshe Farjoun is Professor of Strategy and Organization at the Schulich School of Business, York University and is currently Visiting Research Fellow at the Judge School of Business, Cambridge University. Moshe received his PhD from the Kellogg School of Management, Northwestern University. His research is mainly conceptual and histor-ical and focuses on strategy, organization, and adaptation in novel, complex, and dynamic contexts in processes such as organizational learning, discovery, strategy making, managerial cognition, and institutional and strategic change. His current projects explore themes such as the interplay of routine and non-routine, as well as stability and change, in and around organizations, coevolution and shaping, endogen-ous change and discontinuities and surprises, and draws on pragmatism, evolutionary theory, and dialectics.

Frédéric Gilbert is Associate Professor at the École des sciences de la gestion, University of Quebec at Montreal. His research explores the transformation and governance of healthcare services at system, organizational, and individual levels. Gilbert has pub-lished in various journals, including *Journal of Health Organization and Management*, *International Journal of Environmental Research*, and *Public Health and Personality and Individual Differences*.

Paula Jarzabkowski is Professor of Strategic Management, Cass Business School. Her research focuses on strategy-as-practice in complex and pluralistic contexts such as regulated infrastructure firms, third-sector organizations, and financial services, par-ticularly insurance and reinsurance. She has conducted extensive, internationally com-parative audio and video ethnographic studies in a range of business contexts. Her work has appeared in leading journals including *Academy of Management Journal*, *Journal of Management Studies*, *Organization Science*, *Organization Studies*, and *Strategic Management Journal*. Her first book, *Strategy as Practice: An Activity-Based Approach* was published in 2005 and her most recent co-authored book, *Making a Market for Acts of God*, was published by Oxford University Press in 2015.

Ann Langley is Professor of Management at HEC Montréal, Canada, and Canada Research Chair in Strategic Management in Pluralistic Settings. Her research focuses on strategic change, leadership, innovation and the use of management tools in complex organizations with an emphasis on processual research approaches. She has published over fifty articles and two books, most recently *Strategy as Practice: Research Directions and Resources* (with Gerry Johnson, Leif Melin, and Richard Whittington).

Jane K. Lê earned her PhD from the Aston Business School and is Professor of Strategic Management at WHU—Otto Beisheim School of Management, Germany. She studies organizational practices and processes in complex, dynamic, and pluralistic organizations. Jane is particularly interested in understanding how people in organizations balance multiple competing demands. She has published her work in journals such as *Organization Science, Organization Studies, Strategic Organization*, and the *British Journal of Management*. Jane is passionate about qualitative research and qualitative research methods and is currently serving on the editorial board of *Organizational Research Methods* and *Organization Studies*.

Marianne W. Lewis is Dean of Cass Business School and Professor of Management. She is an international thought leader in the field of leadership and organizational paradoxes. Change and complexity accentuate tensions—competing demands, contradictory pressures, and challenging double-binds. Her research applies a provocative paradox lens to such domains as organizational change, governance, and innovation. Her work appears in the leading management journals, including *Harvard Business Review, Academy of Management Journal, Organization Science*, and *Journal of Operations Management*. She was a UK Fulbright Scholar in 2014 and is currently completing two, related books. Her paper, 'Exploring Paradox: Toward a More Comprehensive Guide', received the *Academy of Management Review* Best Paper Award in 2000 and is among the most cited in the field. She joined Cass after a decade as Associate Dean at the University of Cincinnati, having earned her PhD from the University of Kentucky and her MBA from Indiana University.

Esther R. Maier is Associate Professor at the Lazaridis School of Business at Wilfrid Laurier University in Waterloo, Canada. She earned her PhD in strategy from the Ivey Business School at Western University. Her research focuses on the dynamic processes of new product creation in artistic (creative industries) and scientific (pharmaceutical) environments. She is particularly interested in the unfolding nature of collective processes and her work is informed by Science and Technology Studies, particularly the work of Michel Callon.

Valérie Michaud is Associate Professor at the École des sciences de la gestion, University of Quebec at Montreal. Her research focuses on tensions and paradoxes in the management of social enterprises, and more specifically on the roles played by management tools in the mediation of those tensions. Her work has been published in *Organization Studies, M@n@gement, Qualitative Research in Organizations and Management, Journal of Management Education*, and *Revue française de gestion*.

Jenni Myllykoski is a postdoctoral researcher at the University of Oulu Business School, Finland. Her research interests include change, temporality, agency, and narratives in process organization research in general and strategy process and practice research in particular. Her research is informed by process philosophy, particularly by the writings of Henri Bergson and Alfred North Whitehead. In her doctoral dissertation, 'Strategic change emerging in time', she examined strategic change from the perspective of temporality.

Charles W. Nuckolls is Professor and Chair of the Department of Anthropology at Brigham Young University in Provo, Utah. He studies moral causality and explanatory belief systems in India, Japan, New Zealand, and the United States. Nuckolls is the author of *The Cultural Dialectics of Knowledge and Desire* and *Culture: A Problem that Cannot Be Solved.*

Miguel Pina e Cunha is Fundação Amélia de Mello Professor of Leadership at Nova School of Business and Economics, Lisbon. His research deals mostly with the surprising (paradox, improvisation, serendipity, zemblanity, vicious circles) and the extreme (positive organizing, genocide). Miguel co-authored (with Arménio Rego and Stewart Clegg) *The Virtues of Leadership: Contemporary Challenges for Global Managers* and received the 2015 Best Paper Award from the *European Management Review.*

Anniina Rantakari is a postdoctoral researcher at the University of Oulu Business School, Finland. Her key areas of interest are the process and practice perspectives on strategy, narrative research, and the dynamics of power and resistance in organizational research in general and strategy research in particular. In her doctoral dissertation, 'Strategy as dispositive: Essays on productive power and resistance', she examined strategy making from a Foucauldian perspective.

Wendy Smith earned her PhD in Organizational Behavior at Harvard Business School and is Associate Professor of Management at the Lerner School of Business, University of Delaware. Her research on the nature and management of strategic paradoxes has been published in journals such as *Academy of Management Journal, Academy of Management Review, Harvard Business Review, Organization Science, Management Science,* and *Academy of Management Learning and Education.* She is co-founder of the blogsite www.leveragingtensions.com, which seeks to connect scholars and practitioners interested in paradox, dualities, and dialectics.

Haridimos Tsoukas holds the Columbia Ship Management Chair in Strategic Management at the University of Cyprus and is Professor of Organization Studies at Warwick Business School. He obtained his PhD at the Manchester Business School (MBS), University of Manchester, and has worked at MBS, the University of Essex, the University of Strathclyde, and the ALBA Graduate Business School, Greece. He has published widely in several leading academic journals, including the *Academy of Management Review, Strategic Management Journal, Organization Studies, Organization Science, Journal of Management Studies,* and *Human Relations.* He was the Editor-in-Chief of *Organization Studies* (2003–8). His research interests include knowledge-based perspectives on organizations, organizational becoming, the management of organizational change and social reforms, the epistemology of practice, and epistemological issues in organization theory. He is the editor (with Christian Knudsen) of *The Oxford Handbook of Organization Theory: Meta-Theoretical Perspectives.* He has also edited *Organizations as Knowledge Systems* (with N. Mylonopoulos) and *Managing the Future: Foresight in the Knowledge Economy* (with J. Shepherd). His book *Complex Knowledge: Studies in Organizational Epistemology* was published by Oxford University in 2005. He is also the author of the book *If Aristotle Were a CEO* (in Greek).

Juergen Weber is Director of the Institute of Management Accounting and Control of WHU, Germany. In his research, he focuses on organizational change processes and on the dynamics and complexity of controllership. He is co-editor of *WHU Controlling and Management Review* and chairman of the International Controller Association (ICV)

Board of Trustees. He held scientific advisory board positions with BVL International for many years and sits on the Scientific Advisory Board of CTcon.

Nicolás J.B. Wiedemann is a doctoral candidate at the Institute of Management Accounting and Control at WHU, Germany. His research interests are truces and organizational change. Currently, he is focusing on the dynamics of truces in organizational life. In addition, Nicolás conducts research on the change in processes and effects of new information technologies in organizations, using examples from the management accounting practice. His research is funded by the Hanns Seidel Foundation.

Leona Wiegmann earned her doctoral degree from WHU, Germany, and is currently Lecturer of Management Accounting in the Monash Business School at Monash University, Australia. Her research interests relate to the change of management accounting practices, in particular from an organizational routines perspective. Leona's current research is focused on the influence of management information systems on the change of practices and on how actors' use of management accounting information becomes implicated in practices.

Series Editorial Structure

Editors-in-Chief

Ann Langley, HEC Montréal, Canada, ann.langley@hec.ca
Haridimos Tsoukas, University of Cyprus, Cyprus and University of Warwick, UK,
process.symposium@gmail.com

Advisory Board

Editorial Officer and Process Organization Studies
Symposium Administrator

Sophia Tzagaraki, process.symposium@gmail.com

Endorsements

"As we become more willing to convert reified entities into differentiated streams, the resulting images of process have become more viable and more elusive. Organization becomes organizing, being becomes becoming, construction becomes constructing. But as we see ourselves saying more words that end in 'ing,' what must we be thinking? That is not always clear. But now, under the experienced guidance of editors Langley and Tsoukas, there is an annual forum that moves us toward continuity and consolidation in process studies. This book series promises to be a vigorous, thoughtful forum dedicated to improvements in the substance and craft of process articulation."

Karl E. Weick, Rensis Likert Distinguished University Professor of Organizational Behavior and Psychology, University of Michigan, USA

"In recent years process and practice approaches to organizational topics have increased significantly. These approaches have made significant contributions to already existing fields of study, such as strategy, routines, knowledge management, and technology adoption, and these contributions have brought increasing attention to the approaches. Yet because the contributions are embedded in a variety of different fields of study, discussions about the similarities and differences in the application of the approaches, the research challenges they present, and the potential they pose for examining taken for granted ontological assumptions are limited. This series will provide an opportunity for bringing together contributions across different areas so that comparisons can be made and can also provide a space for discussions across fields. Professors Langley and Tsoukas are leaders in the development and use of process approaches. Under their editorship, the series will attract the work and attention of a wide array of distinguished organizational scholars."

Martha S. Feldman, Johnson Chair for Civic Governance and Public Management, Professor of Social Ecology, Political Science, Business and Sociology, University of California, Irvine, USA

"*Perspectives on Process Organization Studies* will be the definitive annual volume of theories and research that advance our understanding of process questions dealing with how things emerge, grow, develop, and terminate over time. I applaud Professors Ann Langley and Haridimos Tsoukas for launching this important book series, and encourage colleagues to submit their process research and subscribe to PROS."

Andrew H. Van de Ven, Vernon H. Heath Professor of Organizational Innovation and Change, University of Minnesota, USA

"The new series—*Perspectives on Process Organization Studies*—is a timely and valuable addition to the organization studies literature. The ascendancy of process perspectives in recent years has signified an important departure from traditional perspectives on organizations that have tended to privilege either self-standing events or discrete entities. In contrast, by emphasizing emergent activities and recursive relations, process perspectives take seriously the ongoing production of organizational realities. Such a performative view of organizations is particularly salient today, given the increasingly complex, dispersed, dynamic, entangled, and mobile nature of current organizational phenomena. Such phenomena are not easily accounted for in traditional approaches that are premised on stability, separation, and substances. Process perspectives on organizations thus promise to offer powerful and critical analytical insights into the unprecedented and novel experiences of contemporary organizing."

Wanda J. Orlikowski, Alfred P. Sloan Professor of Information Technologies and Organization Studies, Massachusetts Institute of Technology, USA

"The recent decades witnessed conspicuous changes in organization theory: a slow but inexorable shift from the focus on structures to the focus on processes. The whirlwinds of the global economy made it clear that everything flows, even if change itself can become stable. While the interest in processes of organizing is not new, it is now acquiring a distinct presence, as more and more voices join in. A forum is therefore needed where such voices can speak to one another, and to the interested readers. The series *Perspectives on Process Organization Studies* will provide an excellent forum of that kind, both for those for whom a processual perspective is a matter of ontology, and those who see it as an epistemological choice."

Barbara Czarniawska, Professor of Management Studies, School of Business, Economics and Law at the University of Gothenburg, Sweden

"We are living in an era of unprecedented change; one that is characterized by instability, volatility, and dramatic transformations. It is a world in which the seemingly improbable, the unanticipated, and the downright catastrophic appear to occur with alarming regularity. Such a world calls for a new kind of thinking: thinking that issues from the chaotic, fluxing immediacy of lived experiences; thinking that resists or overflows our familiar categories of thought; and thinking that accepts and embraces messiness, contradictions, and change as the *sine qua non* of the human condition. Thinking in these genuinely processual terms means that the starting point of our inquiry is not so much about the *being* of entities such as 'organization', but their constant and perpetual *becoming*. I very much welcome this long overdue scholarly effort at exploring and examining the fundamental issue of *process* and its implications for organization studies. Hari Tsoukas and Ann Langley are to be congratulated on taking this very important initiative in bringing the process agenda into the systematic study of the phenomenon of organization. It promises to be a path-breaking contribution to our analysis of organization."

Robert Chia, Professor of Management, University of Strathclyde, UK

"This new series fits the need for a good annual text devoted to process studies. Organization theory has long required a volume specifically devoted to process research that can address process ontology, methodology, research design, and analysis. While many authors collect longitudinal data, there are still insufficient methodological tools and techniques to deal with the nature of that data. Essentially, there is still a lack of frameworks and methods to deal with good processual data or to develop process-based insights. This series will provide an important resource for all branches of organization, management, and strategy theory. The editors of the series, Professors Ann Langley and Hari Tsoukas are excellent and very credible scholars within the process field. They will attract top authors to the series and ensure that each paper presents a high quality and insightful resource for process scholars. I expect that this series will become a staple in libraries, PhD studies, and journal editors' and process scholars' bookshelves."

Paula Jarzabkowski, Professor of Strategic Management, Aston Business School, UK

1

Introduction

Moshe Farjoun, Wendy Smith, Ann Langley, and Haridimos Tsoukas

1.1 Introduction

Contradictions and tensions permeate and propel organizational life, such as reaching globally while focusing locally, competing while also cooperating, performing reliably while experimenting, taking risks and learning, or granting autonomy while constraining freedom. These tensions can give organizational members pause, but also spur them to take action; they may be necessary for preserving the social order, but are also required to transform it (Farjoun, 2017).

Tensions and contradictions remain an important subject for organizational analysis, due to their pervasiveness, their importance to individuals, organizations, and wider social collectives, and their varied, shifting, and regenerative nature (Pondy, 1967; Benson, 1977; Quinn & Cameron, 1988). Over the years, organizational researchers investigated contradictions and tensions in goals, values, identities, beliefs, messages, interests, emotions, practices, relationships, and outcomes (Lewis, 2000; Fairhurst et al., 2016; Schad et al., 2016). Although not the first, Morgan's *Images of Organization* (Morgan, 1986) offered some of the earliest insights to embed the notions of contradictions and mutually sustaining opposites, and the accompanying dialectical and paradoxical thinking, into mainstream organizational analysis, arguing that understanding organizational complexity required insight into paradoxical interventions and dialectical change (Tsoukas & Hatch, 2001).

Recently, scholars have demonstrated a renewed interest in contradictions, evidenced by the growth, systematization, and differentiation in the multiple theoretical domains around organizational contradictions (Fairhurst et al., 2016; Schad et al., 2016). Such resurgence may be due to the increased experience of contradictions within organizations. Smith and Lewis (2011) suggest three intertwined forces which make contradictions salient in organizations: (1) scarcity: the experienced limitation of resources such as time, space, money, talent, etc.; (2) change: the magnitude, pace, and unpredictability in which contemporary environments transform and shift, and the uncertainty and novelty they introduce; and (3) plurality: the multiplicity of perspective, values, goals, and outcomes which can foster clashes between self and others, global needs and local demands, etc. (Jay, 2013; Denis et al., 2001, Ashforth & Reingen, 2014). Indeed, interviews with over 150 CEOs around the world, conducted in collaboration with scholars at the University of Oxford and the executive search firm Heidrick & Struggles (Said Business School & Heidrick & Struggles, 2015), underscore the salience of such tensions at the senior leadership level. CEOs point to a host of contradictions they cannot solve but need to live with over time. More broadly, a recent study by the Executive Board suggests that employees across organizations have experienced an increase in these types of tensions (see http://www.cebglobal.com/blogs).

These various shifts in organizational life fuel further interest in process research to better understand ongoing transformation, shifts, and change at multiple points in history (Benson, 1977; Langley & Tsoukas, 2016). Recent studies offer varied lenses to understand the nature and implications of contradictions in organizations and to link them with process organizational research. We focus here on three lenses in particular: dialectics, paradox, and dualities.

1.1.1 *Dialectics*

Inspired by scholars such as Hegel, Marx, and Engels, dialectics research explores processes of conceptual or social (and sometimes even natural) conflict, interconnection, and change. The generation, interpenetration, and clash of oppositions, leads, sometimes, to their transcendence in a fuller or more adequate mode of thought or form of life (or being) (Bhaskar, 1993) or, in other conceptions, simply to their evolution, reproduction, or continual transformation (Benson, 1977; Langley & Sloan, 2012). In recent years, scholars applied a dialectical lens to a wide range of topics including organizational change (Van de Ven & Poole, 1995), institutional change (Farjoun, 2002; Seo & Creed, 2002), strategic alliances (Das & Teng, 2000; De Rond & Bouchiki, 2004), the development of disciplines (Abbott, 2001), decision making (Denis et al., 2011), identity dynamics (Kreiner et al., 2015), hiring procedures (Murdoch & Geys, 2014), creativity (Harvey, 2014), globally distributed work teams (Cramton & Hinds, 2014) and the evolution of management models (Bodrožić & Adler, 2018).

1.1.2 *Paradox*

Drawing from both Eastern and Western philosophy, paradox scholars emphasize tensions as contradictory and interdependent elements that persist over time and are impervious to resolution (Lewis, 2000; Van de Ven & Poole, 1989; Quinn & Cameron, 1988; Smith & Lewis, 2011). Scholars depict paradox as both absurd and irrational (Chia & Nayak, 2017), as well as prevalent and inherent (Tracey & Creed, 2017). Approaches to addressing paradoxes begin with accepting and engaging competing demands (Huq et al., 2017; Miron-Spektor et.al., 2018; Knight & Paroutis, 2017). Studies highlight two types of practices to address paradox, each in ongoing relationships with one another: (1) differentiating: splitting opposing forces to value their distinctions and differences, and (2) integrating: seeking synergies, linkages, and interrelationships (Smith & Tushman, 2005; Andriopoulos & Lewis, 2009; Smets et al., 2015; Smith, 2014; Miron-Spektor et al., 2011; Salvato & Rerup, 2018). Only differentiating or only integrating practices can fuel vicious cycles, whereas virtuous cycles of engaging paradox depend on the interaction between both practices—emphasizing Quinn and Cameron's (1988) early insight that 'managing paradoxes is paradoxical'.

1.1.3 *Duality*

The duality lens on organizational contradictions highlights the coexistence of opposing and complementary elements, processes, or effects (Ashforth & Reingen, 2014; Farjoun, 2010; Seo et al., 2004). The duality view suggests that the two largely opposing elements may interpenetrate one another such that one includes elements of the other (Dewey, 1922; Farjoun, 2010; Giddens, 1984; Levinthal & Rerup, 2006). As evident in the work of Dewey and Giddens, duality is closely connected to dialectics and shares with it the interest in endogenous and recursive influences (also see Orlikowski, 1992). Indeed, dialectical theory models transformation through conflict between two largely opposing elements, such as agency and structure, that may interpenetrate until one includes elements of the other and they are no longer mutually exclusive.

Though varied in their emphases, these complementary approaches all depict tensions as interconnected contradictions. Distinct from dilemmas and tradeoffs with clearly resolvable contradictions, dialectics, paradoxes, and dualities variously stress the interdependent nature of opposing poles; their persistent, dynamic shifts over time; the role they play in organizational processes, change, innovation, and potential transformation (Tsoukas & Chia, 2002; Van de Ven & Poole, 1995); and the challenges and opportunities they present for organizational actors (Denis et al., 2001).

1.1.4 *Summary of Varied Lenses*

The chapters in this volume, inspired by the Eighth International Symposium on Process Organization Studies, explore three main, connected themes through both conceptual and empirical studies. First, these chapters offer insight into how process theorizing advances understandings of organizational contradictions. Studies depict interconnected contradictions as fuelling and provoking one another, resulting in perpetually changing relationships (Schad et al., 2016; Fairhurst et al., 2016; Sheep et al., 2017). Prototypical questions include how these interrelated contradictions emerge, change, and shift over time (e.g. Langley & Sloan, 2012) and how they spark ongoing cyclical dynamics (Tsoukas & Pina e Cunha, 2017).

Second, these studies shed light on how dialectics, paradoxes, and dualities fuel organizational processes that affect persistence and transformation. The juxtaposition of opposites can intrigue and energize, as well as perplex and paralyze. These contrasting effects require a deeper understanding of how, when, and why some contradictions lead to change or stability (or both), and how these organizational contradictions facilitate or undermine (or both) processes such as creativity and innovation (e.g. Miron-Spektor & Erez, 2017), strategizing (e.g. Smith, 2014), or institutional change (e.g. Farjoun, 2002).

Third, studies in this volume explore how dialectics, paradoxes, and dualities qua lenses for studying organizations converge and diverge (e.g. Fairhurst et al., 2016; Farjoun, 2017; Hargrave & Van de Ven, 2017). How are these lenses distinct? How are they similar? How do they relate to one another? How can research benefit from adopting multiple lenses? What methodologies are most useful to studying organizational contradictions? This investigation can offer scholars greater clarity in studying interrelated contradictions and processes.

In the rest of this introduction, we expand on each of these three themes, as reflected in the various chapters, and provide an overview of each chapter along the way. We end with a discussion of directions for future research that will further the key themes of the volume, develop the three lenses, and strengthen their contributions to organizational and process research.

1.2 Theme 1: A Process Perspective on Organizational Contradictions

Although theories of dialectics, paradox, and dualities emphasize dynamic shifts over time, the details of these dynamics remain relatively underexplored (Schad et al., 2016). Process perspectives offer opportunities for unpacking the nature of these shifts. The chapters in this volume particularly address three main process issues: persistence of opposites, cascading effects, and cyclical dynamics. In addition, since all of these processes occur in time, temporality is a theme that pervades most papers.

The first issue concerns the nature and dynamics of *persistence of opposites*. Studies employing a paradox lens depict the relationship between oppositional poles as persistent, impervious to resolution, and sustaining over time (Lewis, 2000; Clegg et al., 2002). Yet we still know little about the details of persistence. What persists and what does not? What fuels and what inhibits persistence? Persistence may imply stability and permanence, yet scholars of paradox depict opposing poles as perpetually shifting and changing in relation to one another. Paradoxes, therefore, remain locked in a relationship between change (the ongoing shifts between the nature of opposing poles) and stability (some element of the paradox that sustains over time and remains impervious to resolution). This observation evokes the perennial paradox of the (n)ever changing world (Birnholtz et al., 2007): there is nothing new under the sun (Ecclesiastes) and everything flows (Heraclitus). It further begs the question of what is new and what is old, as reflected in the Paradox of Theseus' Ship. If, over time, Theseus proceeds to replace every aspect of his ship—the sail, the boom, the mast, the floor planks, etc.—then is the new ship really the same as the old ship? If, as humans, each of our cells dies and new cells replace them, are we really the same person at 80 that we were as a baby? Such paradoxical perspectives may reinforce the view of stability and change as a duality: rather than being separable and antagonistic, stability enables change and change allows for stability (Farjoun, 2010).

In their chapter, Pina e Cunha and Clegg offer one insight about addressing such tensions between change and stability. Leaders, they argue, can seek to release the energy embedded in such tensions toward beneficial outcomes, without seeking resolution. Drawing from Li's (2016) yin-yang approach, they include insights about responses involving (1) both/and, (2) either/or, (3) neither/nor, (4) both/or, and (5) either/and. As they delineate, each of these responses offers different approaches to the nature of persistence; either understanding persistence as an anomaly in a system, an inability to move forward, an ongoing interaction in a dynamic equilibrium, a transcendent novelty, or as constitutive of ongoing—a 'permanent dialectic'.

In their in-depth study of a healthcare organization, Gilbert, Michaud, Bentein, Dubois, and Bédard, apply a paradox lens to depict a second issue—the *cascading effects* of tensions across hierarchies. As Fairhurst and colleagues (2016) noted, 'to avoid too much complexity, scholars often narrow their foci and study one primary paradox at a particular level, and they often do so by overlooking the role of power and thus [assuming] the equal influence of opposing poles' (p. 6). By tracking tensions through multiple organizational levels and actors, Gilbert and colleagues uncover how tensions are transferred across a hierarchy through discourse as well as the control of specific structures and tools. Their results emphasize how tensions transform and surface as actors, at a higher level, mobilize those at a lower level. They further depict differences in outcomes across levels. Embracing paradox can be beneficial at higher levels of an organization, but create challenges at lower levels.

In his intriguing paper on cooperative cognition and reflexive awareness, drawing on Buddhist epistemology and the yin-yang imagery, Dunn highlights the mutual dependence between individual and group cognition, and subjective-objective awareness. In cooperative cognition, he notes, while individuals are aware of themselves and others' roles in the group, they may also become aware of the group itself and how well it performs a task. Expanding on Buddhist (especially Dharmakīrtian) epistemology, Dunn echoes phenomenological thinking by noting that features of subjectivity are always present in any instance of cognition. Describing the notion of 'reflexive awareness', he remarks that 'every form of cognition includes not only a phenomenal form of the cognition's object, but also a phenomenal form of the subjectivity that occurs with the cognition of any object'. In other words, an awareness of an object simultaneously includes an intransitive awareness of the subject. In cooperative cognition, reflexive awareness enables group members to become aware of the functionality of the group while the group is focusing on its task (rather than, as traditionally assumed, focusing introspectively on itself).

Third, some chapters in this volume explicate *cyclical dynamics* associated with competing demands. In their recent work, Tsoukas and Pina e Cunha (2017) delineate vicious cycles (deviation-amplifying cycles that turns a bad situation worse), virtuous cycles (deviation-amplifying cycles that turn a good situation better), and stabilizing cycles (cycles in which an action counteracts a negative shift and brings about stability). Lewis' chapter in this volume extends this work, using the actions of senior leaders of LEGO to demonstrate how persistent competing demands fuel ongoing cyclical dynamics. Convinced of the value of their interlocking brick, LEGO senior leaders vehemently exploited this technology despite significant shifts in the toy industry. Declining sales led to a major wake-up call and, in response, leaders shifted—emphasizing innovation, exploration, and novelty. Lewis elaborates on the self-reinforcing cognitions, emotions, and behaviours that create defensive dynamics and fuel these vicious cyclical swings between inertial entrenchment and radical innovation. LEGO leaders finally could engage both emphasizing the exploitative base and exploratory innovation by adopting a paradoxical mindset and articulating a motivating and integrative higher purpose. By teasing out the sources of defensiveness, Lewis offers insight about the mechanisms fostering a cyclical relationship between paradoxical demands and how these relationships emerge, change, and shift over time.

1.3 Theme 2: Organizational Contradictions as Fuelling and Depicting Organizational Processes

Scholars view contradictions as a motor for change and transformation. Poole and Van de Ven (1995) depict the juxtaposition of bipolar opposites as one of four archetypal models of change and development, highlighting how dialectic processes can lead to novel opportunities in firms (see also Seo & Creed, 2002; Denis et al., 2011; Kreiner et al., 2015; Farjoun, 2002; Harvey, 2014). The chapters in this volume expand upon several organizational processes and transformations fuelled by contradictions.

Myllykoski and Rantakari depict the processual dynamics fuelled by tensions in understandings of time. Their investigation into the strategic discussions about the growth and internationalization of a Finnish software firm surfaced different temporal conceptualizations: a focus on an in-time approach that emphasized the emergent present and over-time approaches that emphasized the linear, planned future. They argue that both discussions of a structured and planned future interacted consistently with an understanding of the real, experienced present, which together informed the ongoing process of creating strategy, emphasizing how competing demands are embedded within and define processual developments.

Maier's chapter induces insights from an ethnographical study of a dramatic television series production to examine the dialectical tension between financial and creative imperatives of *production* projects. Drawing on the notion of dialectic interplay, she shows how, in this cultural industry, calculative practices enabled middle managers to combine qualitative judgement and intuition with quantitative monetary evaluations, reflecting a process of dynamic interplay. As her evidence shows, entrenched dualisms may affect the way work gets done in temporary organizations and how individuals address the tensions and contradictions they encounter during their everyday work practice.

Wiedemann, Wiegmann, and Weber's longitudinal study also shows how contradictions fuel organizational processes. Studying a leadership team engaged in a strategic management routine in a multidivisional firm, they illustrate how tensions between individual and collective interests break down truces, and subsequently how splitting discussions into distinct spaces devoted to the routine and to a 'meta-routine' enables truces to be renegotiated, restabilizing the routine, though never permanently. The tensions highlighted in the chapter punctuate the process through which truces break and (re)form. The study also revealingly illustrates the unexpected role of artefacts in reshaping tensions, and in disrupting and reforming truces in organizational routines.

Several other chapters mentioned above further elucidate how contradictions fuel processes. Although their work is conceptual, Pina e Cunha and

Clegg relate contradictions and paradoxes to several organizational processes. Power dynamics in particular, as well as control and discourse processes, are also evident in Gilbert et al.'s study. Whereas the focus in Maier's study is on middle-level managers, Gilbert et al. pay particular attention to how tension between quality and efficiency transfer between top-level and front-line employees and through the interaction between managers and professionals.

1.4 Theme 3: Different Lenses for Studying Organizational Contradictions

Scholarship of dialectics, paradox, and dualities offers insights on how these lenses on organizational contradictions converge as well as diverge. Chapters in this volume draw on these lenses in different ways: they interpret each lens more or less broadly, focusing on one lens only or combining several.

In his erudite article, ranging from Kantian philosophy to his anthropological studies of southern Indian villages, Nuckolls explores how paradox and dialectical lenses reinforce, integrate, and inform one another. He discusses knowledge systems, their internal paradoxes, and the dialectics these paradoxes create. Dialectics, he asserts, is the motor of paradox. All knowledge systems contain antinomies (i.e. equally defensible but mutually opposed explanatory accounts). Playing out these persistent tensions fuels a system's development. For example, religion, specifically Christianity, embeds the tension between determinism (an omniscient deity with unlimited power) and free will (the agency of humans to affect their destiny). If a deity is omniscient and unlimited, then that deity is the source to offer humans free will. Yet such free will offers humans agency that limits the expanse of power and diminishes the omniscience of the deity. As Nuckolls suggests, approaches to understanding the tension between determinism and free will inform the writing of multiple theologians and spur varied Christian practices, each often building from, learning from, and responding to one another over time. Such tugs and shifts result in multiple, shifting instantiations of Christianity—a dialectical transformation over time. Underlying this transformation remains the persistent, unsolvable, mysterious paradoxical tension between determinism and free will.

The convergence between process and dialectic lenses is shown by Pina e Cunha and Clegg when they explore the question of how paradoxes persist. The authors situate their contribution within the traditional contours of paradox research, as reflected in the notions of yin-yang (Li, 2016) and in accepted ways to engage paradoxes (e.g. Lewis, 2000). Yet, building on Benson's insightful analysis of how a dialectical lens applies to organizations, they particularly draw on dialectics, not as a short end for tension or interplay but as a full-fledged process perspective. The Bensonian analysis helps the authors situate paradoxes within the totality of other paradoxes within organizations, highlight their shifting nature, and examine their relation to power and interests.

Maier's study draws on a more restrictive, yet productive application of dialectics. Rather than drawing on dialectics as a process perspective, as Pina e Cunha and Clegg have done, Maier mainly draws on dialectics as a way to examine the interplay between seemingly incompatible polarities. She also draws on the notion of duality as a way to overcome conventional and less helpful dualisms such as between art and commerce. Wiedemann, Wiegmann, and Weber, too, identify dialectics less as a comprehensive process perspective in itself and more as synonymous with tension, contradiction, and paradox that can contribute to driving processes forward.

Finally, Jarzabkowski, Bednarek, and Lê offer insight into how to study paradoxes, dialectics, and dualities. Drawing on process and practice theory, they depict organizational contradictions as socially constructed through people's activities, practices, and interactions. Yet as paradox theory suggests, these contradictions can be salient and more easily observable, or latent and less experienced and therefore less observable. Studying salient paradoxes is easier, and they suggest prior work that sets out ways to do so through language, emotions, and actions. By virtue of being less observable, latent paradoxes are more challenging to study. These authors offer suggestions of how to do so, exploring the silences in everyday action, juxtaposing temporal events and linking place and spaces that connect opposing paradoxical poles.

1.5 Reflections and Future Research Directions

This volume has benefited from rich and varied contributions. The different chapters offered philosophical, conceptual, empirical, and methodological contributions and integrated long-standing perspectives with contemporary practical and theoretical challenges. At one level, each of the chapters attests for the usefulness of process approaches to organizations as well as the need to better understand organizational contradictions. Yet, the various studies extend beyond these more familiar linkages to examine how contradictions pervade organizational processes and transformations as well as being imbued by inner dynamics.

Despite the immense progress made in the study of organizational dualities, dialectics, and paradoxes, the contributions in this volume open up a host of new questions and directions. Additional issues are continually surfaced by individuals, groups, and organizations as they struggle to make sense and navigate a multitude of changes and transformations. Just as organizations are continually replenished by tensions and contradictions, research on organizational contradictions seems as open-ended as ever. And yet, some directions may seem more promising, useful, and significant than others. In the spirit of providing some guidance while keeping agendas elastic and emergent we list below several potential avenues for future theorizing in this domain.

First, we need to continue to set higher aspirations. There are many ongoing changes and transformations that can benefit from a sustained effort from our community. Some of these developments are significant in their consequences. We can definitely try to say more about global issues such as poverty, corruption, immigration, and intractable conflicts (see e.g. Tracey & Creed, 2017). Other developments are still in the making. For instance, automation brings with it many interesting contradictions between humans and machines, as manifest in issues of control, learning, accountability, ethics, liberty, and so on. As another example, the ascendance of 'alternative truths' highlights the tension between substance and appearance, the hidden and the visible. These and other examples suggest that contradictions cannot be regarded as neutral phenomena. They often manifest and reveal important dynamics of power and control. Thus, future research can try to better target the types of problems and phenomena surfacing contradictions, and how they are dealt with, and can make a considerable difference to, as well as shed light on, emerging changes in technology, tastes, and policies.

Second, the linkages between organizations, process thinking, and contradictions are manifold. Future research can examine relatively unexplored linkages such as between routines and tensions, capability and choice, bottom-up and top-down developments, and the like. Research efforts may need to be rerouted from studying traditional hierarchies to examining new organizational forms such as social networks, apps, and heterarchies. To better understand how tensions evolve and help transform organizations, we may need to better trace them through historical and comparative studies.

Third, we may need to be more introspective about how we approach the study of organizations. While in this volume we stressed three important lenses, there are other traditions, such as practice theory, pragmatism, and evolutionary theory, that are clearly relevant. Have we as a community drawn on conflict, contradiction, and tensions between different approaches to the best extent? Have we found the 'sweet point' between our shared interests and our divergent approaches to study them?

These are just a few of our own reflections after putting together this volume's contributions. We are hopeful that readers will draw on these directions and add new contributions to this vibrant stream of research.

References

Abbott, A. 2001. *Chaos of disciplines*. Chicago, IL: University of Chicago Press.

Andriopoulos, C. & Lewis, M.W. 2009. Exploitation-exploration tensions and organizational ambidexterity: Managing paradoxes of innovation. *Organization Science*, 20(4): 696–717.

Ashforth, B.E. & Reingen, P.H. 2014. Functions of dysfunction: Managing the dynamics of an organizational duality in a natural food cooperative. *Administrative Science Quarterly*, 59(3).

Benson, J.K. 1977. Organizations: A dialectical view. *Administrative Science Quarterly*, 22(1): 1–21.

Bhaskar, R.A. 1993. *Dialectic: The Pulse of Freedom*. London: Verso.

Birnholtz, J.P., Cohen, M.D., & Hoc, S.V. 2007. Organizational character: On the regeneration of Camp Poplar Grove. *Organization Science*, 18(2): 315–32.

Bodrožić, Z. & Adler, P.S. 2018. The evolution of management models: A neo-Schumpeterian model. *Administrative Science Quarterly*, 63(1).

Cameron, K.S. 1986. Effectiveness as paradox: Consensus and conflict in conceptions of organizational effectiveness. *Management Science*, 32(5): 539–53.

Chia, R. & Nayak, A. 2017. Circumventing the logic and limits of representation: Otherness in east–west approaches to paradox. In W.K.L. Smith, M.W. P., Jarzabkowski, & A. Langley (eds), *The Oxford Handbook of Organizational Paradox*. Oxford: Oxford University Press.

Cramton, C.D. & Hinds, P.J. 2014. An embedded model of cultural adaptation in global teams. *Organization Science*, 25(4): 1056–81.

Das, T.K. & Teng, B.-S. 2000. A resource-based theory of strategic alliances. *Journal of Management*, 26(1): 31–61.

De Rond, M. & Bouchiki, H. 2004. On the dialectics of strategic alliances. *Organization Science*, 15(1): 56–69.

Denis, J.-L., Lamothe, L., & Langley, A. 2001. The dynamics of collective leadership and strategic change in pluralistic organizations. *Academy of Management Journal*, 44(4): 809–37.

Denis, J.-L., Dompierre, G., Langley, A., & Rouleau, L. 2011. Escalating indecision: Between reification and strategic ambiguity. *Organization Science*, 22(1): 225–44.

Dewey, J. 1922. *Human Nature and Conduct: An Introduction to Social Psychology*. London: Carlton House.

Fairhurst, G.T., Smith, W.K., Banghart, S.G., Lewis, M.W., Putnam, L.L., Raisch, S., & Schad, J. 2016. Diverging and converging: Integrative insights on a paradox meta-perspective. *Academy of Management Annals*, 10(1): 173–82.

Farjoun, M. 2002. The dialectics of institutional development in emergent and turbulent fields: The history of pricing conventions in the on-line database industry. *Academy of Management Journal*, 45(5): 848–74.

Farjoun, M. 2010. Beyond dualism: Stability and change as duality. *Academy of Management Review*, 35(2): 202–25.

Farjoun, M. 2017. Contradictions, dialectics and paradox. In A. Langley and H. Tsoukas (ed.), *Sage Handbook of Process Organization Studies*. London: Sage.

Giddens, A. 1984. *The Constitution of Society: Outline of the Theory of Structuration*. Berkeley, CA: University of California Press.

Hargrave, T.J. & Van de Ven, A.H. 2017. Integrating dialectical and paradox perspectives on managing contradictions in organizations. *Organization Studies*, 38(2–4).

Harvey, S. 2014. When accuracy isn't everything: The value of demographic differences to information elaboration in teams. *Group and Organization Management*, 29: 560–87.

Huq, J.-L., Reay, T., & Chreim, S. 2017. Protecting the paradox of interprofessional collaboration. *Organization Studies*, 38(3–4): 513–38.

Jay, J. 2013. Navigating paradox as a mechanism of change and innovation in hybrid organizations. *Academy of Management Journal*, 56(1): 137–59.

Knight, E. & Paroutis, S. 2017. Becoming salient: The TMT leader's role in shaping the interpretive context of paradoxical tensions. *Organization Studies*, 38(3–4): 403–32.

Kreiner, G., Hollensbe, E., Sheep, M., Smith, B., & Kataria, N. 2015. Elasticity and the dialectic tensions of organizational identity: How can we hold together while we're pulling apart? *Academy of Management Journal*, 58(4): 981–1011.

Langley, A. & Sloan, P. 2012. Organizational change and dialectic processes. In D.M. Boje, B. Burnes, & J. Hassard (eds), *The Routledge Companion to Organizational Change* (pp. 261–75). Abingdon: Routledge.

Langley, A. & Tsoukas, H. (eds). 2016. *The Sage Handbook of Process Organization Studies*. London: Sage.

Levinthal, D. & Rerup, C. 2006. Crossing an apparent chasm: Bridging mindful and less-mindful perspectives on organizational learning. *Organization Science*, 17(4): 502–13.

Lewis, M.W. 2000. Exploring paradox: Toward a more comprehensive guide. *Academy of Management Review*, 25(4): 760–76.

Li, P.P. 2016. Global implications of the indigenous epistemological system from the east: How to apply yin-yang balancing to paradox management. *Cross Cultural and Strategic Management*, 23(1): 42–77.

Miron-Spektor, E. & Erez, M. 2017. Looking at creativity through a paradox lens: Deeper understanding and new insights. In M.W. Lewis, W.K. Smith, P. Jarzabkowski, & A. Langley (eds), *Handbook of Organizational Paradox: Approaches to Plurality, Tensions and Contradictions*. Oxford: Oxford University Press.

Miron-Spektor, E., Gino, F., & Argote, L. 2011. Paradoxical frames and creative sparks: Enhancing individual creativity through conflict and integration. *Organizational Behavior and Human Decision Processes*, 116(2): 229–40.

Miron-Spektor, E., Ingram, A.S., Keller, J., Smith, W.K., & Lewis, M.W. 2018. Microfoundations of organizational paradox: The problem is how we think about the problem. *Academy of Management Journal*, 61(1): 26–45.

Morgan, G. 1986. *Images of Organization*. Thousand Oaks, CA: Sage Publications.

Murdoch, Z. & Geys, B. 2014. Institutional dynamics in international organizations: Lessons from the recruitment procedures of the European external action service. *Organization Studies*, 35(12): 1793–811.

Orlikowski, W.J. 1992. The duality of technology: Rethinking the concept of technology in organizations. *Organization Science*, 3(3): 398–427.

Pondy, L.R. 1967. Organizational conflict: Concepts and models. *Administrative Science Quarterly*, 12(2): 296–320.

Poole, M.S. & Van de Ven, A. 1989. Using paradox to build management and organizational theory. *Academy of Management Review*, 14(4): 562–78.

Quinn, R. & Cameron, K. 1988. Paradox and transformation: A framework for viewing organization and management. In R. Quinn & K. Cameron (eds), *Paradox and Transformation: Toward a Theory of Change in Organization and Management* (pp. 289–308). Cambridge, MA: Ballinger.

Said Business School & Heidrick & Struggles. 2015. The CEO report: Embracing the paradoxes of leadership and the power of doubt. Oxford: University of Oxford.

Salvato, C. & Rerup, C. 2018. Routine regulation: Balancing conflicting goals in organizational routines. *Administrative Science Quarterly*, 63(1).

Schad, J., Lewis, M.W., Raisch, S., & Smith, W.K. (2016). Paradox research in management science: Looking back to move forward. *Academy of Management Annals*, 10(1): 5–64.

Seo, M.-G. & Creed, W. 2002. Institutional contradictions, praxis, and institutional change: A dialectical perspective. *Academy of Management Review*, 27(2): 222–47.

Seo, M.-G., Putnam, L., & Bartunek, J.M. 2004. Dualities and tensions of planned organizational change. In S. Poole & A. Van de Ven (eds), *Handbook of Organizational Change* (pp. 73–107). Oxford: Oxford University Press.

Sheep, M.L., Fairhurst, G.T., & Khazanchi, S. 2017. Knots in the discourse of innovation: Investigating multiple tensions in a reacquired spin-off. *Organization Studies*, 38(3–4): 463–88.

Smets, M., Jarzabkowski, P., Burke, G.T., & Spee, P. 2015. Reinsurance trading in Lloyd's of London: Balancing conflicting-yet-complementary logics in practice. *Academy of Management Journal*, 58(3): 932–70.

Smith, W.K. 2014. Dynamic decision making: A model of senior leaders managing strategic paradoxes. *Academy of Management Journal*, 57(6): 1592–623.

Smith, W.K. & Lewis, M.W. 2011. Toward a theory of paradox: A dynamic equilibrium model of organizing. *Academy of Management Review*, 36(2): 381–403.

Smith, W.K. & Tushman, M.L. 2005. Managing strategic contradictions: A top management model for managing innovation streams. *Organization Science*, 16(5): 522–36.

Tracey, P. & Creed, D. 2017. Beyond managerial dilemmas: The study of institutional paradoxes in organization theory. In M. Lewis, W.K. Smith, P. Jarzabkowski, & A. Langley (eds), *Oxford Handbook on Organizational Paradox* (pp. 490–509). Oxford: Oxford University Press.

Tsoukas, H. & Chia, R. 2002. On organizational becoming: Rethinking organizational change. *Organization Science*, 13(5): 567–82.

Tsoukas, H. & Hatch, M.J. 2001. Complex thinking, complex practice: The case for a narrative approach to organizational complexity. *Human Relations*, 54(8): 979–1013.

Tsoukas, H. & Pina e Cunha, M. 2017. On organizational circularity: Vicious and virtuous cycles in organizing. In W.K. Smith, M.W. Lewis, P. Jarzabkowski, & A. Langley (eds), *The Oxford Handbook of Organizational Paradox* (pp. 393–412). Oxford: Oxford University Press.

Van de Ven, A. & Poole, M.S. 1995. Explaining development and change in organizations. *Academy of Management Review*, 20(3): 510–40.

2

Persistence in Paradox

Miguel Pina e Cunha and Stewart Clegg

2.1 Introduction

> Paradoxes are fun. In most cases, they are easy to state and immediately provoke one into trying to 'solve' them.

(Sainsbury, 2009, p. 1)

In the early days of theories concerning management and administration it seemed best to think, organize, and do strictly according to plan—the cycle encouraged by scientific management (Taylor, 1911) and administrative theory (Fayol, 1930). While these are still dominant lay views in practice amongst the professional community of academic research dedicated to management, the dominance of planning has been displaced by the emergence of a paradox theory of organization that is gaining momentum (Schad et al., 2016). It is increasingly recognized that the presence and participation of tension and contradiction in the processes of instituting and organizing (Lewis & Smith, 2014; Seo et al., 2002; Sundaramurthy & Lewis, 2003) is a normal phenomenon. From initial studies focused on the content of paradox as a one-off event, the literature has evolved to consider the paradox *process* as a persistent and thoroughgoing corollary of organizing; opposition in complementarity requires charting to compose an appropriately variegated and rich conceptual map of the dynamics of paradox.

Ontologically, paradox is now considered as constitutive of organization, as structurally rooted (Putnam, 2013, p. 624) and as normal (Putnam et al., 2016, p. 66): experiencing paradox is essentially constitutive of organizational becomings and doings. Contemporary literature explores the unique features and types of paradox, disentangling paradox from related concepts such as tension, dialectic, duality, and contradiction. Multiple layers of contradiction and paradox are seen to be immanent to organizing. A complementary and more *pragmatic* stream explores paradox as a managerial tool with which to engage organizations through tension and contradiction in order to achieve organizational success (Price Waterhouse Change Integration Team, 1996). The pragmatics of paradox respond to *how* they can be used to help organizations in a global, interconnected, competitive landscape. In this case paradox is something an organization *has* rather than being essentially constitutive of what an organization can be considered to becoming.

Contemporary paradox scholars share the view that: (1) doing organization entails being 'inherently paradoxical' (Jarzabkowski et al., 2013, p. 245), incorporating deep paradoxes; (2) paradoxes are complex phenomena, resistant to 'best way' solutions; (3), their management is challenging; (4) they contain an element of unanticipated eventfulness, revealed in sudden and surprising shifts and turns. The language of theory tries to capture these with expressions such as foolishness (March, 2006), crazy systems (Putnam et al., 2016), or strange loops (Hofstadter, 1979). These processes have the quality of seemingly 'often beginning where they end' (Putnam et al., 2016, p. 83). Being in this organizational world, a variant of 'Wonderland' (McCabe, 2016), is as confusing as it is stimulating. One explanation for the elusive, stubborn quality of paradox and strange looping is a lack of resolution: paradoxes cannot be solved in the sense of being tackled effectively, once and for all. Paradoxes persist: persistence is a feature of most recent definitions of paradox. Yet it is an unexplored dimension of it. We focus on the persistence because it has been assumed rather than theorized and elaborated. Persistence, 'the state of continuing to exist for a long period of time' (Oxford Advanced Learner's Dictionary), confers a process dimension to an otherwise episodic phenomenon, a temporary dimension of contradiction. To take paradoxes as persistent means that they should be approached as processes which, although at times they may appear to be 'solved', eventually resurface, bringing action back to 'where it all started'—even though every new start is more than a repletion, a necessarily different start.

Organization scholars have dedicated limited attention to the *persistence* of paradox until recently, despite its pervasiveness. Persistence, as a core definitional dimension of paradox, deserves elaboration in its own right. If paradoxes persist, explaining why they persist is of central importance for a theory of organization. The phenomenon of persistence will be perceived ontologically as a dimension of organization, as immanent. The central question this chapter asks is *why do paradoxes persist?* By considering paradox as the duality of synergy and tradeoff, the focus on 'persistent attempts to explain paradoxes away' (Hughes & Brecht, 1975, p. 1) should, from a process perspective, be replaced by an ontology of persistence.

In asking why paradoxes persist there are, we think, three facets to be explored through addressing these subordinate questions: (1) what is paradox?

With this we debate the introduction of persistence in the definition of paradox. (2) Why do paradoxes persist? Here we focus on insolubility as the ontology of paradox, as captured in the notion of paradox as an infinite loop. (3) How does persistence operate? Benson (1977) provides a conceptual vantage point with which to address this question, provided by his principles of dialectical analysis, putting conflict at the centre of the paradoxical *process*. We complement extant paradox research by focusing on persistence rather than resolution. We defend the thesis that paradoxes cannot be solved and that organizations best deal with them by directing the energies released by tension in potentially beneficial directions *without resolution*.

The chapter is organized as follows. We start by contextualizing persistence as a definitional dimension of paradox. Next we ask *why* paradoxes persist, introducing a yin-yang paradox epistemology, following the work of Li (2016), who considers tradeoff and synergy the core components of paradox. We discuss that paradox persists because tradeoffs and synergy dynamically push and pull over time, countering resolution. We finally discuss how paradox persists. Before closing we advance implications for theory and practice.

2.2 Persistence in the Conceptual Evolution of Paradox

A group of influential authors define paradox in consistent theoretical terms with initial definitions being content-focused while recent definitions become more process-oriented. Pioneers Cameron and Quinn (1988) referred to paradox as a concept embracing contradiction and the clashing of ideas, 'contradictory, mutually exclusive elements that are present and operate equally at the same time' (p. 2). Van de Ven and Poole (1988, p. 22) defined paradox as 'the real or apparent contradiction between equally well-based assumptions or conclusions'. Poole and Van de Ven (1989), before differentiating between modalities of paradox (in rhetorical studies, logic, and social theory), explained that the notion is often used as a loose conceptual umbrella for 'interesting and thought-provoking contradictions of all sorts' (p. 563). For Lewis (2000, p. 760), paradox means 'contradictory yet interrelated elements— elements that seem logical in isolation but absurd and irrational when appearing simultaneously'.

Persistence constitutes a recent definitional vector, one that is more process-oriented, with Smith and Lewis (2011, p. 382) defending the thesis that paradox refers to 'contradictory yet interrelated elements that exist simultaneously and persist over time'. Schad et al. (2016, p. 10) reaffirmed the importance of persistence by conceptualizing paradox as 'persistent contradictions between interdependent elements'. From a process perspective, persistence is the core definitional dimension of paradox inhering in its deep structure rather than being an apparent and surface problem to be solved. It is for this reason that paradoxes should be distinguished from other contiguous processes characterized by tension, such as dilemmas. A dilemma lacks the deep structure of a paradox; it poses a problem, the problem can be solved, and organizing moves on. Dilemmas can be solved without reappearing as paradoxes. What defines a paradox is the persistence of tension: no matter how it is approached a paradox will re-emerge repeatedly as a constitutive and integral element of the organizing process. What makes a paradox paradoxical is its repetitious insolubility and continuity over time. Paradoxes may be managed but, given the constitutive contradictions of organizing, they cannot be solved in the same way that a dilemma can, to disappear and never reappear again, as will be elaborated below.

The central paradox of paradox at the present time concerns the role of persistence: a number of paradox scholars claim that paradoxes cannot be resolved, yet how they treat management and approaches to paradox implies otherwise. They are held captive by the notion of their being a steady state of dynamic equilibrium to be attained. However, the practical appropriation of paradox as a managerial tool risks emptying paradoxes of paradoxical features by making them resolvable (Tse, 2013). If persistence defines paradox, resolution as the end of persistence denies paradox.

Tensions that can be solved, therefore, belong to conceptual domains other than paradox. Paradox, as early intuited by Zeno the Greek and more recently by M.C. Escher, expresses a propensity for infinity and lack of resolution (Hughes & Brecht, 1975; Putnam et al., 2016). In order to situate persistence debates about paradox in theory, we explore the five approaches to tension laid out by Li (2016) premised on what he calls a yin-yang epistemology. The yin-yang, a philosophical orientation based on Laozi's Daoist teachings, was transcribed in the *Daodejing* (Barbalet, 2014). Eastern thinking, with its sophisticated sensitivity to the constitutive nature of contradiction, is visually captured in its iconic graphical depiction (Schad et al., 2016). According to Morgan (1986, p. 256):

> the dark yin and the bright yang [constitute a symmetry], but the symmetry is not static. It is a rotational symmetry suggesting, very forcefully, a continuous cyclic movement: the yang returns cyclically to its beginning, the yin attains its maximum and gives place to the yang. The two dots in the diagram symbolize the idea that each time one of the two forces reaches its extreme, it contains in itself already the seed of its opposite.

Applied to organizing, the yin-yang system is a process-sensitive framework that embeds persistence at its core. Persistence and synergistic resolution are conceptually incompatible, the former neutralizing the latter. The notion of 'resolution' suggests the end of concretization, representing the antithesis of paradox, given its central concern with change, becoming, perturbation, and the rejection of an ontology of being, stages, and sequences, in favour of flux and continuation. To appreciate paradox, therefore, implies the acceptance of persistence.

2.3 Why Persistence? The Yin-Yang Perspective

The paradox literature assumes a dualistic opposition between 'either-or' and 'both-and' streams. Such dualism rests on the understanding that the 'both-and' system is superior to the more traditional posing of 'either-or' dualism in a competitive landscape marked by global challenges, hyper-competition, and opposing demands (Hargrave & Van de Ven, 2017; Smith et al., 2016). As with many dualisms, however, the consideration that managers have to choose between one or the other obscures alternative, equally relevant possibilities, prompting some sort of 'one best way' fallacy, one that is ontologically at odds with the conceptual stream we choose to explore: a process framework that sees the future as open-ended, endless, and circular (Luo & Zheng, 2016).

In order to comply with the definition of paradox as persistent process, one needs to depart from the logics of consistency and resolution and consider dualities for dealing with contradictory demands facing organizing (Farjoun, 2010). To situate this debate in the extant literature we start from Li's (2016) discussion of a yin-yang epistemology of paradox. Instead of two, Li (2016) advances five possible approaches to tension in a yin-yang system of thought. These have to do with how organizations articulate the two core dimensions of paradox, the relations between tradeoff and synergy as endogenous—in the sense that each element contains the seed of its opposite.

Tradeoff, a common characteristic of life in organizations (Weick, 1992), refers to the oppositional side of paradox. Synergy represents a higher-level articulation of opposites that transforms tension into complementarity. Paradox promotes tension and stimulates psychological discomfort, balancing acts, and the permanent risk of unbalancing (Vince & Broussine, 1996). Managerialist approaches emphasize paradox as a potential source of dynamic equilibrium but paradox management constitutes an exercise on the verge of disequilibrium. Paradox also entails synergy. The promise of managing paradox lies in the channelling of tension to maintain organizing that is vital and dynamic, which explains recent emphases on the synergistic effects of paradox. As Hargrave and Van de Ven (2017, p. 324) point out, the paradox perspective 'sees contradiction as addressed through synergy'.

In line with Li (2012, 2016), we study persistence by conceptualizing paradox as involving synergy *and* tradeoff. The five yin-yang possibilities considered by this author are: (1) neither-nor, (2) either-or, (3) both-and,

(4) both-or, and (5) either-and. In this section, we explain the differences between these systems, which are summarized in Table 2.1, and their respective implications for paradox as a persistent process. Three preparatory notes are necessary. First, we represent the yin-yang frame as non-dualistic, thus as consistent with the idea that opposition and complementarity are inherent to and constitutive of social dynamics (Putnam et al., 2016). Second, a yin-yang reading of tension and paradox does not assume the intrinsic superiority of any perspective (Li, 2016). In other words, it accepts that the management of paradox is not necessarily better, functionally speaking, than its dismissal via treating it, for example, as a dilemma. Tensions emerge in context and different contingencies promote diverse paradoxical manifestations (Cunha et al., forthcoming). As such, there is no reason to presume that one approach is inherently superior because of its sensitivity to paradox. It may be; it may be not. In simpler environments, simpler solutions may be applicable (Tsoukas, 2016). Third, recent research on paradox and organization builds on the conceptually constraining grand duality characterizing the 'either-or' and 'both-and' approaches. Dualistic opposition is a conceptual straightjacket, given that the

Table 2.1. Paradox and persistence

Approach	Paradoxical core	Explanation	Persistence of paradox is	Application
Neither-nor	Tradeoff: × Synergy: ×	Tradeoff and synergy are both negated.	Anomaly: variables of interest are approached in isolation.	Remove: contradictions are perceived as anomalies and dismissed.
Either-or	Tradeoff: √ Synergy: ×	The either-or system of thinking recognizes tradeoff while negating synergy.	Irresolution: contradictions are indicators of irresolution, i.e. of incomplete adoption of the right approach.	Resolve: investing in the adoption of the right approach.
Both-and	Tradeoff: × Synergy: √	Opposites can be integrated in harmonious dualities.	Dynamic equilibrium: contradictions can be articulated fruitfully.	Cope: integrate opposites by treating them as synergistic.
Both-or	Tradeoff: √→× Synergy: ×→√	Views on tradeoff and synergy change over time. Sublation is used to suspend the tradeoff.	Transcendence: thesis and antithesis can be articulated as a higher-level synthesis.	Synthesize: persistence can be temporarily suspended until new solutions reveal their limitations and trigger a new cycle.
Either-and	Tradeoff: √ Synergy: √	Paradox involves a dynamic tension between tradeoff and synergy. To keep balance one requires the other.	Constitutive: opposites exist in a state of permanent dialectics.	Embrace: live with paradox. View tension as inherent and a source of change.

two approaches are part of a range of possibilities rather than *the* only approaches to socially constructing paradox.

We next elaborate the systems laid out by Li (2016) and their consequences for the framing of paradox persistence. Each of these systems treats the persistence of paradox differently and the key features of persistence surface differently in each approach. The different systems will be illustrated with the case of a cooperative, with reference to the work of Ashforth and Reingen (2014).

2.3.1 *Neither-Nor System*

The neither-nor perspective denies both tradeoff and synergy. As a cognitive system, it represents a naïve interpretation of the social world, in the sense that it rejects the contradictions and paradoxes constitutive of social systems. The neither-nor system of thought regards the co-existence of opposites as impossible, given the full situation of conflict between them, precluding synergy. Organization theories that ignore the role of contradiction, tension, and paradox belong to this conceptual domain. In organization and management theory, this approach carries an important legacy. Most theories of organization do not assume paradox as constitutive.

NEITHER-NOR SYSTEM: PERSISTENCE AS ANOMALY

In the neither-nor system, persistence, per se, is not a conceptually relevant theme. Paradigmatically, this system corresponds to a worldview in which complex phenomena are approached in isolation from their twin oppositional phenomena. Conceptual separation of opposites is regarded as advantageous, permitting clarity of thinking. The lack of process sensitivity to time, space, interest, local politics, and contradiction limits its conceptual depth, however. Given the clarity of assumptions, persistence should be absent—its presence would be dysfunctional. For example, in a cooperative organization, a purist ethos focused on value-oriented goals would define the organization's identity as the rejection of the profit consideration (Michelsen, 1994) typical of mainstream business firms. Between these two forms there is no tradeoff or synergy, as idealists would define the cooperative as the refusal of enterprise. The emergence of contradictions is revelatory of unsolved issues, anomalies to be removed.

2.3.2 *Either-Or*

The either-or system of thought recognizes tradeoffs and rejects synergy. The choice of one of the poles implies the rejection of the other. Managing organizations according to this system consists of tackling multiple antinomies and making the right choices. In yin-yang logic, by denying synergy this system negates paradox; if synergy is integral to paradox it cannot be denied. Consequently, organizations are conceptualized as facing dilemmas that can be tackled through choice. Opposition is recognized but once a decision is made it ceases to be perceived as an active constraint. Decisions such as to make or buy, explore or exploit, and adopt organic or mechanistic structures exemplify this systematic approach. Managing is taken as a stream of dualistic decisions expected to remove contradiction, as promoted by what has been called 'the church of decision-making theory' (Reed, 1991, p. 566). The either-or system is well suited to dilemmatic choices: those that involve alternatives between opposites but not genuine paradoxes. Once an issue is framed as a dilemma and a choice is made, its consequences can become apparent. In doing so, however, the elements in contradiction are not holistically articulated. If, for example, exploitation is perceived as the core strategic capability supporting a business model geared towards cost and efficiency (Porter, 1985), the preference for exploitation precludes the pursuit of exploration: either one force *or* the other prevails.

'EITHER-OR': PERSISTENCE AS IRRESOLUTION

A bipolar epistemology (Bobko, 1985) anchors this system aimed at resolution of paradoxical tension. Tension is interpreted as implying irresolution, insufficient emphasis, such that, if a paradox persists, it constitutes an indication that a decision or a course of action has not been adopted integrally and consistently enough. For example, organizations may interpret 'stuck in the middle' positioning (Porter, 1985) as an indicator of strategic indecision and the lack of emphasis on the right pole. The stuckedness revealed by persistent contradiction may be perceived as a negative manifestation to be remedied, a strategic flaw resulting from an incomplete adoption of a well-defined approach. In the case of a cooperative, for example, an organization with some level of hybridism resulting from the partial adoption of a business logic would conform to this case. In contrast with the previous system, the interrelation is problematized but persistence is rejected as a viable system.

2.3.3 Both-And

The both-and system recognizes synergy but denies tradeoff (Li, 2016). Smith et al. (2016) defended the power of both-and approaches to paradox management. The reasoning behind the both-and approach is conceptually powerful:

> managers need to shift from an 'either/or' mindset to a 'both/and' one by seeing the virtues of inconsistency, recognizing that resources are not always finite, and embracing change rather than chasing stability. In practical terms, this means nurturing the unique aspects of competing constituencies and strategies while finding ways to unite them. (Smith et al., 2016, p. 65)

In such a system paradox is subordinated and ultimately negated because the elements in contradiction are apparent opposites that in practice are constructed as complementary, at least temporarily (Li, 2016). Complementarity temporarily suspends paradox, as synergy prevails. The 'both-and' system thus corresponds to a view of paradox in which tension is a path to a condition freed from the 'wild' side of paradox (tension, conflict, surprise, impossibility of control). The notion of dynamic equilibrium suggests that the attainment of a state of sustainable balance, the 'reconciliation of the apparent polarities' (Chen, 2002, p. 179), is possible and desirable. In this sense paradox persists as incomplete and unstable synergy but nonetheless as synergy. The role of decision makers is to cope with tradeoffs so as to keep it as a force subordinated to synergy.

Such a harmonious reconciliation of opposites corresponds to a theorization of opposition without tension—or with benign tension. No paradox author defends quite such a simplistic conceptual lens, but the emphasis on synergy renders this system as biased as the 'neither-nor' framework, as it also denies the possibility that paradox is persistent (Li, 2016): the opposites are represented as complementary, which discounts opposition. Managerially, this can appear to be an attractive and powerful proposition because it assumes that managers can balance opposites through coping. The search for managerial application through synergy risks conceptually emptying paradox of tradeoffs, up to the point that it does not constitute paradox anymore, at least temporarily, before opposition and resistance override apparent synergy.

BOTH-AND: PERSISTENCE AS DYNAMIC EQUILIBRIUM

In the both-and system, paradox is approached via synergy. The resolution of paradox has been indicated as a source of competitive advantage (Collins & Porras, 1994; Fredberg, 2014). In such perspective, 'the solving of paradox is inherent in management practices' (Fredberg, 2014, p. 173). Hargrave and Van de Ven concur (2017, p. 324), qualifying paradox management as the path toward synergy and virtuous circularity 'as a process in which managers purposefully iterate between contradictory elements in order to ensure attention to both. This enables them to avoid 'paralyzing and often vicious cycles' and instead initiate 'virtuous cycles' of learning and enhanced organizational performance.' If paradox refers to the persistence of opposition and interdependency, this system emphasizes synergy at the cost of taming persistent push-pulls that carve out contradictions, within organizational systems, beyond managerial control. It frames persistence conceptually as indicative of partial and incomplete synergy. Successful coping with contradiction will transform paradox into persisting synergy but not persisting paradox—managerially this may be a preferable condition but ontologically it constitutes a non-paradoxical state.

In a cooperative this may correspond to organizational hybrids that are expected to balance the oppositions in such a way that tension gives way to peaceful and respectful coexistence between idealists and pragmatists. In such a case, a new, hybrid identity can emerge from the purposeful iterations between contradictory forces, a viable and sustainable 'middle way'.

2.3.4 Both-Or

The both-or system is defined as 'temporarily recognizing but ultimately denying tradeoff between temporarily, but ultimately fake, opposite elements; temporarily denying, but ultimately recognizing, synergy between temporarily true, but ultimately fake, opposite elements'. It corresponds to Hegel's dialectical logic (Li, 2016, p. 28). Via sublation, paradox is initially accepted but ultimately rejected. In this case it is 'recognized as a problem to resolve'. Resolution through sublation shifts emphasis from tradeoff to synergy. The two elements in opposition are eventually articulated in a synthesis that 'solves' the paradox by transporting it to a higher level (Clegg & Cunha, 2017). In this system, the ultimate goal of management consists in bringing oppositions to a superior level of resolution such as in finding synthesis that articulates pre-existing poles in a higher-order solution transcending those poles. Living with paradox and closing it via resolution are faced with hesitation. Paradox is not conceptually embraced as the poles are split instead of being articulated in ongoing balance: it does not pass the definitional test of persistence.

BOTH-OR: PERSISTENCE AS TRANSCENDENCE
The resolution of paradox via transcendence enacted in synthesis that becomes a new thesis, pushing a new dialectical cycle forward, emphasizes the continued, ongoing tension involved in paradox. Pragmatically the 'both-or' system may make conflicts tractable and, in this sense, constitute a viable and functional solution to managerial exercises in contradiction. From a conceptual perspective it does not correspond to an ultimately paradoxical stance. Paradox is transitory rather than persistent. It is only temporarily tolerable. A 'cooperative corporation' such as Mondragón (MCC) may be representative: as it responds to challenges, it epitomizes a new form of sophisticated synthesis that is unparalleled in its innovation and its capacity to combine solidarity and competitiveness (Azevedo & Gitahy, 2010); its nature as a cooperative with a well-defined original mission seems to prevail over a genuinely hybrid identity, making every synthesis a temporary solution with which to navigate the two horns of its dilemma, opposing the social and the entrepreneurial, in the direction of solidarity. As Whyte (1999, p. 480)

pointed out: 'MCC has not lost its original ideals, and there is continuing debate within the system over how to overcome the deficiencies.'

2.3.5 Either-And

The 'either-and' perspective represents paradox as synergy *and* tradeoff, the two core elements coexisting in the same place at the same time, as push-pulls between centripetal and centrifugal forces that exist in a state of relationality rather than of independence (Kassinis & Panayiotou, 2016). The 'either' element expresses the presence of tension, conflict, and tradeoff, whereas the 'and' particle captures harmony, synergy, and complementarity (Li, 2016). In this system, tradeoffs and synergies between opposites are recognized yet appreciated: 'Yin-Yang balancing treats the two opposite elements in a paradox as both partial trade-off and partial synergy within a threshold as a range of holistic and dynamic balancing points for healthy tension' (Li, 2016, p. 28), with balancing referring to the dynamic interplay of the forces in tension. Managers do not aim at 'solving' the paradox, they rather seek to prolong the state of fruitful opposition that renews and reinvigorates. This mode allows agents to feed back persistence by recursively practising and thinking about practice, with reflexivity in action dereifying structures, submitting them to agency and volition, infusing them with dynamism and instability. Because agents do not take structures for granted, they continuously revise them, experimenting at the interface of actuality and potentiality, causing paradoxes to emerge as they act.

Ashforth and Reingen's (2014) study of Natura provides an exemplary illustration of 'either-and' approaches in action. In this cooperative, idealists and pragmatists defend distinct visions for the organization. The visions are opposite and the opposition leads to conflict and to critical views of the counterpart, with each party seeing its own position as inherently superior. The two sides, however, also nurtured an appreciation of the importance of conflict. As the authors explain, 'each group appeared to recognize the other as a necessary evil, as part of a greater whole. Members were prone to liken themselves to a family, implying mutual love in spite of conflict' (p. 493). Love and conflict coexist as push-pulls, preserving both synergy and tradeoff. The groups developed rituals of mutual consideration in order to prevent the transformation of substantial conflict into personal fighting; nonetheless, the differences and the antagonism between the two parties remain active. The synergy/tradeoff balance is ongoing and supported by the cooperative's mission and identity. These overarching goals operate as a supraordinate value that integrates sectional interests and segmented orientations. In turn, the belief that it is possible to prosper *because of* conflict rather than in spite of it is sustained via a permanent relational dialectic of opposition and synergy (Clegg et al., 2002).

EITHER-AND: PERSISTENCE AS CONSTITUTIVE

In this system persistence is fully acknowledged and appreciated as constitutive of the social world. Because tradeoffs and synergies are accepted as core organizational dimensions, tension and contradiction are not regarded as anomalies to be solved but as part of the very fabric of organization, expressions of its inner complexity and dynamism, factors to be accommodated rather than excluded. To manage change, as Chia (2014) points out, it is necessary to 'let go' instead of to seek control. Such a permanent dialectic is integral rather than exceptional to organizational becoming. As the case of Natura suggests, this type of oscillation seems to be a property of the organization as a whole rather than of some of its parts (Ashforth & Reingen, 2014). Natura accepts that a cooperative constitutes a specific institutional form in which pragmatists and idealists should work side by side in a state of hybridity as identity (Chaddad, 2012). Accepting this deep hybridity can be crucial in tackling the weaknesses of the cooperative form in competitive contexts (Whyte, 1995).

Instead of adopting a bipolar attitude and regarding paradoxes as solvable, the nurturing of paradox in the either-and system prompts organizations to assume the potential for 'strange loopiness', meaning that the surprising, frustrating, yet exciting and ironic nature of paradox is inherent, therefore embraced and lived. In itself, persistence is not necessarily positive or harming. It can be circular and complex as reflected in the notion of the strange loop. Following Hofstadter (2007, pp. 101–2), a strange loop is an

> abstract loop in which, in the series of stages that constitute the cycling around, there is a shift from one level of abstraction to another, which feels like an upward movement in a hierarchy, and yet somehow the successive 'upward' shifts turn out to give rise to a close cycle. That is, despite one's sense of departing ever further from one's origin, one winds up, to one's shock, exactly where one had started out. In short, a strange loop is a paradoxical level-crossing feedback loop.

The propensity of paradox to manifest as strange looping means that its management involves the acceptance that paradox will not necessarily lead to a new and higher state but will be recursive, pointing back to some beginning. Such is the meaning of persistence. Strange loops are revelatory of the cyclical, repetitive nature of organizing around paradox. Yet, this repetitive stability comports and accommodates change and deviation (Hussenot & Missonier, 2016). By taking strange loopiness into account, vicious and virtuous circles may be conceptualized as different manifestations of the same ontological deep paradoxical order, one in which stability is temporary and evolution is prone to reversal. Given the tradeoff/synergy of push-pull, 'not only are the paradoxes through which process occurs never resolved, but . . . they continually develop and transmute' (Barbalet, 2014, p. 23); that is, they change nature or shape, hopefully but not necessarily to acquire some superior form. Within the original yin-yang framework, Barbalet points out that 'In Daodejing paradox relates to process inherently and process is understood to occur through a paradoxical generation of paradox' (p. 23).

2.4 How Does Persistence Operate? A Dialectical Perspective

Having discussed why paradoxes persist, we now focus on *how*: how do paradoxes operate from within larger social systems, recursively composing them and being composed by them in a continuous fashion? Benson (1977) elaborates one of the most comprehensive theoretical frameworks in which contradictions are at the core of the becoming. Benson's process-oriented theory of change and transformation is framed by dialectics. As he explained,

> a dialectical view is fundamentally committed to the concept of process. The social world is in a continuous state of becoming—social arrangements which seem fixed and permanent are temporary, arbitrary patterns and any observed social pattern are regarded as one among many possibilities. Theoretical attention is focused upon the transformation through which one set of arrangements gives way to another. (Benson, 1977, p. 3)

Benson's framework is particularly suited to analyse the persistence of paradox given its emphasis on the roles of conflict *and* continuity in the construction and revision of social systems, echoing the synergy/tradeoff tension.

By considering the principles enunciated by Benson (1977), persistence can be explained as follows: as agents reconstruct their social totalities, they open contradictions that cause rearrangements, inviting agents to engage with further rearrangements as they revise their previous forms of involvement with the system. They do so in an ongoing fashion in a process bounded by diverse interests and shaped by agentic positions within power networks. Because any rearrangement produces a reactive re-rearrangement, the process propels towards infinity. As Zeno the Greek warned us, Achilles would never catch up with the tortoise because every movement that Achilles made would be accompanied by a concomitant movement by the tortoise, no matter how long the race lasted (Sainsbury, 2009, p. 1).

The implications of a Bensonian lens to the study of paradox are profound. First, because they exist in totalities, paradoxes should be studied in relation to other paradoxes. Paradoxes persist because they interact with other paradoxes, with one intervention leading to the need to rearrange contiguous parts of a system that respond to intervention in necessarily unpredictable manners, given the system's complexity (Jarzabkowski et al., 2013). Second, paradoxes, or the social construction of them, may change over time: a paradox may mutate to become something different: what starts as a vision of transcendence (Abdallah et al., 2011) may subsequently be reinterpreted as the trigger of a vicious circle (Masuch, 1985; Tsoukas & Cunha, 2017); an orientation favouring relentless and deep exploitation may end up revealing exploratory potentialities, if only because exploitation is more than mere repetition (Piao & Zajac, 2016). Social systems are rich in surprise and unexpectedness (Merton, 1936; Cunha et al., 2012). Longitudinal studies are therefore critical in pursuing a research agenda on paradox as a persistent process, as is evident in the empirical work of Jarzabkowski and her colleagues (2013). Third, paradoxes occur in the context of established social forms and unstable power circuits (Clegg, 2014). The consideration of power is fundamental to understanding the emergence of contradictions as well as their continuity and metamorphosis. Contradictions partly stem from divergent interests, the tension between centre and periphery, what is and what can be. Finally, the social form matters: the type of structure influences the emergence of certain paradoxes instead of others. Organic and mechanistic structures can be predicted to facilitate different sorts of contradictions, in terms of how they stimulate learning by managing the tension between exploration and exploitation (Kessler et al., 2016). Finally, paradoxes have history: every paradox grows over the institutional remains of past paradoxes (Lanzara, 1998), which means that interventions occur not over blank organizational pages but over layers of history that potentially collide with newly designed interventions, thus opening up cleavages and contradictions between the past and the present. As Stoltzfus et al. (2011, p. 362) summarized, 'strategies for coping with paradox often become paradoxical themselves'. Paradoxes are persistent and replenished.

2.5 Implications

Taking paradox as a duality of synergy and tradeoff means that, from a process perspective, focus on resolution should be replaced by an appreciation of persistence. Paradox as persistence has an element of infinity. It has no beginning and no ending, just ongoingness, the endless interplay of opposites: as in a circle, beginnings and endings are common, following the enunciation of Heraclitus (Hughes & Brecht, 1975). Paradoxes solved cease to be paradoxes, as paradoxes lean towards the endless. The managerial zeal to solve paradox thus represents the dissolution of paradox. What renders paradox critical for theory and application is its imperviousness to resolution, its stubborn persistence, reflected, as previously noted in Hofstadter's (1979, pp. 22–3) notion of the strange loop:

the drive to eliminate paradoxes at any cost, especially when it requires the creation of highly artificial formalisms, puts too much stress on bland consistency, and too little on the quirky and bizarre, which makes life and mathematics interesting. It is of course important to try to maintain consistency, but when this effort forces you into a stupendously ugly theory, you know something is wrong.

A theory of paradox without conflict, contradiction, irony, or surprise lacks aesthetic appeal; it is an ugly theory of organizational paradox. The implications of such an ontological stance for management are relevant, as we now discuss.

2.5.1 Implications for Theory and Research

A process framework represents paradoxes as ongoing, time-sensitive, socially constructed, emergent, situated. Instead of seeking to understand how to solve them as episodic eruptions of chaos, process researchers should instead treat paradoxes as conceptual windows over infinity, revelations of process, and continuity. A process research agenda on paradox may ask questions such as: How does persistence shape and change paradoxes? Do 'solved' paradoxes re-emerge anew? Are vicious circles and virtuous circles process-analogues (Nelson, 2014) or are they qualitatively distinct? Exploring the dynamics of persistence with a consideration of time, feedback, looping, and power dynamics can greatly benefit the understanding of paradox as process.

2.5.2 Implications for Practice

Sustaining paradoxical tensions in balance over time can be a daunting task. Tradeoffs, contradictions, and paradoxes can be regenerative but they are difficult to handle and to balance in continuity. Managers may have difficulty in sustaining oppositions, tensions, and contradictory narratives, because stakeholders can express a preference for clarity and unambiguity (Garg & Eisenhardt, 2017). Expectations of clarity and decisiveness may stimulate avoiding the ambiguities of paradoxical thinking. Conveying clear narratives may be a better communication strategy than storytelling around ambiguity and contradiction. Complex thinking may constitute a valuable asset (Tsoukas & Hatch, 2001) but it is also a difficult proposition when stakeholders strive for decisiveness and clarity of focus. Embracing ambiguity, holding tensions in play, creating zones of thirdness or in-betweenness to sustain tensions, may provide concrete ways in which to respond to the push for clarity and decisiveness.

While maintaining and preserving contradictions without resolution can be rewarding (Dodd & Favaro, 2006; Takeuchi et al., 2008), it is also effortful.

As a routine becomes institutionalized as successful, more effort will possibly be invested in its perfecting. Routines that started out containing paradoxical qualities, as vehicles of both stability and change (e.g. Feldman & Orlikowski, 2011; Feldman & Pentland, 2003) may progressively become simpler, more 'narrowly focused versions of their former selves, converting a formula of success into a path toward failure' (Miller, 1993, p. 116). Finally, paradoxes interact with paradoxes and 'tensions often masquerade as one another' (Dodd & Favaro, 2006, p. 64). From a process perspective, today's solutions can become tomorrow's problems and yesterday's problems may constitute the building blocks of tomorrow's solutions (Greiner, 1972). Managing paradox may thus entail dealing with masquerades rather than with resolutions. Managing paradox constitutes a challenge that requires courage, resilience, and resistance to frustration, as well as a problematization of the meaning of resolution. When it involves paradox, resolution is and can only ever be temporary. Awareness of persistence can thus constitute a managerial imperative. Instead of forcing synergies, organizations can approach paradoxes as an organizational facet to be treated as process rather than event: persistent, irremovable, potentially wicked. For practice, this might imply recourse to devil's advocacy, cultivating discomfort with unanimity and paying attention to signals of vicious circles (e.g. solutions that become problems or discourses of change that aggravate rigidity; see Cunha & Tsoukas, 2015). Managerially speaking persistence constitutes an invitation to live with paradox rather than representing it as a puzzle waiting for a solution.

2.6 Conclusion

Paradox and contradiction are deemed to be part of the new normal (Eisenhardt, 2000) rather than organizational aberrations. They persist because they cannot be resolved. For managers, alas, one of the crucial and intriguing features of paradox is their dynamic persistence (Keller & Lewis, 2016; Smith & Lewis, 2011). Thus far persistence has been affirmed more than theorized. We discussed paradox persistence and elaborated how persistence should constitute an explicit object of study on its own. We did so from a yin-yang theory of organization. It is because 'contradictoriness *is* one of the essential characteristic properties of man, groups, organizations, and institutions' (Mitroff, 1983, p. 393, emphasis in original) that contradictions are not logical fallacies to be removed but entrenched manifestations of the deep order of organizing. As Luo and Zheng explained, 'since contradiction or inconsistency always exist in reality, it is still possible that the opposites-in-unity may produce more endogenous trade-off than synergy' (2016, p. 390). Paradox is thus deeply ingrained in social totalities (Michel, 2014).

Where agents do not take structures for granted, they continuously revise them, experimenting at the interface of actuality and potentiality, causing paradoxes to emerge as totalities are acted upon. To appreciate paradox is to assume that tradeoffs can become synergies and that synergies can untap tradeoffs, only before they rotate their order, in a circular movement with no end in sight. The appreciation of paradox entails an acquired taste for infinity; hence, paradoxically, it is in part the persistence of paradoxes that, as Sainsbury (2009) said, makes them 'fun'.

Acknowledgements

We are grateful to our editor Moshe Farjoun, and to Horia Moasa, Linda Putnam, Luca Giustiniano, and Patrícia Pedrosa for their feedback to earlier versions. Remaining errors or misinterpretations are our sole responsibility. Miguel Pina e Cunha received support from National Funds through the Fundação para a Ciência e Tecnologia under the project Ref. UID/ECO/00124/2013 and by POR Lisboa under the project LISBOA-01-0145-FEDER-007722.

References

Abdallah, C., Denis, J.L., & Langley, A. 2011. Having your cake and eating it too: Discourses of transcendence and their role in organizational change dynamics. *Journal of Organizational Change Management*, 24(3): 333–48.

Ashforth, B.E. & Reingen, P.H. 2014. Functions of dysfunction: Managing the dynamics of an organizational duality in a natural food cooperative. *Administrative Science Quarterly*, 59(3): 474–516.

Azevedo, A. & Gitahy, L. 2010. The cooperative movement, self-management, and competitiveness: The case of Mondragón Corporacíon Cooperativa. *WorkingUSA: The Journal of Labor and Society*, 13: 5–29.

Barbalet, J. 2014. Laozi's Daodejing (6th century BC). In J. Helin, T. Hernes, & R. Holt (eds), *The Oxford Handbook of Process Philosophy and Organization Studies* (pp. 17–31). Oxford: Oxford University Press.

Benson, J.K. 1977. Organizations: A dialectical view. *Administrative Science Quarterly*, 22: 1–21.

Bobko, P. 1985. Removing assumptions of bipolarity: Towards variation and circularity. *Academy of Management Review*, 10: 99–108.

Cameron, K.S. & Quinn, R.E. 1988. Organizational paradox and transformation. In R.E. Quinn & K.S. Cameron (eds), *Paradox and Transformation* (pp. 1–18). Cambridge, MA: Ballinger.

Chaddad, F. 2012. Advancing the theory of the cooperative organization: The cooperative as a true hybrid. *Annals of Public and Cooperative Economics*, 83(4): 445–61.

Chen, M.J. 2002. Transcending paradox: The Chinese 'middle way' perspective. *Asia Pacific Journal of Management*, 19: 179–99.

Chia, R. 2014. In praise of silent transformation: Allowing change through 'letting happen'. *Journal of Change Management*, 14(1): 8–27.

Clegg, S.R. 2014. Circuits of power/knowledge. *Journal of Political Power*, 7(3): 383–92.

Clegg, S. & Cunha, M.P. 2017. Organizational dialectics. In M.W. Lewis, W.K. Smith, P. Jarzabkowski, & A. Langley (eds), *The Oxford Handbook of Organizational Paradox: Approaches to Plurality, Tensions, and Contradictions*. New York: Oxford University Press.

Clegg, S., Cunha, J.V., & Cunha, M.P. 2002. Management paradoxes: A relational view. *Human Relations*, 55(5): 483–503.

Collins, J.C. & Porras, J.I. 1994. *Built to Last: Successful Habits of Visionary Companies*. New York: Random House.

Cunha, M.P. & Tsoukas, H. 2015. Reforming the State: Understanding the vicious circles of reform. *European Management Journal*, 33(4): 225–9.

Cunha, M.P., Clegg, S.R., & Rego, A. 2012. Surprising organization. In T. Pitsis, A. Simpson, & E. Dehlin (eds), *Handbook of Organizational and Managerial Innovation* (pp. 295–316). Cheltenham: Edward Elgar.

Cunha, M.P., Fortes, A., Gomes, E., Rego, A., & Rodrigues, F. Forthcoming. Ambidextrous leadership, paradox and contingency: Evidence from Angola. *International Journal of Human Resource Management*.

Dodd, D. & Favaro, K. 2006. Managing the right tension. *Harvard Business Review*, 84(12): 62–74.

Eisenhardt, K.M. 2000. Paradox, spirals, ambivalence: The new language of change and pluralism. *Academy of Management Review*, 25: 703–5.

Farjoun, M. 2010. Beyond dualism: Stability and change as duality. *Academy of Management Review*, 35: 202–25.

Fayol, H. 1930. *Industrial and General Administration*, translated by J.A. Coubrough. London: Sir Isaac Pitman & Sons.

Feldman, M.S. & Orlikowski, W.J. 2011. Theorizing practice and practicing theory. *Organization Science*, 22(5): 1240–53.

Feldman, M.S. & Pentland, B.T. 2003. Reconceptualizing organizational routines as a source of flexibility and change. *Administrative Science Quarterly*, 48(1): 94–118.

Fredberg, T. 2014. If I say it's complex, it bloody well will be: CEO strategies for managing paradox. *Journal of Applied Behavioral Science*, 50(2): 171–88.

Garg, S. & Eisenhardt, K.M. 2017. Unpacking the CEO–board relationship: How strategy-making happens in entrepreneurial firms. *Academy of Management Journal*, 60(5), 1828–58.

Greiner, L.E. 1972. Evolution and revolution as organizations grow. *Harvard Business Review*, 50(4): 37–46.

Hargrave, T.J. & Van de Ven, A.H. 2017. Integrating dialectical and paradox perspectives on managing contradictions in organizations. *Organization Studies*, 38(2–4): 319–39.

Hofstadter, D.R. 1979. *Godel, Escher, Bach: An Eternal Golden Braid*. New York: Vintage Books.

Hofstadter, D.R. 2007. *I Am a Strange Loop*. New York: Basic Books.

Hughes, H.P. & Brecht, G. 1975. *Vicious Circles and Infinity: An Anthology of Paradoxes*. New York: Penguin.

Hussenot, A. & Missonier, S. 2016. Encompassing stability and novelty in organization studies: An events-based approach. *Organization Studies*, 37: 523–46.

Jarzabkowski, P., Lê, J.K., & Van de Ven, A.H. 2013. Responding to competing strategic demands: How organizing, belonging, and performing paradoxes coevolve. *Strategic Organization*, 11(3): 245–80.

Kassinis, G. & Panayiotou, A. 2016. The helix of change: A visual metaphor. *European Management Review*, 14(2):143–63.

Keller, J. & Lewis, M. 2016. Moving towards a geocentric, polycultural theory of organizational paradox. *Cross Cultural and Strategic Management*, 23(4).

Kessler, S.R., Nixon, A.E., & Nord, W.R. 2016. Examining organic and mechanistic structures: Do we know as much as we thought? *International Journal of Management Reviews*. DOI: 10.1111/ijmr.12109.

Lanzara, G.F. 1998. Self-destructive processes in institution building and some modest countervailing mechanisms. *European Journal of Political Research*, 33: 1–39.

Lewis, M.W. 2000. Exploring paradox: Toward a more comprehensive guide. *Academy of Management Review*, 25(4): 760–76.

Lewis, M.W. & Smith, W.K. 2014. Paradox as a metatheoretical perspective: Sharpening the focus and widening the scope. *Journal of Applied Behavioral Science*, 50(2): 127–49.

Li, P.P. 2012. Toward an integrative framework of indigenous research: The geocentric implications of Yin-Yang balance. *Asia Pacific Journal of Management*, 29: 849–72.

Li, P.P. 2016. Global implications of the indigenous epistemological system from the East: How to apply yin-yang balancing to paradox management. *Cross Cultural and Strategic Management*, 23(1): 42–77.

Luo, Y. & Zheng, Q. 2016. Competing in complex cross-cultural world: Philosophical insights from Yin-Yang. *Cross Cultural and Strategic Management*, 23(2): 386–92.

March, J.G. 2006. Rationality, foolishness, and adaptive intelligence. *Strategic Management Journal*, 27(3): 201–14.

Masuch, M. 1985. Vicious circles in organizations. *Administrative Science Quarterly*, 30(1): 14–33.

McCabe, D. 2016. 'Curiouser and curiouser!': Organizations as Wonderland—a metaphorical alternative to the rational model. *Human Relations*, 69(4): 945–73.

Merton, R.K. 1936. The unanticipated consequences of purposive social action. *American Sociological Review*, 1: 894–904.

Michel, A. 2014. The mutual constitution of persons and organizations: An ontological perspective on organizational change. *Organization Science*, 25(4): 1082–110.

Michelsen, J. 1994. The rationales of cooperative organizations: Some suggestions from Scandinavia. *Annals of Public and Cooperative Economics*, 65(1): 13–34.

Miller, D. 1993. The architecture of simplicity. *Academy of Management Review*, 18: 116–38.

Mitroff, I.I. 1983. Archetypal social systems analysis: On the deeper structure of human systems. *Academy of Management Review*, 8: 387–97.

Morgan, G. 1986. *Images of Organization*. Newbury Park, CA: Sage.

Nelson, E.S. 2014. Technology and the way: Buber, Heidegger, and Lao-Zhuang 'Daoism'. *Journal of Chinese Philosophy*, 41(3–4): 307–27.

Piao, M. & Zajac, E.J. 2016. How exploitation impedes and impels exploration: Theory and evidence. *Strategic Management Journal*, 37(7): 1431–47.

Poole, M.S. & Van de Ven, A.H. 1989. Using paradox to build management and organization theories. *Academy of Management Review*, 14: 562–78.

Porter, M.E. 1985. *Competitive Advantage*. New York: Free Press.

Price Waterhouse Change Integration Team. 1996. *The Paradox Principles: How High-Performance Companies Manage Chaos, Complexity, and Contradiction to Achieve Superior Results*. Chicago, IL: Irwin.

Putnam, L.L. 2013. Primary and secondary contradictions: A literature review and future directions. *Management Communication Quarterly*, 27(4): 623–30.

Putnam, L.L., Fairhurst, G.T., & Banghart, S. 2016. Contradictions, dialectics, and paradoxes in organizations: A constitutive approach. *Academy of Management Annals*, 10(1): 65–171.

Reed, M. 1991. Organizations and rationality: The odd couple. *Journal of Management Studies*, 28(5): 559–67.

Sainsbury, R.M. 2009. *Paradoxes*. Cambridge: Cambridge University Press.

Schad, J., Lewis, M.W., Raisch, S., & Smith, W.K. 2016. Paradox research in management science: Looking back to move forward. *Academy of Management Annals*, 10(1): 5–64.

Seo, M., Putnam, L.L., & Bartunek, J.M. 2002. Dualities and tensions of planned organizational change. In M.S. Poole & A.H. Van de Ven (eds), *Handbook of Organizational Change and Innovation* (pp. 73–106). New York: Oxford University Press.

Smith, W.K. & Lewis, M.W. 2011. Toward a theory of paradox: A dynamic equilibrium model of organizing. *Academy of Management Review*, 36: 381–403.

Smith, W.K., Lewis, M., & Tushman, M. 2016. 'Both/and' leadership. *Harvard Business Review*, 94(5): 63–70.

Stoltzfus, K., Stohl, C., & Seibold, D.R. 2011. Managing organizational change: Paradoxical problems, solutions and consequences. *Journal of Organizational Change Management*, 24(3): 349–67.

Sundaramurthy, C. & Lewis, M. 2003. Control and collaboration: Paradoxes of governance. *Academy of Management Review*, 28(3): 397–415.

Takeuchi, H., Osono, E., & Shimizu, N. 2008. The contradictions that drive Toyota's success. *Harvard Business Review*, June: 96–104.

Taylor, F.W. 1911. *The Principles of Scientific Management*. New York: Harper & Brothers.

Tse, T. 2013. Paradox resolution: A means to achieve strategic innovation. *European Management Journal*, 31(6): 682–96.

Tsoukas, H. 2016. Don't simplify, complexify: From disjunctive to conjunctive theorizing in organization and management studies. *Journal of Management Studies*. DOI: 10.1111/joms.12219.

Tsoukas, H. & Cunha, M.P. 2017. On organizational circularity: Vicious and virtuous circles in organizing. In M.W. Lewis, W.K. Smith, P. Jarzabkowski, & A. Langley (eds), *The Oxford Handbook of Organizational Paradox: Approaches to Plurality, Tensions, and Contradictions*. New York: Oxford University Press.

Tsoukas, H. & Hatch, M.J. 2001. Complex thinking, complex practice: The case for a narrative approach to organizational complexity. *Human Relations*, 54(8): 979–1013.

Van de Ven, A. & Poole, M.S. 1988. Paradoxical requirements for a theory of change. In K. Cameron & R.E. Quinn (eds), *Paradox and Transformation* (pp. 19–63). Cambridge, MA: Ballinger.

Vince, R. & Broussine, M. 1996. Paradox, defense and attachment: Accessing and working with emotions and relations underlying organizational change. *Organization Studies*, 17(1): 1–21.

Weick, K.E. 1992. Agenda setting in organizational behavior. *Journal of Management Inquiry*, 1(3): 171–82.

Whyte, W.F. 1995. Learning from the Mondragón cooperative experience. *Studies in Comparative International Development*, 30(2): 58–67.

Whyte, W.F. 1999. The Mondragón cooperatives in 1976 and 1998. *Industrial and Labor Relations Review*, 52(3): 478–81.

3

Creating Production Values in a Dramatic Television Series

Bridging Creative and Financial Imperatives through the Dialectics of Calculative Practice

Esther R. Maier

> Eighty percent of the choices you make are about money. Whether it's about can we afford to hire a particular actress or actor, or can we afford to do this extra shot that's going to put the crew into overtime? If we don't get through this scene by lunch, will we take a meal penalty which will accrue a particular cost? No matter what show I've ever worked on the primary creative discussion we have is about money.
>
> (Showrunner, Series X)

Once overlooked by management scholars as anomalies due to their unique organizing patterns and practices, in recent years the cultural industries have proven to be fertile ground for explorations of the tensions and contradictions of organizational life. Products in this sector are built around an artistic core, with their significance determined by the consumer's coding and decoding of value (Townley et al., 2009). This translates into a high degree of demand uncertainty given the non-utilitarian and experiential nature of these products (Caves, 2000). With the transition to a 'post-industrial' economy, many firms far removed from the cultural industries now focus on the symbolic dimensions to differentiate their products from the competition (DeFillippi et al., 2007). For instance, Eisenman (2013) highlights how the design attributes of products ranging from tea kettles and mobile phones to automobiles convey aesthetic and symbolic information that goes beyond their basic utility. These attributes trigger an emotional response and give rise to second-order meanings that consumers attach to these products. Although these second-order meanings can only be suggested by product designers, they enhance the adoption rates of new products and extend the life of existing ones when shared by consumers. Consequently, the cultural industries are often viewed as templates for organizations struggling to cope with fragmented markets and volatile consumer tastes (Lampel et al., 2000; Lash & Urry, 1994). Firms within this sector must harness knowledge and creativity in the production process in order to enhance the value of their products. This creates a challenge as creative labour is typically characterized as idiosyncratic and difficult to manage (Lampel et al., 2000).

Indeed, much of the literature on the cultural industries is focused on the core tensions between the artists who need creative freedom and the managers that require stability in order to predict and control (DiMaggio, 1977). However, more recent work challenges this stylized view by providing a more nuanced view of the complexities inherent in this sector. For instance, researchers focused on the processes of valuation highlight the reliance on the judgement devices used to signal the quality of the product for consumers (e.g. Hsu et al., 2012; Karpik, 2010). These studies provide considerable insight into the evaluative practices of the multiple actors—ranging from critics to advertisers—that collectively signal product quality to the market, but simplify the sphere of production out of necessity (e.g. Karpik, 2010). Consequently, the internal valuations used in the making of these goods is largely absent in these accounts. This leaves open many questions surrounding the role of calculative practices—both quantitative and qualitative—in the valuation processes of the individuals who actually produce these goods (for important exceptions see Girard & Stark, 2003 and Jeacle & Carter, 2012).

My research interest is in understanding the role of calculation and judgement in the production of one particular cultural good: a dramatic television series. More specifically, my focus is on the creation of *production values* that inhere in the quality of the final product. Although it has received little attention in the management literature on the cultural industries, the concept of production values is not new. It is a term used by industry professionals in their internal assessments of product quality (Mulgan, 1990). The significance of production values will be explained more fully below, but the concept brings together both qualitative and quantitative assessments of quality. This provides a focal point for exploring the dialectical nature of the relations between calculation and judgement in calculative practice. In illuminating these relations, I draw on the notion of dialectic in a limited way, primarily as a synonym for the 'dynamic interplay' between calculation and judgement. This allows us to move beyond the duelling dualisms that are central in much of the literature on the cultural industries to see how the final product emerges through the integration of the creative and financial imperatives. The tensions and conflicts that emerge through this process are not only generative, but necessary for something novel to emerge (Harvey, 2014).

3.1 'Balancing Acts' in the Production of Cultural Goods

Paradox and tensions are recurring themes in the organizational literature on the cultural industries. Whether focused on the production of music, theatre, film and television, or other cultural goods, firms in this sector must navigate the twin poles of art and commerce in order to be successful (Townley et al., 2009). Not only do these firms need to balance the tradeoffs between artistic excellence and financial viability, they also need to find the right blend of the novel and the familiar in the products they create (Jones et al., 2016; DeFillippi et al., 2007; Lampel et al., 2000). Production of these 'experience' goods[1] typically takes place in project-based or temporary organizations that bring together a diverse team of individuals with expertise in specific disciplines (Bechky, 2006). In much of the extant literature, the battle lines on these projects are typically drawn between the individuals that provide artistic labour (i.e. creatives) and those involved in the business functions (i.e. suits or 'humdrum' others) who, in our stylized view, are only concerned with making money (DiMaggio, 1977; Caves, 2000).

However, this formulation of paradox in the cultural industries has increasingly come under criticism for oversimplifying how creative processes unfold, particularly in large-scale, collective undertakings such as film and television production. In these complex projects the emergent nature of the design process requires creativity from conception through to completion (Maier & Branzei, 2014). Since the design process continues through production, it is distributed across many actors and the final product emerges through a self-organized, engineered process that is not directed from above (Girard & Stark, 2003). Further, the mid-level management roles on these projects are frequently inhabited by artists, making it difficult to categorize them as either a creative or a manager. Thus, approaches that draw boundaries along occupational lines to portray creativity and management as antithetical not only reinforce outmoded stereotypes of both artists and managers; they also eclipse other important tensions in the production of these goods (Townley & Beech, 2010).

These approaches are usually based on the notion that artistic freedom requires the absence of any form of constraint. However, artistic creativity is not an 'anything goes' phenomenon but a practice that requires mastery of a specific discipline as well as the management of the self, others, and objects (Townley & Beech, 2010). In collaborative undertakings that rely on creative contributions from multiple artistic disciplines (e.g. film and television), individuals also bring their own personal tastes and ideas regarding the quality or configuration of the product (Caves, 2000). However, their individual inputs

---

[1] These are products whose qualities cannot be accurately assessed by buyers until they are consumed (Caves, 2000).

must also be conjunctive in order for the product to be successful (Adler & Chen, 2011). This requires individual contributors to negotiate a series of settlements among multiple and often conflicting concepts of what is important in the final product (Stark, 2009). Integrating these divergent views results in a 'creative synthesis' that provides a map used by project members to guide the development of the final product (Harvey, 2014). In the transformation from conception to completion, project members also engage in a variety of evaluative practices to assess the state of the work in process along the way. These practices incorporate a broad range of material, stylistic, aesthetic, situational, and financial factors that guide and constrain their actions (Moeran & Pedersen, 2015).

In film and television, industry professionals use the term *production values* to refer to their own assessments of the quality of a product. It is a concept that incorporates aesthetic judgement of their inputs based on a set of professional criteria along with the economic constraints (i.e. budget) of the project. The professional standards of quality include things such as the technical issues of lighting and cinematographic style, the elements that appear within the frame (e.g. sets, props, and costumes), the quality of writing, and the effectiveness of how ideas are conveyed through the unfolding narrative (Mulgan, 1990). Although there is a correlation between the size of the project budget and production values, a large budget is no guarantee that high production values will be achieved (cf. Gil & Spiller, 2007). Rather, high production values emerge through a series of individual and collective (aesthetic) choices over the course of the project.

In their aim to make the best programme possible given the circumstances of production (e.g. the size of the project budget), myriad choices are made by the project team or 'crew' along the way (Nelson, 1997). These aesthetic choices rely on value assumptions, albeit often tacit ones. They are also connected to the monetary and temporal resources available to realize their ideas. In this way, the creation of production values relies on both (aesthetic) judgement and different forms of calculation and highlights the complex relations between them. Yet calculation and judgement, much like the creatives and the suites, have typically been viewed in opposition to each other. However, an alternative perspective inspired by science and technology studies is challenging this conception.

3.2 Calculation and Judgement in Valuation Processes

The separation between calculation and judgement has long served as the disciplinary divide between economics, the science of calculation, and sociology, which is often viewed as a qualitative discipline (Karpik, 2010;

Stark, 2009). The need to move beyond this binary opposition is a central theme in recent studies of markets, be they financial markets (Buenza & Stark, 2004), supermarkets (Cochoy, 2008), or the markets for singularities (Karpik, 2010). For instance, Callon and Muniesa (2005, p. 1231) highlight how both calculation and judgement '[s]tart by establishing distinctions between things or states of the world and proceeds by imagining and estimating courses of actions associated with those things or those states as well as their consequences'. By illustrating how both calculation and judgement require individuals to array and manipulate elements within a single spatial-temporal frame to produce an outcome or reach a conclusion, Callon and Muniesa (2005) aim to break down the opposition between the qualitative and the quantitative. Their broadened conception of calculative practice comprises both qualitative and quantitative elements that are placed within a frame for evaluation. The frame or calculative space can take many forms (e.g. a shopping cart, spreadsheet, factory floor, or court of law) and the particularities of different calculative spaces orient the nature of the calculative practice. Whether the 'calculations' required are qualitative or quantitative depends on the nature of the evaluations required to make a decision. Cochoy (2008) coined the neologism *qualculation* to refer to the form of evaluation made when numerical calculation is not possible. Since both judgement and calculation work by setting boundaries around 'what counts' or what is important, it is the setting of limits that makes qualculation possible (Moser & Law, 2006).

This conception of calculative practice has informed the focus on the processes and practices of valuation in recent studies of social and economic life. In these accounts, valuation is (re)conceptualized as a situated activity that aims to establish 'value' for a particular actor and purpose (Muniesa, 2011). This approach resonates with a pragmatist notion of valuation that emphasizes the processes and practices of valuation rather than the concept of value as a thing in itself (Dewey, 1923). By replacing the notion of value with the action of valuation, another essentializing dualism between value and values is dissolved (Stark, 2009). Instead of being embraced as a purely quantitative exercise, the process of valuation is viewed as a practical action that is socially and materially distributed across a range of actors and devices (Muniesa, 2011; Stark, 2009).

This perspective has not only informed studies of financial markets, it has also been used to explore markets for singularities (e.g. fine wines, music, films, and personalized professional services) where quality is more influential than price in the purchase decision. Singular goods are also characterized by the use of multiple criteria for assessments of value (Karpik, 2010). Given the uncertainty of demand surrounding singular goods, many of these authors focus on the valuation schemes (e.g. judgement devices and quality ratings assigned by critics). For instance, in the market for wines consumers rely on reviews from critics for assessments of product quality (Hsu et al., 2012) and the algorithms of TripAdvisor provide an 'objective' ranking of hotel accommodations based on the experiences of other travellers (Jeacle & Carter, 2011; Orlikowski & Scott, 2015).

These studies highlight the distributed nature of calculative agencies across market actors and devices but these concepts have also been applied, albeit much less frequently, to the study of calculative practices within organizations. For instance, in his analysis of emergent design processes, Stark (2009) notes that the debates and compromises that shape the final product are informed by the different values and perspectives of each of the different disciplines that contribute to the project. In a similar vein, Jeacle and Carter (2012) use the context of a high street fashion retailer to show how the calculative practices of the trinity of designer, buyer, and merchandiser integrate cost management without sacrificing garment design or quality. Although the cost calculations play an important role, they do not take priority over other concerns but are integrated into the complex calculus that is part of the design process.

While these findings are suggestive of the importance of both calculation and judgement in the creation of singular goods, they leave open the question of how these two come together in the daily activities of the individuals who make them. In other words, how do the calculative practices of the individuals involved in the production of singular goods balance calculation and judgement in their assessments of the product they are creating? With very few empirical accounts of how creative work is managed, we have limited insight into how these evaluative and calculative practices guide the choices made by different participants as they go about designing and producing the product.

3.3 Research Setting and Methods

The insights in the paper were generated through an in-depth study of a dramatic television series produced in Toronto, Canada. *Series X*[2] was in its sixth season of production at the time of the study. The series is produced by Series Corp., an independent production company, as qualified Canadian content, which means the show is eligible for a combination of grants and labour-based tax credits as part of its financing. This is a typical financing model in Canada, where content is produced using a hybrid model of public and private sources. Financial incentives cover a portion of the total cost of the product, with the balance raised through sales in the international

---

[2] The name of the series has been changed to preserve the confidentiality granted as a condition of access.

markets once production is complete. With budgets that are typically two thirds of their American counterparts, production crews strive to deliver the same level of production values despite their limited budgets.

Data for the study were collected from multiple sources. Access was granted to observe the crew as their work unfolded over the eighty-two-day schedule of principal photography. During this time, I witnessed thirty-two hours of scheduled planning meetings and observed the shooting crew both in studio and on location. My presence on set also allowed me to observe numerous informal meetings among the crew and the writers in the story department by virtue of being in the right place at the right time. These observations were augmented with data from forty-six semi-structured interviews conducted with key crew members (department heads and assistant department heads) conducted over the course of the study.

Data analysis was inductive and followed a grounded theory approach (Glaser & Strauss, 1967; Dougherty, 2002; Strauss & Corbin, 1990). The process began with careful reading and open coding of interview and observational data as well as other documents collected during the course of the study. This process was iterative and inductive, focusing on the calculative practices and devices used by the crew as well as their formal and informal conversations about production values. Given my prior career in the industry, I anticipated that discussions about costs would be central in creative conversations and would inform the choices made on how to realize the vision the writers set out in the scripts. However, the malleability of the scripts during prep and the willingness of the writers to make changes to resolve the challenges faced by the rest of the crew came as a surprise.

The opening quote in the introduction reveals two distinct moments or calculative spaces generated through the analysis. The first occurs during the planning process or 'prep' that happens before scripts move into production. It is during this process that decisions are made regarding whether 'we can afford to hire a particular actress or actor' and other elements (e.g. locations or elaborate sets) required in order to realize the writers' vision. This calculative space is characterized by the estimates each department head prepares during prep to forecast the costs for each scene. The estimates are shaped by the myriad deliberations that transpire during prep over how best to address the needs of the script within the parameters of the budget and schedule. The second distinct moment happens when the scripts in each shooting block move into production or what the crew refers to as the 'floor'. This is where the shooting crew (see Table 3.1) executes the plans to realize the creative vision set out in each script that was developed in prep. Since the shooting crew is paid overtime when their standard eleven-hour days are exceeded (but the prep crew is not), they are challenged to get through all of the scenes in the schedule on a given day without incurring overtime. The salience of the clock

Table 3.1. Crew structure on *Series X*

Group	Role	Responsibility
Story	Writers	Scriptwriting
Directors	Director	Approach to filming the script(s)
Planning	Showrunner	Overall creative
	Line producer	Overall logistics (including budgeting)
	Production designer	Set design
	Production manager	Crew logistics (including budget support)
	Production accountant	Cost reporting and bookkeeping
	1st AD	Design and executing the shooting schedule(s)
Prep crew	Art director	Set construction
	Costume designer	Wardrobe for cast and background performers
	Locations manager	Find workable locations for each script
	Props master	Prop design and construction
	Set decorator	Furnishing sets
Shooting crew	Director of photography	Cinematography
	Continuity	Scene and dialogue continuity while filming
	Gaffer	Electrics and lighting
	Key grip	Camera rigging (e.g. cranes, dolly tracks)
	Hair and makeup	Prepare performers for camera
	Transportation	Service the transportation needs of cast and crew

is illustrated in the questions, 'Can we afford to do this extra shot?' and 'If we don't get through this scene by lunch, will we take a meal penalty?' These calculations are not written down and despite being rooted in economic concerns, they are not necessarily mathematical in nature. The presence of these two distinct calculative spaces is significant as it highlights how the spatial-temporal frames required shift and unfold over the transformation from the script to the screen. Further, the coexistence of these two spaces shows how crew members can inhabit multiple calculative spaces at the same time. The implications of the two calculative spaces on the relations between calculation and judgement are presented in Section 3.4.

3.4 Findings: Overview of Production Structure

Before diving into the main findings, it is important to provide an overview of some of the key organizing practices of a dramatic series production. First, television is a writer's medium in contrast to film, which is a director's medium. On *Series X*, a different director is used in each of the shooting blocks, which is common in the industry. Leadership of the project is shared by the line producer and the showrunner, an individual who has risen through the ranks of the writers. As detailed in Table 3.1, these two individuals are supported by a crew comprising a number of departments with each representing a specific artistic or technical discipline or support function. The managers of each department, known as department heads, have considerable discretion and autonomy in designing the inputs required and coordinating the tasks of their respective teams. When they commit to work on the series, the department heads agree to deliver their portion of the project within the budget allocated to their respective areas. Since the scripts are not written in advance of production, they make this commitment without knowing the specifics of what will be required.

To accommodate the thirteen scripts that constitute the season, the eighty-two-day schedule of principal photography is divided into eight shooting blocks. Each block comprises either one or two scripts for production and the length varies accordingly (e.g. six and a half days of principal photography for one script or thirteen days for two). An equal amount of time is devoted to 'prep' (i.e. planning) before the scripts move into production. While the scripts go through these two processes sequentially, for the crew they happen in tandem: as the script(s) in one shooting block is in prep, the script(s) in another shooting block is in production. The time spent in planning is essential as each script requires finding new locations, casting new performers, and designing new sets and costumes:

> We're going to be making the same product every week. But, the variables that go into the creation of . . . to make each product an individual unit could be anywhere from we need 50 horses and a skyscraper in this episode, [in] the next episode we just need a boat, and the next episode, we just need a jail cell and two guys [guest performers]. But, that can also bite you in the ass because then you have to get two guys that are good enough to carry it, and all of a sudden they cost three or four times as much as you thought they were going to be. Then, the lighting effects and the staging to make those two guys interesting may end up costing more than renting 50 horses. (Showrunner)

Not only are the 'variables' that go into the creation of each episode different, but the costs of creating the elements are unknown until each department head has the opportunity to analyse the scripts. The writers may draft the initial stories, but they rely on the expertise of the director and the different department heads to transform the text on the page for the screen. The design of the final product is a collective undertaking that begins with the cycle of scheduled planning meetings that the crew enacts during prep for each shooting block (see Table 3.2). As these meetings unfold a creative synthesis emerges that integrates different interpretations of the script. This synthesis both arises from and informs the estimates of costs that are prepared during prep. During production, this synthesis is subject to revision as the crew grapples with the tensions of how to realize the vision given the pressures of time.

Table 3.2. Scheduled planning meetings

Meeting*	Attendees**
Concept meeting	All
Art department	Art director, production designer, writer
Costumes department	Costume director, writer
Background	Costume director, casting director
Props	Props master, writer
Technical survey (tour of locations for shooting block)	All (except writer)
Production meeting	All
Read through	Writers, cast members

* Additional meetings are scheduled when needed to coordinate inputs for more complex scenes such as those involving digital effects or requiring choreography (e.g. fight scenes)
** The line producer, 1st AD, and director attend all planning meetings

3.5 Integrating Content and Production Values: Estimating Costs in Prep

> The reality is that you establish a level of production values on the show, or the movie, or whatever you're shooting. So once that's established, and it's harder in the beginning because when you first start off in season one—I mean you have a sense—but when you establish what the show is going to ultimately be in the end...everything is a reaction to the script. So everything you do is reacting to words on the page. (Line producer)

The aspirational level of production values may be established in the first season, but it is not something that can be taken for granted as this level of quality must be (re)created and sustained for each of the thirteen episodes. By Season 6, the series concept and the visual language that guides the conception and design of the creative elements (e.g. costumes, sets, and props) required to realize the stories set out in the scripts are well established. Yet even within these limits, individual creative interpretations can go in many different directions and both the characters and visual language evolve over the course of different seasons. In order to achieve a high level of production values, the individual inputs from the different departments (e.g. set design and lighting) must come together as a cohesive whole. The shared vision required to make this happen begins to emerge in the concept meetings, the first of the scheduled planning meetings:

> [The concept meeting] is the first pass at the script. Everybody has had a chance to look at it and everyone raises their concerns in terms of how you are actually going to make it happen. You know, it's at that point that you get more notes from the Showrunner too, because it's [the script] still at that stage where it's evolving. It may not work to have a character in a certain scene, or where they're going to be; whether it's day or night in that scene; or all that kind of stuff which all gets a bit more ironed out there. (Costume designer)

The planning process is characterized by the need to make a series of pragmatic choices regarding how best to realize the words on the page (e.g. casting decisions, location selection, set design options, and scheduling constraints). Since these decisions are ultimately reflected in the scripts, everyone understands that the scripts will continue to evolve during prep. While there are multiple feasible trajectories for realizing the vision within each script, the path selected is also influenced by the director for each shooting block. In addition to providing the department heads with the opportunity to raise their creative and logistical concerns regarding the materialization of the script, the concept meeting is where the team assembled hears how the director is planning to approach each scene. This information helps them refine—and sometimes dramatically alters—their ideas of what is required. As ideas are discussed through the lively exchange, the conversation sometimes strays into the cost of realizing them, but this is largely left to the individual department meetings that follow:

> And then from my perspective there is the wardrobe meeting where I can fine tune from those notes. So that involves the money part of it. So like I'll say, 'Well, this is going to cost this much. If you want to do this scene, it's going to be that much money.' (Costume designer)

Preparing these cost estimations is not simply a mechanical process; rather, they are informed by individual interpretations of the script. When the scripts are released to the crew for prep, each department head reads them several times before the concept meeting. As each department head moves from their first light read of each script into a more detailed analysis, they begin to visualize the details of each scene. These imaginings of where the characters are located, how they move through the space, what they are wearing, and the traces they leave behind in these spaces become the basis for their estimations. Their ascriptions to the characters in the scripts are reflected in their emerging designs for the props, sets, and costumes required for each scene. These value judgements also influence the nature of the materials used and how elaborate the design is, which are then used in the calculations of materials, manpower, and time required to make the elements needed for each scene. They are also guided by the level of production values that the crew is aiming to achieve. Inevitably, the first informal and provisional tally of the emerging estimates provokes a moment of reckoning for the writers regarding what is or is not possible within the scripts:

> Things do change when you have the Concept Meeting and you have the money people, 'ch-ch-ch-ch. Oh no!' Then obviously you get your best wishes and fantasies brought down to earth. That happens pretty quickly those first couple of days, 'We can't do this. We can't do that. You can't have two face masks.' And that's where there's a negotiation process . . . It's a negotiation of content and also where you sit in the shooting schedule. (Writer 1)

Each individual understands production values from the perspective of his or her discipline: what matters to the writers is different from what matters to the director of photography, production designer, or art director. The negotiations over content revolve around the writers' conceptions of 'what is important' to the story, but they must also integrate the department heads' concerns about the level of quality. In this way, the scripts do not simply flow from the writers to the crew to be 'built' as specified; the conversations about the preliminary estimates shape the emerging design of the product. Since production values are equally as important as content, one of the writers attends each of the individual department meetings to clarify and preserve the essence of the story. However, the collaborations between the writers and the department heads are mediated by the 'money people' (i.e. line producer and production manager). They may be the messengers, but the expertise and judgement of each department head is required to perform the calculations of expected costs.

By their own admission, the writers are often surprised by how some scenes that they think will be easy to execute are actually far more complex and costly. However, expensive scenes (e.g. a crowd scene that needs a hundred extras or a night scene that requires complex and costly lighting setups) are not dismissed out of hand. These choices are informed by a complex calculus that integrates the value of a particular scene to the story with the time and money required to realize it. Deliberations over the importance of a particular scene rely on value judgements of the writers and there are many scenes in each script that they can change to make it work with the schedule and the budget. However, when a consensus is reached on the importance of an 'expensive' scene, the department heads have a number of options. They may move money from one episode to another, or they may collaborate with the director to find ways to utilize their limited resources for maximum impact on screen. For instance, if the director can capture the desired emotion in a scene by shooting from close angles, they may only need to build a two- or three-walled set instead of a full set that provides a 360-degree view. These choices rely on the aesthetic judgement of the director, and they also shape the estimates of costs.

Given the tight timelines in series production, time is also a scarce resource. During prep, the 1st AD designs the shooting schedule that will be followed when the scripts in that block move into production. When designing the schedule, scenes are not scheduled in the order they appear in the scripts, but in a way that makes the most sense for the workflow of the crew. This process involves considerable judgement on the part of the 1st AD. Not only does he need to ensure that each prep department has sufficient time to complete their work, he also needs to ensure that each scene is allocated sufficient time in production for the director to realize his or her vision. There is a rule in film that 'you can make it with no money, but with time and staff, or you can make it with lots of money, and no time or staff' (assistant art director). The first part of this rule is evident when scenes that require special builds are scheduled towards the end of the shooting block to give the prep departments more time to complete their work. For instance, when renting an ultralight airplane that was central to one of the scripts proved to be cost-prohibitive, this form of temporal shifting provided the time necessary for the props department to design and build a replica. The second part of this rule is seen in the hiring of additional labour or the reliance on more costly, ready-made materials to create the elements needed for scenes scheduled earlier in the shooting block. However, this rule does not hold for the shooting crew. When the scripts move into production, the crew is faced with another set of challenges as they aim to realize the vision developed during prep.

3.6 Realizing Production Values: Fluidity and Flow in Calculative Practice

We were a bit late arriving on location but thanks to a lift from one of the drivers, we made it from base camp to the video tent on location just as the crew was finishing the setup for the first shot of the day. It's a scene where [George] goes for a swim in the river where he will meet [guest star] and an awkward conversation ensues. [George] is already in the water and the guest star is on the shore waiting for his cue to jump in. The headset is silent as we wait for the crew, but suddenly [George] exclaims, 'Production values! Start rolling!' As I look up into the monitor beside the camera, a duck swims into the frame followed by a bunch of ducklings. The Director exchanges glances with the Director of Photography and then the gives the signal to the 1st AD to call the shot. The cameras start rolling but one of the two performers stumbles over his lines so the Director cuts the shot. 'Reset!' instructs the 1st AD over the headset. As the crew spring into action to restart the shot, a male voice comes through the headset in a deadpan response, 'Ah, we can't reset the ducks.' Everyone in the video tent bursts into laughter.   (Field notes)

The above passage illustrates how the desire to create production values is instilled in the performers as well as the crew. Production values can be enhanced in serendipitous moments such as these, but for the most part they are built into the plans developed during prep. In order to take advantage of spontaneous events—or to overcome any obstacles encountered—the crew must maintain the flexibility required to adapt in the moment. Despite the time and attention devoted to developing the detailed plans for production, the crew also expects that nothing will proceed according to plan when the cameras start rolling. The shooting crew is under intense pressure to get through all the scenes in the schedule on a given day without incurring overtime, which they refer to as 'making the day'. The time the director requires to achieve the imagined ideal for each scene is ostensibly incorporated into the shooting schedule; however:

> You're compromising all the time because we sort of give them more work than can reasonably be done in a day. It's fairly constant that it's … even if you do the math. If you do the math, we generally have 11 scenes to do in a day. That means you have an hour a scene and it takes 15 minutes to do a shot, so you're never going to make the math work. So, somewhere around hour eight, you're giving up something because nothing ever goes completely according to plan.   (Showrunner)

When the scripts move into production, the constraints of the budget are substituted by the constraints of the schedule. Time becomes the currency of their calculations and is central in their evaluations of possible compromises. These calculations are not written down and, unlike prep, there is no time for lengthy deliberations over alternative solutions. This immediacy shifts the spatial-temporal frame and alters the nature of the relations between calculation and judgement. In the face of time pressures, the aesthetic judgements required to sustain and enhance production values are fleeting and fluid:

> It can be a bit crazy on set sometimes, especially when it comes to decision-making. But, I think there's a big difference between when you're visualizing something in your head and then when it's actually in front of you: it's not quite the same and so we just have to adapt to it.   (Gaffer)

Production is characterized by moments like this where the crew is confronted with the physical manifestation of their imagined ideal, whether that takes the form of a fully dressed set or in the way that a performer delivers his or her lines. In this moment of reckoning, the ideal must be reimagined as whatever is captured by the camera becomes the basis for the quality of the product. The shooting crew does not have the luxury of time for lengthy deliberations or comparing alternatives against established criteria. With the clock ticking, each individual must find a way to work with what they have. For instance, the gaffer may respond in the moment by using lighting to cast shadows that mask imperfections on the set, or even to conceal the effects of age on a performer. The use of sophisticated lighting techniques is one of the hallmarks of high production values and they are also integral to the aesthetic of the series. The gaffer instinctively draws on his expertise in deploying technology to deliver the desired effect despite the imperfections of the inputs. In a similar vein, the art director uses 'forced design' when confronted with a not quite finished set. By drawing on his understanding of how the physical elements 'perform' for the camera, he can reimagine the original ideal and rearrange the existing elements to create the desired atmosphere for the scene.

The Director of Photography (DP) brings yet another perspective on how to create the desired atmosphere in less than ideal circumstances by using the movement of camera. When 'hour 8' rolls around and the inevitable compromises must be made, they usually come in the form of revised plans for the remaining scenes in the schedule. In order to 'make up' time, scenes that were initially scheduled for multiple camera angles (shots) are often reimagined in order to achieve the same emotional impact, albeit with fewer shots:

> I had a scene where...I had to have their eye-lines. There's no [speaking] lines, but I had to have their look. So, I explained this to [the DP] and I know what this means. I know we can't do all the eye-lines. So he said, 'Let's do a French reverse.' I thought, 'Great. Never heard of it.' It's a kind of cheating where you get that [the character] is looking to two different places. It's not the same as it would be if you were having establishing shots and two separate eye-lines, but for the kind of scene that I was doing, it was appropriate. It worked. (Director 3)

In this instance the director wanted to have the facial expressions (eye-lines) of the two key characters as they engaged in a conversation with a third person to capture the different emotions being conveyed in the scene. However, she also understands that they do not have enough time to shoot the scene from the multiple camera angles that this requires. Knowing that they only have time to do the shot from one perspective or camera angle, the DP suggests a 'trick' that dates to the early days of film-making. By positioning the performers in a specific way, the DP uses the movement of the camera to create the illusion of multiple sight lines with a single shot. In this instance, the director relies on the aesthetic judgement that the DP has built through years of experience to find an approach that will not compromise the essence of the emotion she desires to convey through the scene.

Given the speed in which these decisions happen, the movement between calculation and judgement may be imperceptible to the uninitiated observer, but it is second nature to the crew. The judgement of which technology to deploy or how to manipulate the physical elements—including the performances of the cast—to provide the desired level of production values in the finished product is informed by time. The non-numerical calculations inherent in this process are rooted in experience and expertise in a specific film craft. They must also incorporate the desired aesthetic (mood, atmosphere) and emotion of each scene. If the crew overlooks any of these factors, they risk compromising production values in the final product. At the same time, their ability to adapt in the moment highlights how the plans developed during prep are not rigid but have a great deal of fluidity. As the crew encounters issues when enacting these plans, they reform the creative ideal that they are working towards in response to the exigencies of production.

3.7 Discussion

In this study of a dramatic television series production my focus was on the nature of the calculative practices the crew engages in to create and sustain production values. This is a practical activity that requires both (in)formal calculation and aesthetic judgement. The latter is subject to a plurality of perspectives and evaluative criteria (Karpik, 2010), while the former arises within two distinct calculative spaces. Reflecting on the calculative practices outlined in Section 3.6, the dialectical nature of the relations between calculation and judgement become apparent. Aesthetic judgement informs the numerical calculations required for estimates of cost, but the initial estimates can also prompt the need to reimagine their initial ideas. The creation of a high level of production values requires a concerted effort to not let either the creative or financial imperatives take priority over the other:

> If you don't produce something where the creative needs are met, for the sake of staying on budget, the reality is you're probably going to incur additional expenses anyhow, because there is generally going to be negative feedback which will create a situation where you have to shoot additional stuff. And so those are the two things...balancing those two things over the course of the whole calendar and then on the day-to-day operations. (Line producer)

This balancing is the ongoing integration of the creative and financial imperatives over the course of the season. During prep, this takes place through the calculative space that takes the form of the emerging estimates. On the one hand, the cost estimates prepared for each shooting block highlight the centrality of the continuous forecasting required to deliver the series on time and on budget (DeFillippi & Arthur, 1998). On the other, preparing these estimates requires the aesthetic judgements of individuals with expertise in a specific film craft. In other words, each artistic discipline informs the judgement required for numerical calculation. The estimates of cost are also estimates of quality as they reflect the level of production values that the crew is striving to achieve. A significant proportion of ascription, ground in the lived experience of the individual crew members, is attached to these aesthetic judgements (Nelson, 1997). This gives rise to the diverse views or interpretations of the script that need to be integrated through the series of negotiated settlements. The creative synthesis that emerges through the integration of these divergent views (Harvey, 2014) is also informed by these estimates and continually updated as new information emerges.

At the same time that the crew is engaged with the estimates that denote the spatial-temporal frame of planning, they also are involved in another set of calculative practices for the scripts in production. Here the calculative space is more cerebral than material as these calculations are not written down.

While they may ultimately be informed by economic concerns (e.g. avoiding overtime), these calculations are not necessarily mathematical in nature. This calculative space is characterized by the tensions between the work required to achieve the imagined ideal and the hours available on the clock. These tensions are exacerbated by the need to reconcile the imagined and the realized. Artistic practice almost always involves a moment of reckoning between these two states (Moeran & Pedersen, 2015) and during this process the creative ideal shifts in response to the reality of the circumstances at hand. This fluidity is made possible through the myriad and fleeting aesthetic judgements made by the crew as they reconfigure the limits as to what is possible given the bounds of time. As noted by Moser and Law (2006, p. 67), 'this limit setting is indeed practical: how the limits are done depends on the task at hand'. It is through this practical setting of limits that both calculation and 'qualculation' are made possible.

In his articulation of the concept of qualculation, Cochoy (2008) argues that judgement follows the cold, hard arithmetic calculations. However, for Callon and Muniesa (2005) judgement precedes calculation as it is necessary to qualify the entities that are thrown into the calculative space. In contrast, the findings in this study suggest there is a dialectical nature to the relations between calculation and judgement, with a creative synthesis emerging from the dynamic tensions between the two. In their concerted efforts to not let either the creative or financial take priority over the other, the crew finds novel solutions to the challenges they encounter. In this way, the relations between these two contradictory forces are a source of inspiration—sometimes experienced as frustration—for their artistic practice. These two elements are interdependent rather than separate or opposed (Farjoun, 2010), as evidenced in the impossibility of disentangling the creative and the financial in the opening quote from the showrunner. The numerical calculations performed by the crew, whether rooted in the currency of time or money, are intertwined with their aesthetic judgements of what is required to create and sustain the level of production values associated with the series.

When it comes to the production of singular goods, Karpik (2010, p. 42) notes that 'Calculation impinges on each judgement or evaluation criteria.' He draws this conclusion from an admittedly simplified (by necessity) view of the production process. This in-depth exploration of those processes affirms this view, but it also draws our attention to the fact that the aesthetic judgements made by the crew shape these calculations. Further, given the collective nature of their undertaking, individuals are not isolated in their calculative practice. The constant (re)defining of limits is an important mechanism that works to connect and coordinate the disparate disciplines and their interdependent creative contributions. The coexistence of multiple calculative spaces allows for the multiple modes of relations between calculation and judgement (Moser & Law, 2006) needed to integrate the creative and financial imperatives from an overall project perspective as well as within the day-to-day operations.

The literature on calculative practice highlights the distributed nature of calculative agency across actors and the material devices or tools that actors draw on to perform their calculations (Callon & Muniesa, 2005). The findings in this study illuminate how the (aesthetic) judgement required for qualculation is also distributed. For instance, a director may have the expertise and ability to choose the right shot, but he or she relies on the tacit support of the crew to make that shot work (DeFillippi & Arthur, 1998). This support begins with the plans developed in prep for the material elements required to transform the script and the allocation of sufficient time for each scene in the shooting schedule. One of the key insights that emerged over the course of this study was that no single individual possessed the knowledge of the full set of tasks required to transform the text on the page to a finished product. The full picture only emerges through the planning meetings as each individual describes what is required from his or her specific creative discipline and department. Thus, each of the semi-autonomous groups actively participates in the conception, design, and production of singular goods.

3.8 Conclusion

To illuminate a more nuanced understanding of the central organizing tensions in the cultural industries, Townley and Beech (2010) push for the need to dig deeper than the surface manifestations of the apparent paradox between the commercial and the creative. By focusing on the creation of production values in a dramatic television series production, this study highlights how the aesthetics of cultural production are ground in everyday commercial practice (Entwistle, 2002). The artistic practices that bring calculation and judgement together in the creation of production values are not performed by 'humdrum' others in backrooms using calculators and ledger sheets. Rather, they are integrated into the different artistic disciplines and practices of the individuals contributing to the project.

When it comes to their own assessments of the product they are making, value is measured in multiple registers that encompass the technical, aesthetic, and social (cf. Stark, 2009). Individuals do not make these evaluations in isolation but need to calibrate their numbers and aesthetic judgements with the collective. It is through the complex calculus of their ongoing evaluative practices that the creative and financial concerns of the project become indistinguishable from each other. The interpenetration of these seemingly opposing forces allows project members to integrate different conceptions of 'what counts' in the final product without the need to make them commensurable. This process allows project members to fluidly redefine what their options might be as the creative aspirations of the scripts are challenged by the inevitable exigencies of production.

As Farjoun (2010) notes when concepts such as exploration and exploitation are viewed as dualisms, it requires a separation of seemingly incompatible functions. When these same concepts are viewed as dualities, it becomes possible for organizations to merge routine with novelty and commitment with flexibility. In a similar vein, when we move beyond the separation of calculation and judgement it becomes possible to develop a more nuanced understanding of creativity as something that resides in the web of relations and heterogeneous practices that produce the social and the material (Moser & Law, 2006). From this vantage point, it becomes possible to identify the connections between the economic and the cultural in the evaluative practices that are central to the production of singular goods.

References

Adler, P. & Chen, C.X. 2011. Combining creativity and control: Understanding individual motivation in large-scale collaborative creativity. *Accounting, Organizations and Society*, 36: 63–85.

Bechky, B. 2006. Gaffer, gofers, and grips: Role-based coordination in temporary organizations. *Organization Science*, 17(1): 3–21.

Buenza, D. & Stark, D. 2004. Tools of the trade: The socio-technology of arbitrage in a Wall Street trading room. *Industrial and Corporate Change*, 13(2): 369–400.

Callon, M. & Muniesa, F. 2005. Peripheral vision: Economic markets as calculative collective devices. *Organization Studies*, 26(8): 1229–50.

Caves, R.E. 2000. *The Creative Industries: Contracts between Art and Commerce*. Cambridge, MA: Harvard University Press.

Cochoy, F. 2008. Calculation, qualculation, calqulation: Shopping cart arithmetic, equipped cognition and the clustered consumer. *Marketing Theory*, 8(1): 15–44.

DeFillippi, R.J. & Arthur, M.B. 1998. Paradox in project-based enterprise: The case of film making. *California Management Review*, 40(2): 125–39.

DeFillippi, R.J., Jones, C., & Grabher, G. 2007. Introduction to the paradoxes of creativity: Managerial and organizational challenges in the cultural economy. *Journal of Organizational Behaviour*, 28: 511–21.

Dewey, J. 1923. Values, liking, and thought. *Journal of Philosophy*, 20(23): 617–22.

DiMaggio, P. 1977. Market structure, the creative process, and popular culture: Toward an organizational reinterpretation of mass-culture theory. *Journal of Popular Culture*, 11: 436–52.

Dougherty, D. 2002. Grounded theory building: Some principles and practices. In J.A.C. Baum (ed.), *Companion to Organizations* (pp. 849–66). Oxford: Blackwell Publishing.

Eisenman, M. 2013. Understanding aesthetic innovation in the context of technological evolution. *Academy of Management Review*, 38(3): 332–51.

Entwistle, J. 2002. The aesthetic economy: The production of value in the field of fashion modelling. *Journal of Consumer Culture*, 2(3): 317–39.

Farjoun, M. 2010. Beyond dualism: Stability and change as duality. *Academy of Management Review*, 35(2): 202–25.

Gil, R. & Spiller, P.T. 2007. The organizational dimensions of creativity: Motion picture production. *California Management Review*, 50(1): 243–60.

Girard, M. & Stark, D. 2003. Heterarchies of value in Manhattan-based new media firms. *Theory, Culture and Society*, 20(3): 77–105.

Glaser, B.G. & Strauss, A.L. 1967. *The Discovery of Grounded Theory: Strategies for qualitative research*. Chicago, IL: Aldine.

Harvey, S. 2014. Creative synthesis: Exploring the process of extraordinary group creativity. *Academy of Management Review*, 39(3): 324–33.

Hsu, G., Roberts, P.W., & Swaminathan, A. 2012. Evaluation schemas and the mediating role of critics. *Organization Science*, 23(1): 83–97.

Jeacle, I. & Carter, C. 2011. In TripAdvisor we trust: Rankings, calculative regimes and abstract systems. *Accounting, Organizations and Society*, 36(4–5): 293–309.

Jeacle, I. & Carter, C. 2012. Fashioning the popular masses: Accounting as a mediator between creativity and control. *Accounting, Auditing and Accountability Journal*, 25(4): 719–51.

Jones, C., Svejenova, S., Strandgaard Pederson J., & Townley, B. 2016. Misfits, mavericks and mainstreams: Drivers of innovation in the creative industries. *Organization Studies*, 37(6): 751–68.

Karpik, L. 2010. *Valuing the Unique: The Economics of Singularities*. Princeton, NJ: Princeton University Press.

Lampel, J., Lant, T., & Shamsie, J. 2000. Balancing act: Learning from organizing practices in the cultural industries. *Organization Science*, 11(3): 263–9.

Lash, S. & Urry, J. 1994. *Economies of Signs and Space*. London: Sage.

Maier, E.R. & Branzei, O. 2014. On time and on budget: Harnessing creativity in large-scale projects. *International Journal of Project Management*, 33: 1123–33.

Moeran, B. & Strandgaard Pedersen, J. 2015. *Negotiating Values in the Creative Industries: Fairs, Festivals and Competitive Events*. Cambridge: Cambridge University Press.

Moser, I. & Law, J. 2006. Fluids or flows? Information and qualculation in medical practice. *Information Technology and People*, 19(1): 55–73.

Mulgan, G. 1990. Television's holy grail: Seven types of quality. In G. Mulgan (ed.), The question of quality (pp. 4–32). London: British Film Institute.

Muniesa, F. 2011. A flank movement in the understanding of valuation. *Sociological Review*, 59(Suppl. 2): 24–38.

Nelson, R. 1997. *TV Drama in Transition: Forms, Values and Cultural Change*. New York: St Martin's Press.

Orlikowski, W.J. & Scott, S.V. 2015. Knowledge eclipse: Producing sociomaterial reconfigurations in the hospitality sector. In P.R. Carlyle, D. Nicolini, A. Langely, & H. Tsoukas (eds), *How Matter Matters: Objects, Artifacts and Materiality in Organizations* (pp. 119–41). Oxford: Oxford University Press.

Stark, D. 2009. *The Sense of Dissonance: Accounts of Worth in Economic Life*. Princeton, NJ: Princeton University Press.

Strauss, A.L. & Corbin, J. 1990. *Basics of Qualitative Research*. London: Sage.

Townley, B. & Beech, N. 2010. The discipline of creativity. In B. Townley & N. Beech (eds), *Managing Creativity: Exploring the Paradox* (pp. 3–21). Cambridge: Cambridge University Press.

Townley, B., Beech, N., & McKinlay, A. 2009. Managing in the creative industries: Managing the motley crew. *Human Relations*, 62(7): 939–62.

4

Unpacking the Dynamics of Paradoxes across Levels

Cascading Tensions and Struggling Professionals

Frédéric Gilbert, Valérie Michaud, Kathleen Bentein,
Carl-Ardy Dubois, and Jean-Luc Bédard

4.1 Introduction

Healthcare organizations are urged to improve services in a context of labour shortages and spending cutbacks. Consequently, healthcare managers develop and implement change initiatives to improve both the quality and efficiency of care. As previously argued, the dual focus on quality and efficiency generates contradictions and ambiguity in health organizations (for instance, Beech et al., 2004; Iedema et al., 2004). These two elements can be considered paradoxical because, even though they appear contradictory (i.e. quality care usually costs more) (Heracleous & Wirtz, 2014), they are also interdependent (i.e. reducing cost of care allows an increase in the quantity of services, thereby improving their accessibility, which is a dimension of quality in the public health sector). Unquestionably, both are essential for long-term organizational performance (i.e. cost control and high quality of care are expected from healthcare organizations) (Lewis, 2000).

It has been shown that managers' ability to deal with paradoxical tensions is related to their ability to implement change and innovation (Vince & Broussine, 1996) and improve organizational performance (Smith & Lewis, 2011). Indeed, acceptance of both poles of the paradox ('embracing' paradox) 'is critical toward sustaining and maximizing the outputs from organizational life' (Jules & Good, 2014, p. 124) as well as for fully exploiting tensions' 'creative potential' (Papachroni et al., 2015, p. 88). While most paradox research has adopted managerial and organization-centred views, we need to better understand how paradoxical tensions evolve beyond manager- and organization-centred perspectives (Jarzabkowski, 2003; Jay, 2013; Lewis & Smith, 2014; Schad et al., 2016; Stoltzfus et al., 2011). As clearly expressed by Fairhurst and colleagues (2016, pp. 5–6), 'to avoid too much complexity, scholars often narrow their foci and study one primary paradox at a particular level', and they often do so by overlooking 'the role of power and thus [assuming] the equal influence of opposing poles' (see also Sheep et al., 2016). This chapter specifically addresses the need for multi-level research.

More precisely, we seek to better understand how paradoxical tensions transfer between actors at different levels. We define the transfer of tensions as the process through which actors at one organizational level engage others in the management of tensions through different means—whether by sharing them or, deliberately or not, handing them over to others. As we will put forward, while the literature that addresses paradox transfers has often studied these transfers from upper to lower management (i.e. Knight & Paroutis, 2017), the design of our study allows for a broader view to clarify the dynamics from a higher level (starting with governmental targets) to a lower level (the health professionals whose work experience gets transformed).

We unpack the dynamics of paradoxes interwoven across levels through the longitudinal case study of a healthcare organization called HealthOrg (a pseudonym). Building primarily on the contributions of Smith and Lewis (2011), Jarzabkowski et al. (2013), and Knight and Paroutis (2017), we adopt a processual view (Langley, 2007) to analyse how managers and employees act and interact in multiple tension–response cycles sparked by an initial paradox. More specifically, we pay special attention to a process launched by the health ministry to increase efficiency of care and to the way it unfolds downward—first to top managers' embrace of paradox, then to lower-level managers, and finally to health professionals.

Following the management of a top-down strategy to deal with the quality–efficiency paradox, exacerbated by new targets imposed on HealthOrg by the health ministry, we see how this initial performing paradox evolves and moves down through the organization, bringing various consequences and new tensions for actors along the way. We show how, through a mix of actions, tension among actors at a higher level transfers to those at a lower level, shaping their perceptions and behaviour. In addition to unpacking paradox dynamics from a multilevel and multiactor perspective, our results offer a more nuanced outlook, one that takes us beyond the contrasting (e.g. vicious versus virtuous cycles, dilemma versus paradox), static (Schad et al., 2016), and power-neutral views (Fairhurst et al., 2016) often found in paradox literature.

4.2 Paradoxical Tensions

Paradoxes 'denote persistent contradiction between interdependent elements' (Schad et al., 2016, p. 2) that are perceived as 'two sides of the same coin' (Lewis, 2000, p. 761) (autonomy–control, quality–cost, stability–change, exploitation–exploration, etc.). The presence of paradox is associated with tensions. Paradoxical tensions refer to 'the clash of ideas, principles, and actions as well as any subsequent feelings of discomfort' (Fairhurst et al., 2002, p. 506) where paradoxes are present. Paradoxical tensions may be viewed 'as an inherent feature of a system or as social constructions that emerge from actors' cognition and rhetoric' (Smith & Lewis, 2011, p. 385). Here, like Smith and Lewis (2011), we acknowledge that they are both. Some paradox can be inherent in specific contexts but paradoxical tensions become salient through actors' perceptions of their environment. According to Smith and Lewis (2011), paradoxes can be classified under four non-mutually exclusive categories. First, performing paradoxes are linked to contradictions faced by actors trying to meet competing demands that are perceived as conflicting. Examples of such paradoxes include those between social–financial performance or, as is the case with HealthOrg, quality–efficiency of services. Second, organizing paradoxes emerge from conflicting elements because 'complex systems create competing designs and processes to achieve a desired outcome' (Smith & Lewis, 2011, p. 384). Typical organizing paradoxes include control–flexibility and collaboration–competition. Third, belonging paradoxes refer to frictions between individuals and groups, or between group identities. Identity tensions often take the form of clashes between individuals and groups or between competing values and loyalties (Reay & Hinings, 2009; Smith & Lewis, 2011). Finally, learning paradoxes relate to the tensions between 'building upon, as well as destroying, the past to create the future' (Smith & Lewis, 2011, p. 383).

A paradox perspective foregrounds the value of supporting paradoxical elements simultaneously, through active responses, despite a natural tendency to favour one element over the other. Active responses do not aim at resolving or eliminating the paradox but rather at accepting and embracing the simultaneous presence of opposing elements (Smith & Lewis, 2011). Active response, i.e. 'embracing' paradox, has largely been favoured, given its potential for fuelling virtuous cycles that promote learning, creativity, and sustainability (Smith & Lewis, 2011), and allowing actors to find better ways to live with both poles simultaneously (Lewis & Smith, 2014; Lüscher & Lewis, 2008). Defensive responses seek to isolate the poles through separation or to resolve the tension between the two poles through synthesis. Defensive responses can offer short-term relief by putting greater emphasis on one pole or the other, which can fuel vicious cycles (Lewis, 2000). Vicious cycles are driven by the anxiety and discomfort that individuals feel when faced with paradox and organizational inertia (Smith & Lewis, 2011), and such patterns aim to avoid the paradoxical tensions at play (Jarzabkowski et al., 2013). It is also possible to adopt defensive responses temporarily while still pursuing active responses in the long run (Smith & Lewis, 2011).

While numerous paradox studies focus on how different actors—usually managers—can better deal with paradoxes, those untangling how tensions transfer across levels and actors are less frequent (Schad et al., 2016). This is a key issue, considering that managing tension at one level can spur tension at others (Raisch & Birkinshaw, 2008). Andriopoulos and Lewis (2010) draw attention to the multilayered nature of paradoxes and related tensions perceived at the company, group, team, and individual levels. They emphasize managerial practices that support both exploration and exploitation at each of these levels. In a similar vein, Knight and Paroutis (2017, p. 423) show how top management practices can shape the interpretive context (instrumental, relational, and temporal) and render paradoxes salient for lower-level managers by priming their sense making and 'orchestrating attention to a repeated and converging constellation of cues', including the use of artefacts (e.g. plans and targets). While Knight and Paroutis provide us with a detailed model of how paradoxes are rendered salient from one organizational level down to another, their focus lies on managers' practices and does not elucidate the manner in which paradox is actually experienced by non-managerial actors. Huq et al. (2016) go one step further and analyse the way in which professionals and managers deal with paradoxical tensions in collective decision making. Their research shows how managers influenced two groups (low and high status) of professionals, each representing one pole of the paradox, to work together to protect the paradox. Managers did so by supporting equality of the two poles, 'strengthening the weaker pole' and focusing on common goals (Huq et al., 2016, p. 522).

To some extent, studying paradoxes across multiple levels and actors raises the question of power. Indeed, 'power is foundational to the functioning and manifestations of paradoxes in all organizations' (Fairhurst et al., 2016, p.177). And, as distinguished by Fairhurst and colleagues, while power can be conceived of as the push-pull force between competing poles (as in Schad et al., 2016), power can also be considered, in paradox research, as 'embedded in a struggle for meaning linked to understanding organizational circumstances' (as in Putnam et al., 2016). This second take on power in paradoxical situations resonates with Knight and Paroutis' (2017) contribution, which, although not framed around power, nonetheless outlines how top managers shape their context through sense making to render paradoxes salient for lower management. While this might be true when managerial actors influence other managerial actors, the extent to which this applies to other relationships remains to be uncovered.

Further, while multiple studies have focused on identifying different types of paradoxes and the responses to them, fewer have sought to explore their dynamic nature or the relations between different paradoxes. As Schad et al. (2016, p. 38) put it: 'How do nested paradoxes interact with one another?' Similarly, little is known about how tensions transfer across actors at different organizational levels. Again, this transfer has been largely approached by examining how top managers can influence other managers' cognition (Lüscher & Lewis, 2008). In an action research process conducted to support managers struggling for meaning at the LEGO company, Lüscher and Lewis showed how paradoxes can fuel each other. For example, when managers face systemic contradictions (organizing paradox), they may respond by sending mixed messages, thereby fuelling a performing paradox for others. For their part, Jarzabkowski et al. (2013, p. 245) showed how managers faced belonging and performing paradoxes when their firm was coping with 'an organizing paradox between market and regulatory demands'. Presenting the recursive relationships between paradoxes, Jarzabkowski and her colleagues' (2013, pp. 264–6) model suggests that different types of paradox operate at different organizational levels:

> The model locates performing at the microlevel of actors interacting over their roles, belonging at the mesolevel of identity with groups and divisions (Lewis, 2000; Lüscher and Lewis, 2008), and organizing at the macrolevel of organizational procedures (Clegg et al., 2002; Lewis, 2000; Smith and Lewis, 2011). This is an important element of our model, as it demonstrates that paradoxes occur simultaneously but at different levels.

Yet aside from these rare exceptions, there has been little empirical research on how paradoxical tensions interact and shift between different levels of managers and non-managers (Andriopoulos & Lewis, 2009; Huq et al., 2016; Jarzabkowski et al., 2013; Putnam et al., 2016). As argued by Andriopoulos and Gotsi (2016, p. 521), we need to 'further understand not only how senior management experience and manage paradoxes, but also how these practices are consumed and influenced by those in lower organizational levels and translated into their daily practices'. We address this gap by unpacking the dynamics of paradoxes interwoven across levels and actors, which also allows us to capture the multiple experiences generated by a top-down 'embracement' of a performing paradox.

4.3 Research Methods and Design

4.3.1 *Case Setting*

This study is based on the in-depth case study of an organizational change initiative aimed at improving the efficiency of home-care programmes offered by HealthOrg, a Canadian public healthcare organization. We focus on this case for two reasons. First, one of the authors was involved in a training programme for high-level executives taken by one of HealthOrg's top managers, providing the access and trust required for such research. Second, healthcare organizations are ideal settings to study paradoxical tensions. Paradoxical tensions can be triggered by resource scarcity, organizational change, and conditions of plurality (Smith & Lewis, 2011), which are prevalent issues in most large healthcare organizations. Indeed, cost inflation and the constant search to improve the quality of clinical care keep tensions salient. Moreover, health professionals' autonomy is perceived as both a prerequisite for the provision of high-quality care and a barrier to managerial control. Knowledge-based work requires significant discretion, i.e. autonomy, which, in turn, leads professionals to work more and to feel pressured in their work (Putnam et al., 2014; Taskin & Devos, 2005). This context entails limited external control and participative processes, which can dilute the overall control over implementation of change initiatives in pluralistic settings like health organizations (Denis et al., 2007). Moreover, managers implement organizational changes which, though intended to address these tensions, can also exacerbate them (Stoltzfus et al., 2011). Thus, the context of organizational change in healthcare organizations offers an ideal research setting to better understand how paradoxical tensions evolve when different actors deal with them.

HealthOrg is a public organization with over 1,000 employees and multiple divisions and points of service that provide acute care, long-term care, home-care, and social services. HealthOrg is part of a publicly funded healthcare system in which the health ministry plays the role of sole purchaser of care. In response to targets set by the health ministry to improve the efficiency of home-care services, managers have initiated organizational changes (i.e. work reorganization, introduction of new performance management tools, etc.). Four levels were considered in the study (see Figure 4.1). Under the health ministry, the CEO of HealthOrg and the director of the home-care division were considered top managers, while team leaders were considered lower-level managers. Finally, front-line professionals (nurses, social workers, clinical supervisors, etc.) and clinical supervisors involved in the provision of home-care services were considered professionals affected by the organizational change. Table 4.1 presents the main characteristics of HealthOrg.

4.3.2 Data Collection

The case study was informed by interviews and document analysis. Semi-structured interviews were conducted with division managers, team managers, consultants, and health professionals (nurses, nursing assistants, social workers, and clinical supervisors) at different levels (see Figure 4.1). A total of twenty-two interviews were conducted at two points in time (T1: introduction of the

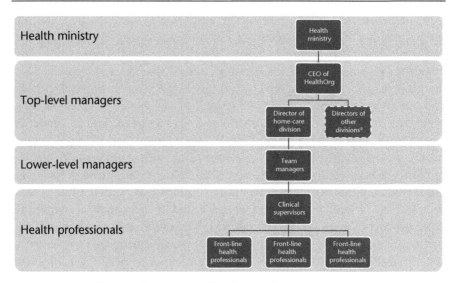

Figure 4.1. Actors and levels considered

Note: *directors of other divisions not included in our study

Table 4.1. Main characteristics of the organization

Organization characteristics	HealthOrg
Territory	Urban
Sites: Hospitals (acute care)	2
Community health centres	2
Long-term care centres	4
Number of employees affected by the change in home-care division	130
Number of employees of the healthcare organization	1,250
Population served	120,000

change; T2: eighteen months into the change). Conducted at the organization, and lasting between 1 hour and 1 hour 40 minutes, the interviews were recorded and transcribed verbatim. Interview questions related to the organizational change and the experiences of actors involved in the change initiatives. Archival analysis of a range of documents relating to the organizational change supplemented the data. These secondary data sources helped us understand the organizational changes and provided a richer analytical context for examining interviewees' responses. Table 4.2 presents the data sources.

4.3.3 *Data Analysis*

Data analysis entailed three distinct steps, beginning with a full transcription of the interviews. This was followed by chronological organization of documents and verbatim transcriptions to build a narrative, allowing for temporal

Table 4.2. Data sources by participant type and data type

Interviews	HealthOrg	
	T1	T2
Health professionals (mainly nurses)	7	4
Managers (top and lower levels)	3	7
Consultants	0	1
Total per time period	10	12*
Total number of interviews	22*	
Documents	Meeting summaries and reports from all committees, action plans, organizational chart, internal communications, project organization manual, etc.	

Note: *six individuals were interviewed at both T1 and T2

bracketing of the data (Langley, 1999, 2007). Two of the authors then shared the chronological account of the case with a group of organizational actors at HealthOrg to validate the content. We synthesized the final narrative to capture the main events, actors, actions, and perceptions throughout the change process under study. The two authors who were most familiar with the data noted the presence of multiple paradoxical tensions in this final narrative.

The second step consisted of concrete coding of paradoxical tensions and actors' responses to them. The coding proceeded as follows: with the help of two research assistants, we undertook an independent, step-by-step systematic coding of all content of the documents and verbatim transcriptions, following the temporal sequence of the material. After each step, discrepancies in coding were resolved through discussions and by moving back and forth between the data and relevant literature.

In terms of coding, paradox identification is a concrete challenge and, as clearly argued by Andriopoulos and Gotsi (2016, p.513), 'there is still confusion around where one can find evidence of paradoxes'. We defined paradoxical tensions as episodes during which latent paradoxes became salient for the actors. We considered these paradoxical tensions to be evidenced when actors referred to conflicting elements or to how they developed responses to address these tensions. Concretely, such elements typically emerged when actors talked about the challenges and constraints generated by the change process triggered by the health ministry's new targets. For example, evidence of paradoxical tensions was noted when professionals reported that managers focused on efficiency at the expense of quality of care. While humour and irony have been described as cues for identifying paradox (Hatch, 1997; Jarzabkowski & Lê, 2016), they did appear regularly in HealthOrg interviewees' comments. However, paradoxical tension was frequently identifiable in statements displaying emotion.

For each paradoxical tension found in the interviews, we systematically identified the two poles of the paradox (which had to be both contradictory and interdependent), the actors involved, and the period during which tensions were salient for participants. We also identified types of tensions and responses, using Smith and Lewis' (2011) paradox typology, i.e. performing, organizing, belonging, and learning. Although we did not find any examples of learning tensions, we found clear performing and organizing tensions, and some form of belonging ones. For example, the initial performing tension (quality–efficiency) was explicitly associated with the health ministry's targets, which relate directly to 'competing goals as stakeholders seek divergent organizational success' (Smith and Lewis, 2011, p. 383). The organizing paradox was labelled as such since organizational actors' actual descriptions clearly referred to issues and tools that triggered the control element of the control–autonomy paradox. Finally, identity tensions relatable to the belonging paradox were identified among health professionals, as the changes challenged their very professional identity. We also categorized the responses of the actors as either active (when they tried to embrace both poles of the paradox) or defensive (when they favoured one pole over another or saw the two poles as being in opposition with each other) (Poole and Van de Ven, 1989). Types, poles, actors, period of salience, and responses were illustrated in a graphical representation (visual mapping, Langley, 1999) which revealed tension variations over time.

Finally, in the third step, we clarified the patterns in which paradoxical tensions shifted between actors at different levels, independently identifying the processes depicted in the graphical representation developed in the previous step. We then shared and counterposed our views to build a consensus on the process by which paradoxical tensions were transferred through discourse and the control of specific structures and tools. This stage of analysis led us to re-examine the data and to refine some of the codes (e.g. control over other actors, control over resources or tools). The cascading of tensions across actors and patterns of transfer is summarized in Figure 4.2.

4.4 Findings

This section sheds light on how paradoxical tensions evolve across organizational levels for top managers, lower-level managers, and health professionals. We start by describing the context in which the research took place. Our results illustrate how the initial tension perceived by the health ministry cascaded down, first to top- then to lower-level management, and finally to health professionals (see Figure 4.2).

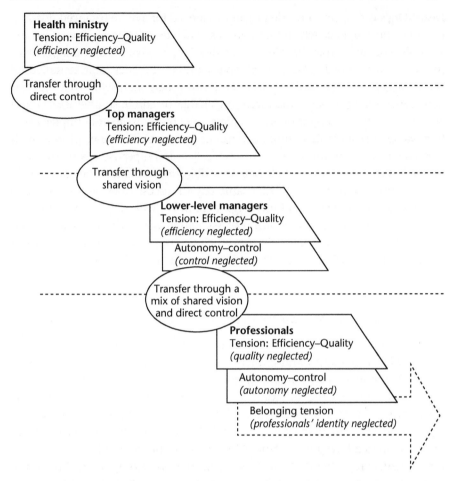

Figure 4.2. Cascading, transformation, and surfacing of tensions between actors

4.4.1 *Research Context*

In the year and a half prior to the period studied, professionals and managers worked together to improve professionals' clinical supervision. Often alone on the road, professionals regularly struggle with issues both personal (i.e. stress related to compassion) and clinical (i.e. patients' needs and care), as they offer home-care services without the support of an on-site clinical team and clinical supervisors. Managers recognized that professionals needed better clinical support.

> The staff felt that they didn't have the clinical support; they didn't know where to ask. [When you do] on-the-road care, you're on your own; you're facing visits and sometimes you don't know what to do in these cases and they have to be able to discuss that isolation with some of the same professionals, just to be able to get that support.   (Lower-level manager)

HealthOrg's managers concluded there was a need for a more balanced distribution of clinical support, which for them was associated with better service quality. They also concluded that the roles of lower-level managers and clinical supervisors (professionals) needed to be clarified. To respond to this issue, representatives of the managers and the professionals developed a new framework that set clear boundaries for lower-level managers (in charge of administrative issues) and clinical supervisors (professionals, in charge of clinical care issues). Implementation was gradual and raised minimal tensions at this point. Overall, professionals seemed satisfied with the adjustments made: '[clinical supervisors] are now more available. Whenever we need help or if we're doing an evaluation, they can usually find a 20-minute [window] in that same day to discuss cases with us. Prior to the changes, they always had meetings, here or elsewhere. Their availability is now remarkable' (Front-line health professional). It was in this context, marked by a quest for quality through improved clinical supervision, that new health ministry targets sparked the quality–efficiency paradox at HealthOrg.

4.4.2 *Tracking Tension from the Health Ministry to HealthOrg*

Managers and professionals were still adapting to recent changes in the roles of lower-level managers and clinical supervisors when the health ministry required all public health organizations to increase the volume of home-care services. To address the situation and strengthen efficiency, top managers were compelled by the health ministry to increase output within existing resource levels. Top managers perceived that the health ministry's control over resources allowed it to impose its goal of improving efficiency. Indeed, top managers reported that the health ministry was not going to invest any more financial resources until the new targets were reached: '[the new targets] represent an increase of almost 20% in the volume of services. [The health ministry] will not fund any development until we reach that goal' (Top manager). Faced with this challenge, HealthOrg's top managers first unsuccessfully tried to negotiate a lower target with the health ministry. However, as they were unable to avoid the targets without being financially penalized, they were forced to embrace the paradoxical tension and decided to strengthen efficiency, which they too began to consider as the weak pole of the quality–efficiency paradox. Top managers jointly decided to hire external consultants for advice on how to meet the health ministry's demands.

According to the consultants, outputs could be increased through closer supervision of professional work done by clinical supervisors who were, in the consultants' view, focusing too much on quality of care at the expense of cost control and efficiency: '[clinical supervisors] were focused on quality at the clinical level and acted more like advisors. However, they weren't necessarily there to ensure that the visits were planned, that they were actually taking place and that care was being delivered' (Consultant). Thus, assisted by consultants, top management concluded that a major shift toward efficiency and performance monitoring was required.

In sum, top managers quickly complied with and embraced the government's goal of strengthening efficiency, considering it to be the neglected pole of the quality–efficiency paradox. We will now see how the tension transferred from top to lower-level managers.

4.4.3 *Tracking Tensions between Top and Lower-Level Managers*

Supported by the consultants, the top managers met with lower-level managers to discuss the shift toward efficiency. After getting the impression that some were questioning the possibility of meeting the new efficiency targets without compromising quality, the director of the home-care division met with all lower-level managers to reaffirm that efficiency would be increased without threatening quality. They discussed their concerns until lower-level managers' support was forthcoming.

> We discussed it, and the meeting was necessary because I didn't want to continue with the implementation without everybody's support. I didn't want to insist for a change that was difficult for [health professionals] . . . We clarified the project after explaining the goal of change. I asked if they were on board and if I could count on their support. Everybody raised their hands.   (Top manager)

Thus, after a few meetings, lower-level managers reached consensus and expressed the same concerns as top managers: 'We were not closely monitoring performance. We did not have the tools to do so. At the beginning, we did not even have statistics. So, what were our health professionals doing? We know they are working hard, but that's the only thing we could say' (Lower-level manager). Once managers at all levels confirmed their support for the necessary change, lower-level managers then had to engage with professionals to implement the change, a shift that represented a more complex process.

4.4.4 *Tracking Tensions between Managers and Professionals*

Like the health ministry, managers had to find a way to increase service efficiency without compromising quality (adjusting response). With the support of consultants, top- and lower-level managers' plan was to shift the focus of professionals (clinical supervisors and front-line professionals) from quality of care to efficiency and performance monitoring. '[The consultants are helping us to] really focus on the [clinical coordinators'] competencies and skills' (Top manager). Managers engaged professionals, in part, through persuasion and respect for professionals' autonomy. Managers explained the need for change to professionals at various informational meetings. The consultants organized meetings with clinical coordinators to communicate the situation and help them conclude that improving efficiency was necessary.

> Everybody must realize the need for change. This communication workshop is meant to describe the structure that we have right now [and then raise the questions], 'What's missing?' The observation is that we have a lot of space in which to talk about clinical supervision, but nowhere to address performance. (Consultant)

Professionals were strongly encouraged to go further to achieve results. 'Even when [the clinical supervisors] incorporate efficiency, we push them to go further. They are responsible for achieving the results and they must show results. We've got tools. [Clinical supervisors] must work harder with low-performance professionals, and if it leads to disciplinary measures, the [lower-level manager] will intervene' (Top manager). Indeed, the shift toward efficiency was imposed by managers before professionals were fully convinced to change:

> If I go back to basics . . . the first part is simply to create the mechanics. I want [a clinical supervisor] to meet her team and create a routine. After that comes the stage where she really understands why she is doing it. At the beginning, she's doing it for the sake of doing it. At one point, she realizes that results improve, that her people get more support. Then, for the whole post mortem, they tell us 'Now I understand what is expected from me.' (Consultant)

This pressure for efficiency came mainly from a review of the clinical supervisors' role and the introduction of new performance-monitoring instruments. '[The greater focus on performance was supported by] all the tools we can put in place to support [clinical supervisors] and enable them to play their role. They will then seek out performance from front-line professionals' (Top manager). More specifically, supervising the professionals' output was now being prioritized on a more regular basis with more precise monitoring tools. Clinical supervisors had to meet with front-line health professionals twice a week to discuss services. The meetings served not only to monitor output but to provide (at least theoretically) an opportunity for clinical support. But since performance monitoring had to be prioritized in brief (15-minute) and frequent meetings, it seemed that there was insufficient time for clinical support:

> [The goal of these meetings] was to meet the supervisor twice a week for 15-minute meetings, to review our plans and also for clinical supervision, but that did not happen. People say that we meet, but that's not really beneficial for the employee. It is rather for managers so they can see what employees do.
>
> (Front-line health professional)

Specific tools also contributed to the observed shift toward efficiency. Front-line professionals now had to meet a very precise schedule for the services they intended to deliver and to confirm what they had accomplished: '[The schedule] is a plan to predict the tasks we are going to do for planning and updates. We have to create this plan every week and to update it' (Front-line health professional). Clinical supervisors confirmed that front-line health professionals' outputs were monitored mainly through monitoring the professionals' schedules.

> We also have an agenda of what must be covered during the meeting...We must address the action plan, performance, and next week's planning based on last week. We also have to look at our intervention plans, but in only 15 minutes, there is no time for that. (Clinical supervisor, professional)

The clinical supervisors' new roles and the monitoring instruments were not blanketly imposed on professionals. Some adjustments were negotiated:

> We've been involved a bit in the conception phase. The tools were ready except...they had to be accepted by the [health professionals]...We sit down and look at the activities that we do, write down a list, and then evaluate how much time [each task] takes on average. We also look at the statistics, and that's being done with the [health professionals], the [clinical supervisors] and [managers]. The task force groups have 7 to 8 people. We set standard time durations that the committee members test in the real world. (Clinical supervisor, professional)

The duration and frequency of meetings for clinical supervision were also discussed. For instance, the consultants' initial optimal scenario of holding meetings every day had to be modified to meeting twice a week. The time spent by clinical supervisors on these scheduled meetings eroded the time available for front-line professionals' ad hoc requests: 'But [my] door is no longer as open as before [for front-line professionals]...because if I meet someone [in the scheduled meetings], I shut it' (Clinical supervisor, professional). Overall, the shift toward efficiency was driven by more frequent and shorter meetings with clinical supervisors and by the use of monitoring instruments focused on outputs in terms of quantity of services. Together, these changes emphasized efficiency and left little room for concerns regarding the quality of clinical care.

Top- and lower-level managers described this shift toward efficiency as temporary. For them, this emphasis on efficiency through performance measurement was essential to rebalance the efficiency–quality paradox in favour of its neglected pole.

> I think that we were lacking this element of supervision of care, and this explains that we have put a lot of emphasis on [the element of supervision]. So yes, [professionals] did improve that aspect, but they dropped the other end. Now, I feel like we focus a lot on the performance dimension because there is so much to learn, but I hope we can put everything back into balance. (Top manager)

At the end of the studied period, the method for reintroducing greater focus on quality had not yet been defined.

> But the issue is to find out how to do that, because time is lacking...I must find time for that, to discuss their work when, at this moment, they are so busy with the performance tools. That's pretty much the issue. But I don't have a problem with a focus on performance tools, as long as later we find a new balance.
>
> (Top manager)

In sum, managers introduced a change process in response to the perceived tension associated with the quality–efficiency paradox that became salient through targets imposed by the health ministry. The new focus of clinical supervision placed greater emphasis on performance monitoring to increase efficiency. We will now see how professionals' perceptions of the paradoxical tension and responses partly differ from those of managers.

4.4.5 *Professionals' Experience of the Process*

If the managers saw themselves as responding to a tension by respecting both poles of the paradox, professionals viewed both the process and the nature of such change in a somewhat different way. Regarding the process, lower managers described the consultant-led process as open and participative: '[According to the consultants], we must feel involved and feel like it is not imposed. That's how they work to develop the tools, to follow up' (Lower-level manager). Professionals, however, expressed a different perception of the same process:

> We must accept the change, but there is very little room for critique or discussion about the change. Why do we go through these changes? Where does this come from? When we ask questions, we're seen as troublemakers.
>
> (Front-line health professional)
>
> They want me to meet with nurses in the morning, but I can't. I tell them that a lot of my time is taken up planning my meeting schedule. They want to have the last word. (Clinical supervisors, professional)
>
> I like the idea of [the consultants], but not how...they think they know more and that their way of thinking is worth more than our opinion. If they were more flexible...I think they would have a lot of good things to contribute, but it's the rigidity [that is] frustrating. (Clinical supervisors, professional)

Professionals and managers also had different views regarding the impact of change on the tensions of the quality–efficiency paradox. Managers advanced a vision that integrated both quality and efficiency. For them, the shift towards efficiency wasn't a threat to the quality of care.

> A lot of [clinical supervisors and front-line professionals] see it as numbers; they don't see quality. But quality has such a broad definition; it's not the quality of

your one-on-one [relation with patient], quality of efficient service, fast service, wait times, the type of service you're getting, the right person. So quality has evolved, and I think the [clinical coordinators] ... see quality of the clinical care, not the quality of the whole thing.   (Lower-level manager)

Health professionals also considered that service efficiency and volume were not inherently incompatible with quality of care. However, they felt that the actually occurring shift towards efficiency reduced the focus on quality, which chafed at the professionals' values:

[W]hat matters for them is the number of visits and the number of interventions. It seems to me that they focused more on quantity than on quality ... I was thinking that 'no, quantity also comes with quality'. I don't have time to look at quality AND quantity ... [Right now], I think that the focus is more on quantity, less on quality. I disagree.   (Front-line health professional)

I am worried about the clinical dimension. [Managers] say that performance is part of quality. Yes, I agree, but to me, that's one part.   (Clinical supervisor, professional)

It completely changes our way of working. It's all about quantity. I'm a clinician, and to me, quality is more important.   (Front-line health professional)

Some professionals (front-line professionals and clinical supervisors) perceived the shift towards efficiency as a threat to quality, but they reported no actual reduction in the quality of services. They even saw some improvements, which they described as a victory. As a clinical supervisor explained: 'I used to hear all the time "you're not here enough, we need you here". So I find it positive because nurses are more present. Yes, there are days when I do have appointments, but I am more here with the [front-line professionals]. We won on that' (Clinical supervisor, professional). Despite these cautious but positive signs of reduced tension, professionals nonetheless reported additional tensions from the changes implemented to improve efficiency. Clinical supervisors managed to protect quality of care, but the new work organization affected the quality of their work experience.

[We receive] lots of feedback from staff: 'We're not in a factory or on an assembly line.' We receive this negativity [from front-line professionals].
                                                (Clinical supervisor, professional)

You have to meet your quota. It can go really fast when you have minor cases, but for the major cases, fatigue sets in and things start to go downhill. It's less enjoyable ... It's enough to make you look forward to retirement.
                                                (Clinical supervisors, professional)

In sum, our results show how paradoxical tensions cascaded first from the health ministry to the organization, and then from the organization's managers to professionals providing and coordinating services. We saw that the health ministry imposed new targets to reinforce the efficiency of home-care services. Top managers quickly agreed and convinced lower-level managers to engage in the pursuit of efficiency. Managers improved efficiency by a process that relied partly on convincing their staff and partly on imposing change and monitoring tools. While lower-level managers were preoccupied with insufficient efficiency and control over professionals, professionals expressed concerns about the opposite pole of both the efficiency–quality and autonomy–control paradoxes. Indeed, professionals were concerned by both quality and their own autonomy, the two poles in which their professional identity as care givers is rooted.

4.5 Discussion: Unpacking the Dynamics of Paradoxes Interwoven across Levels

Our analysis offers insights into how paradoxical tensions transfer and evolve as they cascade down through actors and levels. Together, these results provide two main contributions. First, they allow us to better understand the dynamics of intertwined paradoxes as they transfer between, and are dealt with by, actors at different levels. Second, we show how managers' and professionals' perspectives and experiences differ regarding both the neglected poles underlying the tension and the corresponding responses.

As shown in Figure 4.2, the HealthOrg case study demonstrates how patterns followed as paradoxical tensions shifted from actors at one level to those at a lower level varied depending on the actors' levels of consensus and power. We saw that paradoxical tensions cascaded from higher- to lower-level actors through actions aimed at both shaping others' perceptions and exerting more or less direct control over others' behaviours. We saw that top-level managers (the CEO of HealthOrg and the director of home-care services) transferred the performing tension through relational practices to shape the perceptions of lower-level managers so that they corresponded to those of their superiors. Top managers were able to increase lower-level managers' attention to efficiency through dialogue and interactions. Gaining support from lower managers was perceived by top management as mandatory in pursuing the transformation they wished to accomplish. These results are consistent with those of other authors who have shown how managers' practices shape interpretive contexts for lower-level managers so that the latter come to share the former's understanding of the tension that has to be addressed (Fairhurst & Putnam, 2014; Knight & Paroutis, 2017). But our study's examination of tensions from the health ministry to managers and then to health professionals—both up and down managerial levels—offers further explanations regarding the key role of control in the transfer of tension between actors at different levels and the way in which tensions cascade and transform during this transfer.

4.5.1 *The Key Role of Control in Shifting Tensions*

As shown in the Results section, these actors mobilized their control over resources, time, work organization, and instruments to make other actors engage with the pole perceived as being neglected. We have seen that actors' power was pivotal to shifting tensions from the health ministry to HealthOrg, and from lower-level managers to professionals. The tension first moved down from the health ministry to HealthOrg when the ministry imposed new targets by tying them to future funding. Since top managers could not get around the health ministry's request, the focus quickly switched to the pole perceived by the ministry as neglected (i.e. efficiency of services).

These results extend previous studies focused on the transfer of tension between actors by showing the key role of power not only in favouring one's vision but in affecting behaviour regardless of the presence of a common understanding. Although the role of power and dialectics in organizational change has long been studied and recognized (Van de Ven & Poole, 1995), power is often associated with the struggle over meaning between actors trying to promote their particular view of how each pole of the paradox should be considered, which shapes future actions and interactions over paradoxical tensions (Fairhurst et al., 2016). Without having framed their analysis around the notion of power, Knight and Paroutis (2017) nevertheless showed how top managers' capacity to shape their context through various activities provides cues that build a shared sense of context and renders tensions salient for lower-level managers. Our results go one step further by showing how control over others can compel actors at lower levels to change their practices whether or not they actually share perceptions about the tension. Thus, power struggles exist not only over meanings but also over specific actions one can take to force others to act according to a vision, regardless of the others' reservations. Yet, as we will now discuss, control over others is not always as clear as that of the health ministry over health organizations, which can catalyse mixed processes when control over others is limited due to professional autonomy.

4.5.2 *Mixed Process*

The health ministry's control over financial resources allowed it to impose its view on HealthOrg, but top and lower-level managers could not exercise the same sway over reluctant professionals. Control over others is not always as clear as that deployed by the health ministry, and actors do not always come together around a common vision as easily as top and lower-level managers do. While top managers used dialogue on a number of occasions to convince professionals to improve efficiency, managers intended to get professionals to change their behaviour whether or not they supported the managers' perspective. Managers urged professionals to favour efficiency through mixed processes that included actions to influence both their vision and, more directly, their behaviours. The mix of influence and control crystallized while managers dealt with the performing tension related to the efficiency–quality paradox of performing (efficiency neglected). Managers used control to compel professionals who were more or less reluctant to accept their view.

With the help of consultants, managers augmented their control over professionals to force them to increase their attention to efficiency through time management, work organization, and instruments. As we saw in the Results section, a new role in performance monitoring was imposed on clinical supervisors and the professionals they worked with. Greater efficiency was achieved through more frequent but shorter meetings so that efficiency would be a priority. In practice, professionals and their clinical supervisors spent the vast majority of their time discussing performance and efficiency monitoring. Also, new follow-up tools, focused on the volume of planned and delivered services, were implemented to monitor professionals' work, and these became the focus of the meetings. The tools incorporated patients' clinical conditions, a hallmark consideration for quality of care, but mainly as a way to justify the number and duration of patient visits. Though managers put pressure on professionals, that control was not absolute. For example, the monitoring instrument underwent adaptation, as did the duration and frequency of the meetings, to take into account the professionals' demands and recommendations as well as to track performance.

These results contribute to the paradox literature by showing how different patterns can coexist in the same organizational context, building on previous studies that focus on transfer of tension between actors who share a similar identity (often managers) (Knight & Paroutis, 2017; Lüscher & Lewis, 2008) or actors with a high level of autonomy (Iedema et al., 2004). Our study shows how power can be used in contexts of total (i.e. health ministry control over HealthOrg's resources) or partial control (managers' control over professionals) to engage others, whatever their level of support for the change.

In short, tensions cascaded between actors through different patterns. Some were transferred through discourse and development of a shared vision, as illustrated by the shift from top managers to lower-level managers. But tensions were also transferred through direct control, as evidenced by the transfer from the health ministry. We also showed that the shift toward efficiency cascaded from managers to professionals through a mixed process involving actions to alter both professionals' perceptions and, more directly, their behaviours, no matter what their level of support for the managers' view. As we will see, tracking tensions as they are experienced by different actors also offers significant insight into how tensions are transformed at the level of professionals and the consequences of this process on the emerging tension of belonging.

4.5.3 *Cascading and Transformation of Tensions: the Contrasting Perspective of Professionals*

Our second contribution relates to the consequences of the managers' endeavour to improve efficiency and engage professionals who did not always share their perception of tension salience. Our results show how paradoxical tensions transformed and emerged while being transferred across actors at different levels. When the health ministry shifted the tension to HealthOrg, top managers agreed that efficiency was being neglected. But as we will now see, managers shifted the tension to professionals, who often did not share their perception, so that tensions became salient for professionals, but not as managers intended them to be. We observed that active manager-led responses converted into different tensions for professionals. Indeed, managers' increasing satisfaction with efficiency coincided with professionals' growing concerns over the other pole of the paradoxical tension. In the view of some professionals, quality was threatened by the manager-led shift toward efficiency. Tension related to the efficiency–quality paradox shifted from managers—for whom efficiency was the neglected pole—to professionals, who feared that quality was being neglected.

We observed a similar mutation as managers perceived their control to be outweighed by professionals' autonomy. The initial tension perceived by managers involved gaining minimal control over professionals, a situation caused by managers' perception that professionals' autonomy was excessive. The managers acted to make the control pole salient for professionals but for professionals, the threatened pole was autonomy.

These contrasting perceptions of paradoxical tensions suggest that what managers viewed as an adjusting response associated with virtuous cycles was seen by professionals as a defensive response threatening the opposite pole of the paradox and fuelling vicious cycles. Indeed, the managers' perception of the tension decreased following their adjusting response and positive confrontation of the two poles, and they reported satisfaction regarding the quality–efficiency paradoxical tension that they initially dealt with. These results are consistent with previous studies focusing on managers which showed that responding actively to paradoxical tensions seems to offer several benefits (Andriopoulos & Lewis, 2010; Lüscher & Lewis, 2008). Embracing paradox could reduce the usual anxiety that stems from working through paradox (Lüscher & Lewis, 2008) and support organizational performance and sustainability (Andriopoulos & Lewis, 2009; Lewis & Smith, 2014; Schad et al., 2016). But professionals' tensions revealed that they had a less positive view of how managers were handling the tensions.

Managerial and organizational perceptions of positive outcomes and virtuous cycles associated with an active response should not obscure other actors' experiences and the potentially darker side of embracing paradoxical tensions. As Vince and Broussine (1996) showed in their study of how managers deal with organizational change, positive and negative perceptions of change can coexist. The surfacing of tensions among professionals revealed by our study is consistent with researchers outside of the paradox stream who suggest that the ongoing quest to improve performance can lead to tradeoffs that improve certain aspects of the employee work experience while threatening others (Grant et al., 2007). The observed transfer of paradoxical tensions from managers to professionals suggests that studies focusing solely on one actor might lead to excessively positive conclusions that fail to acknowledge how acting at one level might 'spark new tensions at another' (Putnam et al., 2016, p. 80; Raisch & Birkinshaw, 2008).

These results may clash with the often extremely optimistic view associating active response (embracing paradox) with virtuous cycles that favour organizational peak performance and sustainability (Lewis & Smith, 2014). Like Jay (2013, p. 155), we wonder: 'Could a narrowly cognitive–interpretative approach to paradox—getting people to see the "both-and" nature of the organization, perhaps through action research intervention—overcome organizational conflict and transform power struggles identified in prior scholarship?' When managers adopt a 'both-and' vision and mobilize active strategies 'to embrace, cope with, and thrive through tensions' (Lewis & Smith, 2014, p. 135), cycles might appear virtuous from a managerial perspective, but studying the process outside of this scope revealed different experiences. It could be beneficial to further investigate the longer-term effects of ongoing active or adjusting responses led by managers who are promoting their vision of the attention required for each pole of a paradox.

4.5.4 *Managers as the Neutral Guardian of Both Poles of the Paradox*

Our results also question the prevalent view in studies depicting managers as the guardians of both paradox poles. For example, Knight and Paroutis explained that 'when leaders perceive too much emphasis on one pole they support the alternate pole' by raising the attention of lower-level actors, adding that 'repeated sensemaking encounters in order to [get lower-level actors to] appreciate the complex relationship between poles' might be necessary (Knight & Paroutis, 2017, pp. 432, 434). Similarly, Huq et al. (2016) showed how managers can support different groups of professionals associated with specific poles by acting as mediators who balance the power of each group while they grapple with the paradox. Our results contrast with this somewhat 'neutral' view of managers. In pluralistic environments where actors pursue diverging goals (Denis et al., 2007), the widely held view that managers must shape others' meanings to match theirs might be problematic. In our study, the managers' view could hardly be considered neutral.

Our results further suggest that the observed shift in the perception of tensions between managers and professionals might actually trigger a belonging paradox. Indeed, managers first perceived a tension with efficiency, which transferred to a tension related to quality perceived by professionals. Managers then perceived a tension related to control, which mutated into a tension over autonomy for professionals. The tension related to goals (efficiency–quality performing tension) and the tension related to work organization (autonomy–control) brought to the surface a belonging tension in the form of clashes between managers and professionals that stemmed from their respective core occupational identities (Reay & Hinings, 2009; Smith & Lewis, 2011). We did not collect data specifically dealing with professional identities, but the results nonetheless highlight frictions between the managers' and professionals' identities. The managers' discourse did not favour one identity per se, but their focus on efficiency was evident, and they also used expressions like 'they don't see it as quality' while referring to professionals as a group. For their part, professionals did not hesitate to claim that, as health professionals, quality of care was their dominant concern, and referred to managers as a group that was biased toward quantity (i.e. 'Their only concern is numbers'). The managers' perception of neglected poles (efficiency and control) is consistent with their own identity, in contrast to the rooting of the professionals' identity in the opposite poles (quality and autonomy) (Freidson, 2001). The belonging tension prevented managers from acting as mediators, as observed by Huq et al. (2016). Instead, at HealthOrg, they acted as promoters, although they always recognized both poles of the paradoxes.

Altogether, the transfer of tensions between actors and the emergence of further tensions observed among individuals shed light on the dynamic of paradoxical tensions and their evolution at multiple levels. These are two central but understudied themes for scholars who adopt a paradoxical framework (Schad et al., 2016). Our results suggest that closer attention must be paid to non-managers and to the potential cascading of tensions when higher-level actors' initiatives to deal with tensions transform and surface further tension in the course of engaging actors at lower levels in their endeavour (Jay, 2013; Smith & Lewis, 2011). Although scholars have recognized that a paradox perspective is not a panacea (Lüscher & Lewis, 2008), the drawbacks or alternative perceptions of active responses to paradoxical tensions are rarely evoked in this line of research. The focus rests mainly on the negative outcomes of defensive responses and the positive outcomes of adopting a paradoxical 'both-and' view (Schad et al., 2016). While our study did not focus on the evaluation of outcomes at the organizational level, it does suggest that actors experience very different processes depending on their roles and capacities within the organization.

4.6 Conclusion

Our initial objective for this chapter was to gain better understanding of how paradoxical tensions and responses evolve over time as managers and professionals act and interact to deal with them. Our results offer two novel contributions to the literature on organizational paradoxes and tensions. First, they help clarify the way in which paradoxical tensions are transferred across actors at different levels via various combinations of influence and control. The actors' power was determinant in the observed pattern of transfer and was sometimes effective in engaging actors at lower levels without their approval. Second, we showed how paradoxical tensions interact across levels while actors' diverging perceptions can lead to mutations and the emergence of tensions. More specifically, our decentred approach showed how tensions were transformed and surfaced for the professionals. What appeared as an active response in favour of a neglected pole (i.e. efficiency) of the paradox from the managers' perspective could be perceived as a defensive response threatening the other pole of the paradox (i.e. quality), from the professionals' perspective. We showed that dealing actively with paradoxical tensions is a more complex endeavour than a recipe for a virtuous cycle. These observations do not challenge the recurring assumption that embracing paradox leads to positive outcomes, but they do suggest that positive and negative outcomes can coexist and differ, depending on the adopted standpoints. The results call into question the somewhat neutral view of managers' perceptions and reaffirm the importance of studying tensions in a broader context that considers organizations and actors at different levels over time. Our results also suggest that greater attention should be paid both to the external context, which can be a source of surfacing tension (as was the case with the health ministry), and to non-managers, who may experience tensions differently from managers.

As Lewis and Smith (2014) clearly explained, using the paradox perspective as a tool to manage tensions differs from using it as a framework to better understand these issues. When used as a framework, the paradox perspective should not be reduced to a tool to build engagement for the unconditional pursuit of goals that may actually be in tension with one another. Future research could therefore be mindful of the actors' range of capacities, of their contrasting views of paradoxical goals, and of their specific experiences. A framework for understanding paradoxical tension dynamics should take into account actors' unequal capacities to promote their views and to impose or respond to specific demands (Huq et al., 2016; Putnam et al., 2016). The optimistic language found in much of the paradox literature regarding an active response to paradoxes may need to be tempered to make room for more nuanced—and paradoxical—observations.

Admittedly, our study has certain limitations. We investigated one large public healthcare organization, in which operations are carried out by professionals with considerable autonomy, albeit less than other professionals, such as physicians (Iedema et al., 2004). However, although the patterns we found could be considered context-specific, we believe they can apply to other pluralistic environments where managers and professionals at different levels interact in order to deal with paradoxical tensions.

Acknowledgements

We would like to express sincere thanks to Wendy Smith and the two anonymous reviewers for their constructive and very helpful comments throughout the review process. We would also like to thank colleagues who generously provided us with feedback and support on earlier versions of this chapter, especially Nesrine Sedoud, Xavier Parent-Rocheleau, Ewan Oiry, and participants at the 2016 PROS Conference and 2014 EGOS paradox track (special thanks to Camille Pradies and Vanessa Pouthier).

Funding

This work was supported by the Canadian Institutes of Health Research, grant PHE-101868.

References

Andriopoulos, C. & Gotsi, M. 2016. Methods of paradox. In M.W. Lewis, W.K. Smith, P. Jarzabkowski, & A. Langley (eds), *Handbook of Organizational Paradox: Approaches to Plurality, Tensions and Contradictions* (pp. 513–27). Oxford: Oxford University Press.

Andriopoulos, C. & Lewis, M.W. 2009. Exploitation-exploration tensions and organizational ambidexterity: Managing paradoxes of innovation. *Organization Science*, 20(4): 696–717.

Andriopoulos, C. & Lewis, M.W. 2010. Managing innovation paradoxes: Ambidexterity lessons from leading product design companies. *Long Range Planning*, 43(1): 104–22.

Beech, N., Burns, H., de Caestecker, L., MacIntosh, R., & MacLean, D. 2004. Paradox as invitation to act in problematic change situations. *Human Relations*, 57(10): 1313–32.

Denis, J.L., Langley, A., & Rouleau, L. 2007. Strategizing in pluralistic contexts: Rethinking theoretical frames. *Human Relations*, 60(1): 179–215.

Fairhurst, G.T. & Putnam, L.L. 2014. Organizational discourse analysis. In L.L. Putnam & D.K. Mumby (eds), *The SAGE Handbook of Organizational Communication: Advances in Theory, Research, and Methods* (pp. 271–96). London: Sage.

Fairhurst, G.T., Cooren, F., & Cahill, D.J. 2002. Discursiveness, contradiction, and unintended consequences in successive downsizings. *Management Communication Quarterly*, 15(4): 501–40.

Fairhurst, G.T., Smith, W.K., Banghart, S.G., Lewis, M.W., Putnam, L.L., Raisch, S., & Schad, J. 2016. Diverging and converging: Integrative insights on a paradox meta-perspective. *Academy of Management Annals*, 10(1): 173–82.

Freidson, E. 2001. *Professionalism, the Third Logic: On the Practice of Knowledge*. Chicago, IL: University of Chicago Press.

Grant, A.M., Christianson, M.K., & Price, R.H. 2007. Happiness, health, or relationships? Managerial practices and employee well-being tradeoffs. *Academy of Management Perspectives*, 21(3): 51–63.

Hatch, M.J. 1997. Irony and the social construction of contradiction in the humor of a management team. *Organization Science*, 8(3): 275–88.

Heracleous, L. & Wirtz, J. 2014. Singapore Airlines: Achieving sustainable advantage through mastering paradox. *Journal of Applied Behavioral Science*, 50(2): 150–70.

Huq, J.-L., Reay, T., & Chreim, S. 2016. Protecting the paradox of interprofessional collaboration. *Organization Studies*, 38(3–4), 513–38.

Iedema, R., Degeling, P., Braithwaite, J., & White, L. 2004. 'It's an interesting conversation I'm hearing': The doctor as manager. *Organization Studies*, 25(1): 15–33.

Jarzabkowski, P. 2003. Strategic practices: An activity theory perspective on continuity and change. *Journal of Management Studies*, 40(1): 23–56.

Jarzabkowski, P. & Lê, J.K. 2016. We have to do this and that? You must be joking: Constructing and responding to paradox through humour. *Organization Studies*, 38(3–4), 433–62.

Jarzabkowski, P., Lê, J., & Van de Ven, A.H. 2013. Responding to competing strategic demands: How organizing, belonging, and performing paradoxes coevolve. *Strategic Organization*, 11(3), 245–80.

Jay, J. 2013. Navigating paradox as a mechanism of change and innovation in hybrid organizations. *Academy of Management Journal*, 56(1): 137–59.

Jules, C. & Good, D. 2014. Introduction to special issue on paradox in context advances in theory and practice. *Journal of Applied Behavioral Science*, 50(2): 123–6.

Knight, E. & Paroutis, S. 2017. Becoming salient: The TMT leader's role in shaping the interpretive context of paradoxical tensions. *Organization Studies*, 38(3–4): 403–32.

Langley, A. 1999. Strategies for theorizing from process data. *Academy of Management Review*, 24(4): 691–710.

Langley, A. 2007. Process thinking in strategic organization. *Strategic Organization*, 5(3): 271–81.

Lewis, M.W. 2000. Exploring paradox: Toward a more comprehensive guide. *Academy of Management Review*, 25(4): 760–76.

Lewis, M.W. & Smith, W. 2014. Paradox as a metatheoretical perspective: Sharpening the focus and widening the scope. *Journal of Applied Behavioral Science*, 50(2): 127–49.

Lüscher, L.S. & Lewis, M.W. 2008. Organizational change and managerial sensemaking: Working through paradox. *Academy of Management Journal*, 51(2): 221–40.

Papachroni, A., Heracleous, L., & Paroutis, S. 2015. Organizational ambidexterity through the lens of paradox theory building a novel research agenda. *Journal of Applied Behavioral Science*, 51(1): 71–93.

Poole, M.S. & Van de Ven, A. 1989. Using paradox to build management and organizational theory. *Academy of Management Review*, 14(4): 562–78.

Putnam, L.L., Myers, K.K., & Gailliard, B.M. 2014. Examining the tensions in workplace flexibility and exploring options for new directions. *Human Relations*, 67(4): 413–40.

Putnam, L.L., Fairhurst, G.T., & Banghart, S. 2016. Contradictions, dialectics, and paradoxes in organizations: A constitutive approach. *Academy of Management Annals*, 10(1): 65–171.

Raisch, S. & Birkinshaw, J. 2008. Organizational ambidexterity: Antecedents, outcomes, and moderators. *Journal of Management*, 34(3): 375–409.

Reay, T. & Hinings, C.R. 2009. Managing the rivalry of competing institutional logics. *Organization Studies*, 30(6): 629–52.

Schad, J., Lewis, M.W., Raisch, S., & Smith, W.K. 2016. Paradox research in management science: Looking back to move forward. *Academy of Management Annals*, 10(1): 1–60.

Sheep, M., Fairhurst, G.T., & Khazanchi, S. 2016. Knots in the discourse of innovation: Investigating multiple tensions in a reacquired spin-off. *Organization Studies*, 38(3–4): 463–88.

Smith, W.K. & Lewis, M.W. 2011. Toward a theory of paradox: A dynamic equilibrium model of organizing. *Academy of Management Review*, 36(2): 381–403.

Stoltzfus, K., Stohl, C., & Seibold, D.R. 2011. Managing organizational change: Paradoxical problems, solutions, and consequences. *Journal of Organizational Change Management*, 24(3): 349–67.

Taskin, L. & Devos, V. 2005. Paradoxes from the individualization of human resource management: The case of telework. *Journal of Business Ethics*, 62(1): 13–24.

Van de Ven, A.H. & Poole, M.S. 1995. Explaining development and change in organizations. *Academy of Management Review*, 20: 510–40.

Vince, R. & Broussine, M. 1996. Paradox, defense and attachment: Accessing and working with emotions and relations underlying organizational change. *Organization Studies*, 17(1): 1–21.

5

Reflexivity in Buddhist Epistemology

Implications for Cooperative Cognition

John D. Dunne

5.1 Introduction

Contemporary human life is made possible by human cooperation. Even the simple endeavour of shopping for vegetables in the market requires the complex cooperation of many humans. To produce vegetables in sufficient quantity to be commercially viable, several humans must cooperate just in the process of farming itself. The transportation of the vegetables to the market requires yet more coordination and cooperation, ranging from the task of scheduling to the proper delivery of items to specific merchants. When one further considers the vast array of cooperatively produced affordances that all this presupposes—automobiles, roads, tools, telecommunications, financing, and more—the extensive and profound degree of human cooperation required for our contemporary life is clearly undeniable. Human cooperation, however, is nothing new. On at least some accounts, the very capacity for robustly cooperative action—rooted in key features of cognition that no other primates managed to develop—is central to the evolution of humans.

In his persuasive book, *A Natural History of Human Thinking* (2014), Michael Tomasello proposes a version of this evolutionary story, and setting aside the details, one can retell it in simple terms. Tomasello's central claim is that, at some point, our earliest ancestors moved beyond the rudimentary forms of social cognition observed in the non-human primates that most resemble us now. Great apes such as chimpanzees and orangutans, for example, appear to have the capacity for many features of social cognition, including the ability to infer the intentions and likely actions that others will take based on those intentions. Uniquely, however, our distant ancestors moved beyond the competition-based model that typifies the social cognition of these non-human primates; instead, our earliest ancestors developed the capacities for truly cooperative cognition. With these capacities, our ancestors could effectively 'outsource' some of their cognitive tasks to a wider group in which each individual was embedded. For example, when engaged in foraging for food, the vigilance required to keep each individual safe from predators and other dangers could be performed by some members of the group, while others could focus on the task of gathering food. As they gathered food, these individuals could devote more of their cognitive resources to that task, while the 'guards' could focus on safety without any concern for going hungry. Even the simple task of foraging, when performed cooperatively, could thus become highly efficient, especially in contrast to the cognitive and physical resources that each individual would otherwise need to devote to both gathering and guarding. Offspring that were talented at this type of cooperative activity were favoured in evolutionary terms, and as our ancestors evolved, they eventually developed the capacity for enhancing their cognitive connectivity through language and through the development of cultural practices that enhanced cooperation.

Whatever one might think of this evolutionary story, the end point is clear: modern humans can cooperate in highly complex and flexible ways to produce farms, markets, highways, and trucks, and they do so by developing and transmitting elaborate cultural practices and social structures that facilitate cooperative cognition. This aspect of human cognition has inspired recent and groundbreaking work in multiple disciplines. In addition to Tomasello's work, key strands of related research and interpretation emerge in the writings of many authors, including: Edwin Hutchins (Hutchins, 1996, 2008, 2010) with his work on cognitive ecology; Andy Clark and David Chalmers (Clark, 2008; Clark & Chalmers, 1998) with their notion of extended cognition; Sean Gallagher on socially distributed cognition (Gallagher, 2013); Jim Coan and colleagues (Beckes & Coan, 2011; Coan & Sbarra, 2015) with their social baseline theory; and Gerry Stahl with his work on group cognition in computer-supported cooperative work and computer-supported cooperative learning. In various ways, these authors—and many others—articulate a similar vision of the unique human capacity for thinking in a way that is distributed across multiple, embodied minds that are deeply embedded in social and cultural networks. Despite notable differences in these approaches (see Hutchins, 2010 for a discussion), one thread that runs through all these various approaches is precisely the motif of cooperation. To emphasize this common thread, and in the interest of simplicity, I will thus speak of 'cooperative cognition', with the understanding that 'distributed cognition' and the other terms mentioned here inform this discussion.

The aim of this chapter is to raise some questions about a specific feature of cooperative cognition that figures, explicitly or implicitly, in all the scholarly work mentioned above. Briefly, in order for cooperative cognition to be distributed over multiple minds, each mind must maintain—at least implicitly—a model of the cooperative network in which the individual is embedded. It seems likely that such a model is highly task-specific, such that the model dynamically shifts in relation to the array of relevant tasks and goals. Maintaining a highly detailed model would consume many cognitive resources, so it also seems likely that the model provides only enough detail to allow individuals to act effectively in the cooperative tasks at hand. The model itself is also both facilitated and constrained by the various norms, habits, and cultural practices that regulate cooperative cognition. Applying all this to the comparatively simple example of foraging for food, each individual engages in actions guided by cognitions that require a tacit understanding of their role in the group's overall task of foraging, as guided by the style of foraging developed by the group over multiple generations. To put it another way, to cooperate in such a task, each individual must at least tacitly maintain an ongoing representation of the overall cooperative network—the task-oriented 'group'—in which they are embedded.

The key question posed by this chapter emerges from the central role played by the individuals' representations of the group in which they are embedded: the 'we' in the phrase, 'We are working toward this goal together.' In particular, that representation of the 'we' of the cooperative enterprise must also involve a monitoring of the state of that 'we'. For example, are we collaborating effectively toward our goal, or are we exhibiting some dysfunction that is inhibiting cooperation? Additionally, cooperative cognition must include some means not only to monitor the state of the network that constitutes the group, but also to sometimes make that network an explicit object of cooperative cognition itself, so that it can be regulated and adjusted when needed. All this raises several questions, but perhaps the most salient question is simply this: in cooperative cognition, how does the group itself become an explicit object of cognition in a way that allows the group to regulate itself? This simple question is actually quite challenging, and my suggestion is that, drawing on a cautious analogy with cognition in an individual, some type of reflexivity may be part of the answer to this question. To clarify the challenges here and the way that some notion of reflexivity may help us to understand cooperative cognition, I will now make a foray into Buddhist epistemology and some key features of its account of cognition in individuals. At the end of this chapter, I will return to the question of cooperative cognition to see what this brief exploration of Buddhist theories might help us to see more clearly in that context.

5.2 Some Methodological Caveats

Before launching into a discussion of Buddhist epistemology, two methodological issues require clarification. First, some of the material presented here, especially in relation to the key notion of reflexivity, remains an ongoing focus of research by scholars of Buddhism, and while the interpretations posed here will largely agree with the current research, I will also disagree with some current claims, most notably those by Dan Arnold (2012) and Christian Coseru (2012). The technicalities of these disagreements would lead us too far into the Buddhist epistemological weeds, so I will simply recommend that the interested reader consult their works for alternative accounts. Along these same lines, many of the sources for the discussion below have not yet been translated into any European language, and constant references to passages in Tibetan and Sanskrit texts would seem superfluous in this context. I will thus just refer briefly in the notes to the key texts.

Second, the Buddhist model discussed below applies to cognition in a single individual, and it does not address cooperative or distributed cognition; thus, the feature of particular interest in the individual—namely, reflexivity—is not theorized as an explicit aspect of cognition beyond the individual. Extending the unit of analysis beyond the individual to the social group has facilitated the previously cited work relevant to cooperative cognition, but that extension might encourage the notion that models of cognition operating beyond the level of the individual can treat these larger units of analysis (such as a family or other human grouping) as if they were just individuals on a larger scale. Social groupings, however, lack the type of connectivity found within individuals, paradigmatically illustrated by the astounding number of connections within the human brain. For this and other reasons, such as the time course of signals sent across socially mediated connections, it seems unwise to simply expand models of individual cognition and apply them to cognitions distributed across individuals. The discussion of reflexivity below is thus not meant to suggest that reflexivity at the level of the individual can simply be translated directly to the level of the group. Rather, my claim is that, by attending to certain features of reflexivity at the individual level, we may come to appreciate key aspects of cooperative cognition that might otherwise go unnoticed. These aspects of cooperative cognition, in turn, have implications for research and for the conceptualization of best practices in working groups.

5.3 Basic Buddhist Model of Cognition: the Case of Visual Recognition

To appreciate the role of reflexivity—and to use it for inciting questions about cooperative cognition—we must first explore some central features of the relevant Buddhist model of cognition, namely, the model articulated in the work of the Buddhist philosopher Dharmakīrti, who was active during the seventh century CE in South Asia.[1] Let us consider especially the paradigmatic case of explicitly categorizing the contents of visual cognition in an act that Dharmakīrti calls visual 'recognition', but that Western philosophers will often call 'perceptual judgement' in visual perception. This type of cognition occurs when, for example, one explicitly categorizes a visual object as being 'blue' or 'yellow', or when one recognizes the object as a 'cup' or 'car'.

According to Dharmakīrti and the many Buddhist theorists who later elaborated on his theories, visual recognition is a causal process that occurs in two basic phases. In the first phase, the visual sense faculty comes into contact with an object, and with some basic attentional features in place, that contact induces a representation of the object in awareness. This representation, called the 'phenomenal form of the object' (Sanskrit, *grāhyākāra*), is initially presented as the contents of visual awareness. In the second phase, which does not necessarily occur, that phenomenal form undergoes a type of conceptual processing that constitutes an act of 'recognition', where the object is categorized as being the same kind of thing as something previously experienced.

Focusing now on the first phase when the initial phenomenal form of the visual object arises in awareness, one might be tempted to say that this phenomenal form is like a 'picture' of the object in that it is a mental representation that emerges from the interaction of the mind, the senses, and the object itself. However, if the phenomenal form of the object is a picture, it is a picture taken with a most peculiar camera, especially since the phenomenal form is not simply some kind of mirror image of the object. Rather, these phenomenal forms vary across individuals, such that no two observers have the same phenomenal form appearing in their visual awareness, even if they are looking at the same object from the same angle. And even within an individual, differences in the immediately preceding mental states—including expectations and affective states—can impact this initial presentation of the object in awareness. Likewise, this initial 'picture' or phenomenal form of the visual object is actually the causal effect of the interaction of the mind, the visual faculty and the material object. As such, this 'picture' reflects the properties of that causal process, including the causal limitations of the visual faculty. For example, according to one standard Buddhist account, visual objects are composed of infinitesimally small bits of constantly fluctuating matter, and the human visual sense cannot detect something that small. Thus, the phenomenal form of the visual object is a kind of amalgam that emerges from the interactions among those bits of matter, the conjunction of that

---

[1] For more details on the issues discussed here, see Dunne (2004, 2011a). For similar accounts, see Dreyfus (1997), Coseru (2012), and Ganeri (2011).

matter with the visual sense, and the various causes and conditions operative within the mind and body where the phenomenal form of the object will be presented as the phenomenal content of visual awareness. Notably, this initial phenomenal presentation of the visual object lasts for a very short period of time, perhaps less than 50 milliseconds. It can be refreshed by further visual contact with the object, but each of these 'pictures' will be slightly different, and each will appear only briefly.[2]

As noted above, the second phase of the process of visual recognition involves a type of conceptual processing that constitutes an act of 'recognition', and this second phase is directly relevant to the organism's deliberate, conscious actions in relation to that visual object. In short, in order for an organism to act deliberately on the visual information, the initial phenomenal form must be processed further so as to categorize the object in a way that makes it an explicit object of action. This act of categorization essentially interprets the object as 'the same kind of thing' as something previously experienced. And while this categorization may involve language in humans, this recognitional process occurs even in organisms, such as pigeons, that lack the capacity for language.[3] Indeed, for Dharmakīrti and his followers, this recognitional process—the action-oriented categorization of the initial visual information that appears briefly in awareness—is the way that all conscious beings organize their sensory information in a way that facilitates action in the world. Additionally, according to this model, the type of concept formation involved in an act of visual recognition can only occur in the context of an organism that is engaged in goal-oriented behaviour. Thus, to put it another way, deliberate action on the visual object only occurs if the object is categorized in a way relevant to action, and that act of categorization involves a process of concept formation that only occurs when the organism is seeking to act in a goal-oriented fashion in the world.

A final basic feature of this act of recognition concerns the 'reportability' of the visual event. Humans can report on their visual experience by saying, for example, 'I just saw a water bottle there.' For Dharmakīrti and his followers, one can make such a report only if one has engaged in the type of categorization involved in the aforementioned act of recognition. Without the type of conceptualization involved in that act of recognition, the initial 'picture' or phenomenal form of the object can arise briefly in phenomenal awareness, but ordinary persons, at least, will have no conscious access to it. A good

---

[2] For some speculations on the temporal dimensions involved here, see Thompson (2014). Note that this model may involve some features that are compatible with a predictive account of perception, but it does not align with a strong version of a predictive account (for more on predictive accounts, see Clark, 2013).

[3] See, for example, the work on concept use in pigeons that dates back to the 1960s (e.g. Herrnstein & Loveland, 1964).

example from contemporary psychology is the notion of 'inattentional blindness' (Mack & Rock, 1998). A well-known demonstration of this phenomenon involves a film of persons passing a ball between them (Simons & Chabris, 1999). When subjects watch the film, each is asked to focus on counting how many passes are made by a particular team. Following Dharmakīrti's theory, the subjects are caught up in a goal—counting the passes. While they are focused on that task, other visual information is entering their visual awareness at the first, initial level of processing discussed previously. However, if that information is not relevant to their goal, the second phase of processing that involves recognition will not occur; as a result, they will not be able to report on that goal-irrelevant visual information, even though it did enter their visual awareness at that first level of the 'picture' or phenomenal form. This theory suggests that, in order to report on goal-irrelevant visual cues, the subject would have to suspend the goal of counting the passes because another goal (such as being aware of anomalies in the visual space) overrides the counting. With all this in place, it is not surprising that, when a person in a gorilla suit wanders through the film of people passing a ball around, about 50 per cent of subjects do not report seeing the 'gorilla' in the film, even though the gorilla-suited person walked directly through the group of people passing the ball. The Invisible Gorilla Test illustrates well this aspect of Dharmakīrti's model—namely, that, even when a visual object has been presented as a phenomenal form in sensory awareness, one can report on that object (by saying, for example, 'I saw a gorilla') only if one has engaged in the goal-oriented act of conceptualization involved in visual recognition.

5.4 Intentionality, Subjectivity, and Reflexivity

Thus far, this account has focused on the process for recognizing an object in visual awareness. In the first phase of that process, a phenomenal form of the object arises in awareness due to the complex causal interactions of the material object, the visual sense faculty, and the various attentional and affective features present in the mind. Under some circumstances, that phenomenal form of the object then goes through the second phase, whereby it is characterized for the purpose of goal-oriented action by a conceptualization that 'recognizes' or categorizes the object in a way that makes it available for deliberate action. That recognition not only enables deliberate action in relation to the object; it also allows a report to be produced, as when one says, 'I see a flower.' At this point, to introduce the notion of reflexivity, another set of features in the model must be explored. These features concern not the object, but rather the subject.

According to the Dharmakīrtian model of cognition under discussion here, every moment of cognition includes not only a phenomenal form of the cognition's object, but also a phenomenal form of the subjectivity that occurs with the cognition of any object. Thus, in visual awareness, when one sees an object that one recognizes as a 'flower', the visual perception includes a sense of a cognitive subject as the apparent agent who is doing the seeing. In vision and other forms of sensory awareness, this presentation of the object in relation to a sense of subjectivity is indicated by the 'out-there-ness' (Sanskrit, *bāhyatā*) of the object. In other words, the object is presented in awareness as being 'for' a subject, such that the object seems to be 'over there' in relation to a subject who is 'in here'. This is so even though the phenomenal form of the object in visual awareness—the shapes, colours, and so on that are phenomenally presented in visual awareness—is not outside of the mind at all. As noted previously, the above qualities are the products of our visual system's interactions with material objects that are then represented phenomenally as colours, shapes, and so on. Yet even though the phenomenal content of visual awareness is not outside the mind, it is presented as being 'over there' in relation to a sense of subjectivity 'in here'. That sense of subjectivity is called, in Buddhist technical terms, the 'phenomenal form of the subject' (Sanskrit, *grāhakākāra*).

For the Buddhist epistemological tradition, this relationship between the phenomenal forms of the object and subject is a necessary feature of any mental state in which an object is presented. In other words, whenever an object is presented in awareness, it must be presented in relation to a sense of subjectivity. In the Western phenomenological tradition, this relationship between object and subject is described as 'intentionality', and as with the Buddhist epistemological tradition, Western phenomenologists see it as necessarily present in any cognition of an object.[4]

One especially striking feature of this model is that, while the phenomenal forms of the object and subject must always occur together, only the object form is presented as being 'for' the subject form that occurs with it. The subject form itself does not appear to be presented as being 'for' some other sense of subjectivity. If the phenomenal form of the subject were presented as an object for some other second-order subject, then in order for that second-order subjectivity to be presented phenomenally, it would also need to be presented for some third-order subject, and so on. In this way, an infinite regress would ensue. Instead, the phenomenal form of the subject—the sense of subjectivity that occurs in a cognition of an object—is *reflexively* presented.

---

[4] For a compelling account from the Western phenomenal perspective, see Zahavi (2005) and, more recently, Zahavi and Kriegel (2015). Note, however, that for Western phenomenologists, consciousness is necessarily structured by intentionality, whereas the Buddhist tradition would maintain that there are some special cases of awareness that are 'non-dual' in that they do not present with the subject–object structure of intentionality.

A straightforward way to understand the term 'reflexive' here is that it points to the use of the reflexive pronoun *sva* in Sanskrit, where awareness of the phenomenal form of the subject is said to involve *sva-saṃvitti* (literally, 'self-awareness'). To understand the grammatical reflexivity operative here, one might consider any language with reflexive pronouns. For example, in Spanish, if I say, 'Yo hablo español' (I speak Spanish), then the verb hablar (to speak) is transitive, with an agent (yo) performing the action of speaking in relation to the grammatical object (español). In contrast, when one says, 'Aquí se habla español' (Spanish is spoken here), the pronoun 'se' is reflexive such that the transitive verb 'hablar' (to speak) is now rendered intransitive. There is no longer a grammatical subject or agent acting on a separate object. In the same way, the sense of subjectivity that occurs in any awareness of an object is presented reflexively, in the sense that it is self-presenting without being taken as the object of some other subjectivity. This is why it is said to involve *sva-saṃvitti*, 'self-awareness' or, in a more precise translation, 'reflexive awareness', In short, the phenomenal form of subjectivity is presented in an intransitive fashion, without it being the object of some other subjectivity.

5.5 Reflexive Awareness in Action

Reflexive awareness serves various roles in the Dharmakīrtian model of cognition within an individual, but two of its functions are especially relevant here.[5] First, reflexive awareness presents an implicit model of the perceiving agent that is crucial for action in the world; and second, it allows one to become explicitly aware of emotions and other background features of one's cognitive state in a way that makes them available for regulation or other deliberate actions. Soon, I will suggest how these two features of reflexivity may shed some light on key aspects of cooperative cognition, but first, I will unpack these two functions of reflexivity in Dharmakīrti's system.

5.5.1 *Reflexivity and Implicit Awareness of the Subject*

As noted above, according to this style of Buddhist epistemology, any awareness with an object must simultaneously include an intransitive awareness of the subject. For example, as I am gazing at a patch of colour, a representation of that colour patch occurs in my visual awareness, and along with it occurs a

---

[5] This section is based on the account of reflexive awareness (*svasaṃvitti*) articulated by Dharmakīrti and his commentators, especially Devendrabuddhi (seventh century) and Śākyabuddhi (eighth century), as found in Dharmakīrti's *Pramāṇārttika*, chapter 3, verses 194–224 and 322–540. Most of these materials have not been the focus of scholarly work, but see Dunne (2004, 2011b, 2012, 2015), Coseru (2012), and Arnold (2010, 2012).

sense that the image or phenomenal form of the colour patch in my visual awareness is being seen by a subject, a perceiver that is doing the seeing. Again, this awareness of subjectivity in visual awareness occurs 'intransitively' or 'reflexively' because the subject itself is not presented as an object for some other subject. Instead, it is simply included in the visual perception of the object.

This reflexive awareness of subjectivity occurs with any phenomenal appearance of an object, and this means that a sense of subjectivity is present even before the second phase of perception, when the object is 'recognized' in a way that makes it available to deliberate action. The clear implication here is that even in the first phase of perception, the object is already presented not just for a passive subject, but rather for a subject that is embedded in a goal-oriented context, minimally defined as obtaining affordances and avoiding dangers. By being presented as an object 'for' a goal-oriented subject, the object is contextualized by the features of the subject, including the subject's spatial and temporal location. And these features are precisely what constitute the model of the subject as an agent—or, indeed, a 'self'—engaged with the world.

One way to understand the role of reflexivity here is to consider the implications of its absence. In other words, let us suppose that the phenomenal form of the object were presented without any sense that it is the object of some subject. In that case, how would the cognitive system specify the object's location in space and time? The Dharmakīrtian interpretation is apparently that the object's spatiotemporal location can only be specified in relation to the sense of subjectivity included with the perception of the object. And this points to a key feature of reflexive awareness: it provides a spatiotemporal reference point for the object by keeping track of the subject's spatiotemporal location, but it keeps track of the subject's location implicitly. In other words, reflexive awareness intransitively presents the subject as the spatiotemporal reference point ('in here') for objects ('over there') without turning the subject itself into another object.

When the object is 'recognized' and thus becomes an explicit focus of goal-oriented action, it is perhaps even clearer that the awareness of the subject must remain implicit in this way. If I see something that I recognize as a door and then attempt to open it, my explicit focus is on the door (or perhaps the door handle). If instead, I turn my explicit focus inward toward my own subjectivity, I will lose my focus on the door until I return my focus to it. Yet without keeping track of the subject's spatiotemporal location, movement relative to the door will be impossible. The Dharmakīrtian claim is thus that, even while maintaining explicit focus on the door, an awareness of embodied subjectivity is continuously but implicitly presented as an essential feature of the cognitive context. In other words, even while fully absorbed in action toward an object, a model of subjectivity as the agent of the action is implicitly maintained through reflexive awareness.

A short exercise can illustrate the point that is being made here. As a thought experiment, focus as intently as possible on the black dot below for five or so seconds:

●

A simple question that can be asked now is this: in the experience of focusing on the dot, was the dot perceived by you, or someone else? According to the account given here, even while you were fully engaged in the simple task of focusing on the dot, the sense that the dot was being seen by someone— namely, you—is included as part of the experience of looking at that dot. Indeed, the question just asked may seem almost ridiculous. That is, the visual experience of the dot 'over there' on the page or screen so obviously requires some sense of a subjectivity 'in here' that it may seem absurd to even ask, 'Who was seeing it?' It is precisely this sense of subjectivity—so obvious that it seems absurd to question—that is presented by reflexive awareness. In short, without any need to attend to the sense of subjectivity that occurs with any focus on an object, that sense of subjectivity is nevertheless presented as an implicit feature of the structure of object-oriented awareness.

5.5.2 *Reflexivity and Explicit Awareness of Subjectivity and Its Features*

The second function of reflexive awareness that may shed light on cooperative cognition is the way that reflexivity does not just provide an implicit or tacit awareness of subjectivity; instead, it also enables explicit awareness of subjectivity and the features (such as emotional states) associated with it. To understand this aspect of reflexive awareness, we must examine some additional aspects of the process of 'recognition' discussed above.

As noted earlier, the Dharmakīrtian cognitive model takes a particular type of cognition as paradigmatic—namely, the cognition that occurs when a sentient being has a sensory perception of an object and then, 'recognizing' that object, performs a deliberate action in relation to it. This theory maintains that all such cases—and, indeed, cognition in general—are embedded in the overall context of a sentient being engaging with sensory experience in terms of goal-oriented action, minimally defined as avoiding dangers and obtaining affordances. Some aspects of this theory, while important, are not fully articulated, and one such aspect is generally known as 'salience'.

In general terms within cognitive science, 'salience' in this context refers to the way that an object emerges as significant in perceptual cognition (Itti & Koch, 2000). Although not clearly articulated by Dharmakīrti or his followers, it seems that the Dharmakīrtian model must also presume some form of salience. The first phase of sensory perception, for example, involves the delineation of objects. Specifically, that phase presents the phenomenal form of an object, and in doing so, it has already selected an object out of a more complex visual field. Presumably, this kind of object selection involves something like salience, but for the Dharmakīrtian model, this first phase cannot involve the interpretation of the object as explicitly relevant to goal-oriented action, precisely because that type of explicit relevance relies on the 'recognition' that occurs in the second phase. Thus, for our purposes here, the term 'salience' will not refer to the process of object selection found in the first phase. Instead, salience refers to the way that an object of perception emerges as significant for goal-oriented action and is thus 'recognized' as explicitly relevant to some goal.

With this notion of salience in place, one can refine the account of the causal process involved in the paradigmatic case of seeing and recognizing an object for the purposes of goal-oriented action. In the first phase, the object is presented in consciousness as a phenomenal form that emerges from the interaction of the object, the sense faculty, and the mind. Simultaneously, a phenomenal form of the subject is presented through reflexive awareness as a phenomenological feature of perceptual awareness in a way that provides a spatiotemporal reference point for the object. Here, it is crucial to note that the phenomenal forms of the object and subject arise together because they are necessary to each other; indeed, they are simply two aspects of the same moment of consciousness. Hence, when (after a very short interval) the moment of 'recognition' occurs, it emerges from that previous moment of consciousness as a whole; that is, it emerges from the complex structure involving both the phenomenal form of the object and the phenomenal form of the subject. Because goal-oriented action generally concerns objects that are taken to be 'out there' in the world, the phenomenal form of the object usually plays the dominant role in the emergence of the moment of recognition. In other words, that object-focused recognition guides action oriented toward the object represented in the phenomenal form. Sometimes, however, the phenomenal form of the subject is the focus of recognition, and this is when an explicit awareness of subjectivity emerges.

By way of example, consider the task of repairing my bicycle tyre. Perhaps I am late for an appointment, and I need to repair the tyre quickly. This task involves a complex series of perceptions that recognize and enable me to engage with many objects relevant to my goal of fixing the tyre. And each of these acts of perceptual recognition involves my focus on the object in question, such as the spot on the tyre where the puncture occurred. Nevertheless, let us suppose that, at a certain point in this series of perceptions, I suddenly notice that I am anxious about completing the task, and that this is hampering my progress. How does this awareness of anxiety emerge? On the Dharmakīrtian model, in my perceptions up to that point in the task, the phenomenal forms of the various objects played the primary causal role in the emergence of the series of recognitions because, given the goal or task that I was holding in mind, these various objects are most salient. But at some point, the phenomenal form of the subject gained salience because it was most relevant to accomplishing that task. Its relevance came specifically through the way that the phenomenal form of the subject presents information about not just the spatiotemporal location of the perceiving subject, but also about other features, including especially the affective features currently active in consciousness. Thus, at a certain point in the process of fixing my bicycle tyre, even though I was focused on some object (such as the spot of the puncture), the phenomenal form of the subject became so task-relevant that, instead of producing another moment of 'recognizing' an object, that moment of consciousness produced a recognition about a task-relevant affective feature within my sense of subjectivity; and thus, the recognition of a goal-obstructing 'anxiety' was produced.

This example of recognizing an affective state as anxiety highlights some crucial features of reflexive awareness. Recall that, when the phenomenal form of the object leads to a moment of recognition about an object, it enables deliberate, goal-oriented action toward that object. Likewise, when the phenomenal form of the subject leads to a recognition such as 'anxiety is occurring', it also enables deliberate, goal-oriented action. In short, by recognizing the anxiety, I now have an opportunity to regulate my affective state in a way that will enable me to fix the tyre more efficiently. In this way, my recognition of the anxiety is directed toward an object, namely, an affective feature of my sense of subjectivity. This means that, at least in relation to that affective feature, one has objectified one's own sense of subjectivity and taken that as a new object. Another way of understanding this objectification of subjectivity is that, prior to the recognition, the previous moment of awareness contained both an object pole (the phenomenal form of the object) and a subject pole (the phenomenal form of the subject). When the moment of recognizing anxiety occurred, the subject pole of that previous awareness is taken as the object of the current awareness. And in keeping with this model, the current awareness has both an object (namely, what has been recognized as 'anxiety') and a simultaneously presented sense of subjectivity. This also helps us to understand one way in which I might fail to regulate my anxiety, in that this process can continue. That is, I can become anxious about my own anxiety, and then I recognize that I am now anxious about my anxiety; continuing this type of iteration, I may spiral into a panic attack. In any case, by this point I am clearly no longer focused on the task of fixing the tyre, since I am by now focusing entirely on my own affective states. Clearly, I will be late for my appointment!

In the way just outlined, reflexive awareness can enable an explicit awareness of the features of one's own subjectivity. This explicit awareness, however, does not depend on somehow moving from a state in which the various features of subjectivity were completely unavailable to a state in which they are now presented. Instead, from the Dharmakīrtian perspective, the various features of subjectivity are *always implicitly presented* in any moment of cognition. These features are presented as the phenomenal form of the subject through reflexive awareness, as discussed previously. Thus, on this model, if one wishes to monitor one's affective states, it is not necessary for one to somehow engage in a constant introspective turn so as to inwardly observe one's emotions and such. Instead, information about one's affective states (and other aspects of one's sense of being a perceiving subject) are constantly presented reflexively. An increased capacity for monitoring affect would thus not come from turning inward; instead, it would be developed by intensifying reflexive awareness, and also by holding in mind a task set or goal that prioritized affective monitoring. In any case, from the perspective of the Dharmakīrtian approach, affective monitoring can and does continue, even to a heightened degree, while still engaging in tasks that are focused on objects in the world (such as repairing a tyre). In contrast, if affective monitoring required an inward, introspective turn, tasks in the world would be severely inhibited, since the focus on an object in the world would constantly be interrupted by an inward focus on one's sense of subjectivity. In short, for the Dharmakīrtian model, an awareness of the subject—which might be explicitly stated as, 'How am I doing?'—is always implicitly available even when fully engaged in some demanding task in the world.

A final point about reflexive awareness of the sense of subjectivity is worth raising here. Since one's sense of subjectivity—along with its various features—is always presented to at least some degree in any moment of object-focused awareness, there is a straightforward way to create opportunities for facilitating one's recognizing (and regulating) subject side features: one may simply use a prompt. Consider this example. A friend and I are admiring a beautiful night sky on an especially clear winter's night, and we are both completely absorbed in that visual scene. When my friend asks whether I am enjoying the night sky, my awareness of the affective features of the experience are immediately available to me because they are encoded with the experience itself. In other words, the prompt does not require me to somehow experience the sky differently; the question simply invites me to notice the affective features that are already included in the experience itself.

5.6 Implications for Cooperative Cognition

5.6.1 *Some Features of Cooperative Cognition*

Before exploring some implications that the Buddhist theory of reflexivity may hold for cooperative cognition, it will be helpful to clarify what is meant by 'cooperative cognition' in this context. As noted earlier, the term 'cooperative cognition' is used here to pick out some common themes in a range of theoretical accounts that overlap significantly, while diverging in ways that are not relevant to the current discussion. All these various approaches, such as 'distributed cognition' and 'group cognition', concern the way that human minds may interact to produce cognitive events together. This perspective stands in contrast to the notion that cognition occurs just 'in the head' of individual humans. Following Tomasello (2014), the main emphasis here is on the way that this type of distributed cognition occurs paradigmatically in the context of humans cooperating in the performance of a task or achievement of a goal.

Examples of the distributed cognition that occurs when humans cooperate include tasks that can only be accomplished by multiple humans working together. In this context, Edwin Hutchins has extensively studied the form of cognition that emerges from the interactions of flight crews in airline cockpits, primarily as observed in realistic flight simulators (e.g. Hutchins, 1995; Hutchins & Klausen, 1998). The complexity of a modern airline cockpit is such that no single human could safely fly this type of airplane without assistance. Much of that assistance comes precisely in the sharing of cognitive tasks, such that tasks are performed in the interaction between humans, rather than occurring 'in the head' of a single human. In one study, Hutchins and Tove Klausen (Hutchins & Klausen, 1998) discuss the distributed cognition that occurs when managing voice communications with Air Traffic Control (ATC). These communications require not just retaining the communication in memory, but also processing that information in a way that leads to appropriate actions. Hutchins and Klausen examine a case in which the captain receives a communication for a new radio frequency. The captain's interactions with the first officer (F/O)—including just a meaningful glance—enable that information to be retained and for the appropriate actions to be taken by both the captain and the F/O. On the analysis proposed by Hutchins and Klausen, the cognitive activities required for the crew to act appropriately emerge from the interactions of the crew as they play their respective roles.

The work of a flight crew illustrates the type of cooperative, distributed cognition that emerges from a group of humans that have learned the roles that must be played to accomplish a complex task that exceeds the abilities of any single human. Cooperative cognition of this type requires a sense of 'shared intentionality' among the humans involved, such that they can maintain a cognitive representation not only of themselves, but also of the various interlocking roles within the cooperating group (Tomasello, 2014). In the above example of the flight crew, the captain and F/O had met only two hours before their training run in the simulator, yet they were able to succeed at their cooperative task because they were highly trained in the overall procedures and the specific roles that each member of the flight crew must play. In the example noted above, when the captain does not give a required response about a radio frequency to ATC, the F/O simply glances at the captain, and when the captain's return look suggests that he cannot recall the number of the frequency, the F/O prompts him verbally (Hutchins & Klausen, 1998). This type of exchange is possible because both the captain and the F/O have a shared sense of the overall procedures and the specific roles that they must play. Thus, even while highly focused on a specific task such as acknowledging a new frequency from ATC, the crew members simultaneously hold in mind a representation of their cooperating group and their roles therein.

In the research on airline flight crews performed by Hutchins and colleagues, the extensive training of flight crews enables a rich form of intersubjectivity that connects the members through cognitive functions such as memory, attention, the interpretation of visual information, and the manipulation of controls. However, intersubjectivity, shared intentionality, and the cooperative cognition enabled thereby can also emerge in contexts that are far less scripted than an airline flight crew. Gerry Stahl (2016), for example, has examined what he calls 'group cognition'—another term for the type of distributed, cooperative cognition under discussion here—in the context of computer-supported cooperative learning. In one instance, Stahl discusses a group of three fourteen-year-old girls engaged in solving a geometry problem about triangles by using the Virtual Math Team (VMT) system. Even though the girls were interacting only remotely through the VMT's interface for texting and online visualizations, Stahl argues that they engaged in a deep form of group (i.e. cooperative) cognition. For Stahl, the type of cooperative cognition that emerges in this type of problem solving is especially marked by the feeling that the participants discover 'thoughts which I had no idea I possessed' (Stahl, 2016, p. 380; Stahl is here quoting Merleau-Ponty). Along these lines, Stahl (p. 378) says:

> The analysis of the team's work concluded that the students' success was an instance of group cognition. None of the students could construct the triangle configuration themselves and the process of construction involved all three exploring, planning and carrying out the construction. Each of the three girls displays a different characteristic behavior pattern throughout their work in the 8 hour-long sessions of our study. Yet, the team is impressively collaborative. This illustrates nicely the notion of individual perspectives within intersubjective group interaction.

Stahl's example clarifies another aspect of cooperative cognition—namely, that it is marked by an intersubjectivity that enables individuals to contribute to a process whose result exceeds their own cognitive capacities. In short, cooperative cognition requires minds to be connected such that cognition is not just happening 'in one's head'.

5.6.2 Implications from Dharmakīrtian Reflexivity

As sketched above, key features of cooperative cognition resonate with the Dharmakīrtian account of reflexivity, and the Dharmakīrtian account thus implies possible areas for research and for best practices in enhancing cooperative cognition within a group. The first implication concerns the capacity for each individual to hold in cognition a representation of the group while the group is focused on a task. The Dharmakīrtian account maintains that, in the case of the individual, reflexive awareness implicitly presents the sense of subjectivity with every object-oriented cognition. The sense of subjectivity is presented as a structural feature of cognition in such an obvious fashion that, as noted earlier, it seems almost absurd to ask, 'Who is reading this now?' Likewise, it would seem that cooperative cognition requires a similar form of implicit awareness that presents the group to each individual without disrupting the group's focus on the task at hand. A research agenda focused on a group's implicit representation of itself follows from this implication of the Dharmakīrtian model.

A second implication concerns the self-awareness of the group that must be in place when the group requires self-regulation, as might happen when a conflict in the group is inhibiting its accomplishment of the task at hand. This situation resembles the example given above when I, in the process of changing my bicycle tyre, become aware of a level of anxiety that is inhibiting my work on the tyre. As noted earlier, the awareness of my anxiety emerges from the ongoing, background presentation of my affective state that is provided by reflexive awareness. In a similar way, even while fully engaged in a cooperative task, the members of a group may become aware of something about the group itself that must be adjusted so as to succeed at their goal. How do members of the group shift their focus from their cooperative work to the group itself in this way? In other words, how do they explicitly ask and answer the question, 'How are we doing?' One obvious option is that some person is tasked with handling these issues for the group; this person monitors the group and makes interventions when necessary. But the Dharmakīrtian model of reflexive awareness sketched above might suggest an entirely different interpretation that would especially apply when the group does not have any top-down supervision, as in the case of a Self-Managing Work Team (SMWT).

In the Dharmakīrtian model, there is no separate part of the mind (or brain) that stands apart from one's experiences of the world and monitors one's subjectivity to make interventions when required. Instead, the reflexivity inherent in one's focus on a task allows one to become aware at appropriate times of subjective features and regulate them as needed. This can happen in a way that allows one to maintain one's overall task; there is no need for some prolonged introspection or outside intervention. Likewise, in the context of cooperative cognition, is something like reflexivity operative? That is, perhaps the members of a cooperatively engaged group not only represent the group implicitly to themselves, but they also implicitly monitor themselves through a similar background awareness. When some dysfunction becomes salient, it emerges as an explicit object for the group's attention so that the dysfunction can be addressed and regulated. Here, the self-managing capacities of SMWTs may be enhanced by considering how team members become aware of a group's dysfunction even while in the midst of a task.

Another key implication of the Dharmakīrtian approach concerns precisely the capacity for self-monitoring and the problem of what I will call the 'illusion of the objectified subject'. As noted above, on the Dharmakīrtian model, reflexivity is what allows the phenomenal form of the subject—the sense of subjectivity in an experience with an object—to lead to a moment of 'recognition' whereby one knows, for example, that anxiety is occurring. This moment allows one to act deliberately on that information so as to regulate the anxiety, but it also comes with a danger. That is, in the moment of recognizing a feature of the subject pole in an experience, one effectively objectifies the subject pole. And as with any experience of an object, that experience also comes with a sense of subjectivity. Thus, it may seem that, by knowing one's objectified subjectivity, one is now knowing one's subjectivity, but this is just an illusion. Instead, one is just knowing a conceptualized version of a previous moment of one's subjectivity, and one is doing so from the standpoint of one's actual subjectivity. A continued pondering of this objectified sense of subjectivity will not give one any additional information about one's actual subjectivity. And of course, by pondering one's objectified subjectivity in this way ('I am anxious!'), the task at hand (e.g. changing the bicycle tyre) will be neglected. Instead, to inquire further into one's state of subjectivity, one must drop the conceptualized 'recognition' of an objectified subjectivity and once again allow reflexivity to do its work by making implicit features of subjectivity become explicitly apparent. In this way, a deep inquiry into the state of one's subjectivity requires an oscillation between the implicit awareness provided by reflexivity and the explicit awareness that occurs with a moment of recognition.

In the context of cooperative cognition, one implication of this aspect of the Dharmakīrtian model is that attempts to understand and regulate a cooperative group's dysfunction may fail if those attempts are focused entirely on the group itself. If something like a Dharmakīrtian model of reflexive awareness applies to cooperative groups, then at some point the group's dysfunction moves from being implicit to becoming explicit, just as my feeling of anxiety while changing the bicycle tyre moved from the reflexively presented background of my awareness to the foreground. In this way, when the group's dysfunction becomes an explicit focus, the group is no longer on its task; instead, it is focused on the group itself and its own dysfunction. Perhaps more importantly, the group's focus on itself involves the same illusion above: when an individual introspects and takes her subjectivity as an object, she is just engaging with a conceptualization of her subjectivity. And while this conceptualization can be useful, it is misleading because it is not one's actual subjectivity. This is so because subjectivity is by nature not an object; it is the standpoint from which objects are known. Likewise, when a group becomes aware of itself, perhaps due to some group-level dysfunction, it can be useful to engage in a kind of 'group introspection', through which the members of the group focus on the group itself. But if the Dharmakīrtian model is applicable here, then the group that is represented as an object for this 'group introspection' is not the actual group at all. Instead, the actual group is the cooperative network of individuals who are now engaged in the cooperative task of examining themselves as a group. Among the many implications here is especially the limited utility of exercises or workshops focused on the collaborative group itself. If the group itself is an explicit object in these activities—as in, 'let's talk about our department'—then the outcome will just be an enhanced conceptualization of the group, but not an enhanced awareness of the group itself.[6]

A parallel implication here is that one would need to acknowledge that the objectified model of the group—the notion of the group that becomes explicit when members become directly concerned with the group itself—is only a heuristic. That is, as with the aforementioned illusion of the objectified subject, the group member's objectified notion of the group could not actually be the model that they hold in mind when they are working cooperatively together. If they were holding an objectified model of the group in mind while working together, then the only object that they could be working on would be the group itself. Instead, the members of the group must hold an implicit model of the group in mind while engaged in cooperative, task-oriented cognition. It is this implicit model of the group that impedes progress toward the group's goal when it becomes dysfunctional, so it is also this implicit model that must occasionally become explicit for the purposes of regulating the group. Again, the implicit model is constantly presented to

---

[6] For the limitations of this type of approach when 'group reflexivity' is understood to involve objectification of the group itself, see Moreland and McMinn (2010).

each member of the group through something like reflexivity, and it is precisely this type of reflexivity that would provide explicit knowledge of the group when needed.

A final implication of the Dharmakīrtian notion of reflexive awareness concerns the enhancement of reflexivity itself. In terms of an individual, if the implicit awareness of subjectivity provided by reflexivity is somehow not up to this task, it cannot be enhanced by turning inward or introspecting, since this will simply provide more objectification of the subject. Instead, the Dharmakīrtian approach would recommend the use of contemplative techniques that enhance reflexive awareness, along with a task set or goal that prioritizes awareness of subjectivity. In this way, one is more likely to become genuinely aware of the subjective features of experience because the phenomenal form of the subject is both stronger (through enhanced reflexivity) and becomes salient more often (due to the modified task set). Various meditative techniques, such as those found in some mindfulness traditions, directly target the enhancement of reflexivity in this way (Lutz et al., 2015).

In the context of an individual, enhanced reflexivity gives one a stronger 'signal', so to speak, from the subjective side of an experience, and this thus provides greater opportunities for becoming aware of emotions, expectations, and other features that may require regulation. If something like the Dharmakīrtian notion of reflexivity in individuals also occurs in collaborative groups, then it too would underlie a group's capacity to regulate itself. But how might this type of intransitive 'group reflexivity'[7] be enhanced? Clearly, a notion of group reflexivity inspired by the Dharmakīrtian account would have something to do with the intersubjective connectivity that the members of the group experience. To some extent, mindfulness and similar contemplative practices that are used to enhance reflexivity in individuals may also be useful for enhancing this type of intersubjective connectivity in groups, inasmuch as these practices can enhance empathy and perspective taking (Dahl et al., 2015). Other strategies focus not so much on explicit training, but on the norms, environment, and styles of interaction that an organization can seek to cultivate in groups. In work that remains fresh even in relation to more recent research documented by Widmer et al. (2009), Vanessa Druskat and

---

[7] It is important to note that the term 'group reflexivity' here is used to suggest that, as in the case of individual cognition, some form of implicit, intransitive awareness of the group is operative in cooperative cognition. This notion of 'group reflexivity' stands in contrast to the same term when used to refer to a group process of deliberately reflecting on the group. This latter usage should properly be called 'group reflection', since it engages with an objectified notion of the group and does not explicitly draw on the form of reflexivity discussed here. Although the term 'group reflexivity' occurs in the research literature in the latter sense of a group's overt reflection about itself, I have chosen to use the same term here in part so as to contest the notion that 'reflexivity' simply means overt reflection on the group. For a review of the literature on 'group reflexivity' in its usage as group reflection, see Widmer et al. (2009).

colleagues (Druskat & Pescosolido, 2002; Druskat & Wolff, 2001) have pointed to a number of best practices in SMWTs that could be construed as enhancing the type of group reflexivity under discussion here. Two of these practices are especially relevant. The first is 'heedful relating'. Drawing on the work of Weick and Roberts (1993), Druskat and Pescosolido note that heedful relating is not about behaviour per se; rather, it concerns the way that one interacts with one's team. Specifically, such interactions are 'attentive, purposeful, conscientious and considerate' (Druskat & Pescosolido, 2002, p. 293). For Druskat and Pescosolido, the group representation that this encourages is one that emphasizes team–member interdependence—a quality that would clearly enhance intersubjective connection and group reflexivity. Along these same lines, Druskat and Wolff (2001) argue that the most effective SMWTs involve mutual trust among members, a sense of group identity, and a sense of group efficacy. Their claim is that all three features are rooted in the affective or emotional aspects of a group's interactions, and thus for Druskat and Wolff, Emotional Intelligence (EI) is a key component of team effectiveness. Given the central role played by reflexivity in the awareness and regulation of emotions in individuals, it seems highly likely that reflexivity in groups, if it exists at all, is at least in part a matter of a group's EI. Norms, environments, and practices that enhance EI—and social connectivity in general—would thus likely enhance a group's reflexivity, and vice versa.

5.7 Conclusion

Some form of reflexive awareness in individuals is well established not only in Dharmakīrtian Buddhist epistemology, but also in the Western phenomenological tradition. While still a target of criticism and a matter of debate, theories of individual reflexivity at least have a long and distinguished history. Group reflexivity, however, is a new and speculative idea that, while implied by theories of cooperative or distributed cognition, has not yet been fully addressed by the formulators of these theories. This chapter suggests a way forward toward formulating a theory of intransitive reflexive awareness in groups, but numerous questions and potential criticisms are necessarily not addressed. A key issue—and one that may be empirically tractable—concerns the modes of connectivity that occur in cooperative, distributed cognition. In the case of a single individual, neuronal connections in the brain and afferent/efferent connections with the body provide a dense array of connectivity to support cognition and sensory-motor functionality, and from a Dharmakīrtian perspective, that dense connectivity would likely be the basis for reflexivity itself. But when cognition moves beyond not only the head, but also the skin, how do individuals connect in a way that can support cooperative, distributed cognition and the 'group reflexivity' that it seems to require? Language obviously plays a central role in providing connectivity, as do facial expressions, physical postures, clothing, and other fairly overt forms of interactive expression. Might there be more? Perhaps physiological synchrony (Konvalinka et al., 2011), or even pheromones (Weller, 1998) play a role? The notion of group reflexivity as an intransitive, background awareness raises not only these, but many more questions. They seem worth exploring.

References

Arnold, D. 2010. Self-awareness (*svasaṃvitti*) and related doctrines of Buddhists following Dignāga: Philosophical characterizations of some of the main issues. *Journal of Indian Philosophy*, 38(3): 323–78. DOI: 10.1007/s10781-010-9095-7.

Arnold, D. 2012. *Brains, Buddhas, and Believing: The Problem of Intentionality in Classical Buddhist and Cognitive-Scientific Philosophy of Mind*. New York: Columbia University Press.

Beckes, L. & Coan, J.A. 2011. Social baseline theory: The role of social proximity in emotion and economy of action. *Social and Personality Psychology Compass*, 5(12): 976–88.

Clark, A. 2008. *Supersizing the Mind: Embodiment, Action, and Cognitive Extension*. New York: Oxford University Press.

Clark, A. 2013. Whatever next? Predictive brains, situated agents, and the future of cognitive science. *Behavioral and Brain Sciences*, 36(3): 181–204. DOI: 10.1017/S0140525X12000477.

Clark, A. & Chalmers, D. 1998. The extended mind. *Analysis*, 58(1): 7.

Coan, J.A. & Sbarra, D.A. 2015. Social baseline theory: The social regulation of risk and effort. *Current Opinion in Psychology*, 1: 87–91.

Coseru, C. 2012. *Perceiving Reality: Consciousness, Intentionality, and Cognition in Buddhist Philosophy*. New York: Oxford University Press.

Dahl, C.J., Lutz, A., & Davidson, R.J. 2015. Reconstructing and deconstructing the self: Cognitive mechanisms in meditation practice. *Trends in Cognitive Sciences*, 19(9): 515–23. DOI: 10.1016/j.tics.2015.07.001.

Dreyfus, G. 1997. *Recognizing Reality: Dharmakīrti's Philosophy and Its Tibetan Interpretations*. Albany, NY: State University of New York Press.

Druskat, V.U. & Pescosolido, A.T. 2002. The content of effective teamwork: Mental models in self-managing teams: Ownership, learning and heedful interrelating. *Human Relations*, 55(3): 283–314. DOI: 10.1177/0018726702553001.

Druskat, V.U. & Wolff, S.B. 2001. Building the emotional intelligence of groups. *Harvard Business Review*, 79(3): 80–91.

Dunne, J.D. 2004. *Foundations of Dharmakīrti's Philosophy*. Boston, MA: Wisdom Publications.

Dunne, J.D. 2011a. Key features of Dharmakīrti's apoha theory. In M. Siderits, T. Tillemans, & A. Chakrabarti (eds), *Apoha: Buddhist Nominalism and Human Cognition* (pp. 84–108). New York: Columbia University Press.

Dunne, J.D. 2011b. Toward an understanding of non-dual mindfulness. *Contemporary Buddhism*, 12: 71–88. DOI: 10.1080/14639947.2011.564820.

Dunne, J.D. 2012. Resources for the study of *Svasaṃvitti* in ultimate contexts. Presented at the National Meeting of the American Academy of Religion.

Dunne, J.D. 2015. Buddhist styles of mindfulness: A heuristic approach. In B.D. Ostafin, M.D. Robinson, & B.P. Meier (eds), *Handbook of Mindfulness and Self-Regulation*. New York: Springer, 251–70.

Gallagher, S. 2013. The socially extended mind. *Cognitive Systems Research, Socially Extended Cognition*, 25–6: 4–12. DOI: 10.1016/j.cogsys.2013.03.008.

Ganeri, J. 2011. Apoha, feature-placing and sensory content. In M. Siderits, T. Tillemans, & A. Chakrabarti (eds), *Apoha: Buddhist Nominalism and Human Cognition* (pp. 228–46). New York: Columbia University Press.

Herrnstein, R.J. & Loveland, D.H. 1964. Complex visual concept in the pigeon. *Science*, 146/3643: 549–51. DOI: 10.1126/science.146.3643.549.

Hutchins, E. 1995. How a cockpit remembers its speeds. *Cognitive Science*, 19(3): 265–88.

Hutchins, E. 1996. *Cognition in the Wild*. Cambridge, MA: MIT Press.

Hutchins, E. 2008. The role of cultural practices in the emergence of modern human intelligence. *Philosophical Transactions of the Royal Society: Biological Sciences*, 363/1499: 2011–19. DOI: 10.1098/rstb.2008.0003.

Hutchins, E. 2010. Cognitive ecology. *Topics in Cognitive Science*, 2(4): 705–15. DOI: 10.1111/j.1756-8765.2010.01089.x.

Hutchins, E. & Klausen, T. 1998. Distributed cognition in an airline cockpit. In *Cognition and Communication at Work* (pp. 15–34). Cambridge: Cambridge University Press.

Itti, L. & Koch, C. 2000. A saliency-based search mechanism for overt and covert shifts of visual attention. *Vision Research*, 40(10–12): 1489–506. DOI: 10.1016/S0042-6989(99)00163-7.

Konvalinka, I., Xygalatas, D., Bulbulia, J., Schjødt, U., Jegindø, E.-M., Wallot, S., Orden, G.V. et al. 2011. Synchronized arousal between performers and related spectators in a fire-walking ritual. *Proceedings of the National Academy of Sciences*, 108(20): 8514–19. DOI: 10.1073/pnas.1016955108.

Lutz, A., Jha, A.P., Dunne, J.D., & Saron, C.D. 2015. Investigating the phenomenological matrix of mindfulness-related practices from a neurocognitive perspective. *American Psychologist*, 70(7): 632–58. DOI: 10.1037/a0039585.

Mack, A. & Rock, I. 1998. *Inattentional Blindness*. Cambridge, MA: MIT Press.

Moreland, R.L. & McMinn, J.G. 2010. Group reflexivity and performance. In S.R. Thye & E.J. Lawler (eds), *Advances in Group Processes*, Vol. 27 (pp. 63–95). Bingley: Emerald Group Publishing. DOI: 10.1108/S0882-6145(2010)0000027006.

Simons, D.J. & Chabris, C.F. 1999. Gorillas in our midst: Sustained inattentional blindness for dynamic events. *Perception*, 28(9): 1059–74.

Stahl, G. 2016. From intersubjectivity to group cognition. *Computer Supported Cooperative Work*, 25(4–5): 355–84. DOI: 10.1007/s10606-016-9243-z.

Thompson, E. 2014. *Waking, Dreaming, Being: Self and Consciousness in Neuroscience, Meditation, and Philosophy*. New York: Columbia University Press.

Tomasello, M. 2014. *A Natural History of Human Thinking*. Cambridge, MA: Harvard University Press.

Weick, K.E. & Roberts, K.H. 1993. Collective mind in organizations: Heedful interrelating on flight decks. *Administrative Science Quarterly*, 38(3): 357–81. DOI: 10.2307/2393372.

Weller, A. 1998. Human pheromones: Communication through body odour. *Nature*, 392(6672): 126–7. DOI: 10.1038/32283.

Widmer, P.S., Schippers, M.C., & West, M.A. 2009. Recent developments in reflexivity research: A review. *Psychologie Des Alltagshandelns/Psychology of Everyday Activity*, 2(2): 1–62.

Zahavi, D. 2005. *Subjectivity and Selfhood: Investigating the First-Person Perspective*. Cambridge, MA: MIT Press.

Zahavi, D. & Kriegel, U. 2015. For-me-ness: What it is and what it is not. In D. Dahlstrom, A. Elpidorou, & W. Hopp (eds), *Philosophy of Mind and Phenomenology* (pp. 36–53). London: Routledge.

6

Vicious and Virtuous Cycles

Exploring LEGO from a Paradox Perspective

Marianne W. Lewis

LEGO offers a fascinating story of organizational cycles. Hailed the 'Toy of the Century', leaders of the family-held firm had fuelled steady growth since its founding in 1932. Yet in 1988, facing changing markets, technology, and competition, sales flat-lined. Stunned, leaders posed a pivotal question: do we focus on our core traditions, enhancing our brand and 'the brick' *or* do we boldly explore new markets and technologies to spur radical innovation? They chose the latter. Following prescribed techniques, they drastically reshaped their strategy, structure, and practices for flexibility and creativity. They cranked out new products and entered new markets at remarkable rates. Their approach was 'textbook perfect', and failed miserably. The resulting innovation deluge stretched the brand and resources, while straining employees, customers, and retailers. The firm had lost focus on its core. By 2004, burdened by massive debt and losses, LEGO was nearing bankruptcy and hostile takeover. Remarkably, LEGO reversed the vicious cycle. Under new leadership, Jørgen Vig Knudstorp approached the core-explore tension from a different perspective. He rebuilt their core traditions and discipline to guide continuous innovation. Today LEGO is thriving as the largest and most innovative and profitable toy company in the world. How did such a vibrant, long-standing organization fall so far so fast? Just as perplexing, how did LEGO regain its positive energy and fuel such upward momentum in equal, seemingly record time?

A paradox perspective proposes that contrasting approaches to paradox—interwoven and persistent contradictions—fuel vicious and virtuous cycles in organizations (Smith & Lewis, 2011). Smith and Berg (1987) depict paradoxes as a double-edged sword, enabling re-enforcing cycles of stuckness and movement. On the one hand, paradoxical tensions may spark defensive reactions that offer temporary comfort and even apparent progress, but intensify underlying tensions and fuel counterproductive, reinforcing dynamics (Sundaramurthy & Lewis, 2003). In contrast, engaging paradox, working through tensions, can surface novel possibilities and build synergies between competing demands that reinforce their positive potential and spur learning in virtuous directions (Lewis, 2000).

Despite accumulating paradox research, explicit studies of organizational cycles remain scarce and our understanding of their fuel limited (Schad et al., 2016). As Tsoukas and Pina e Cunha (forthcoming) noted, such research challenges existing methods as it requires more holistic, longitudinal, and multicausal views. The dynamics of organizations unfold over time and through the interplay of emotions, cognition, and practice as well as wider organizational conditions and external pressures (Sundaramurthy & Lewis, 2003). Indeed, in the case of LEGO, extant studies have identified an array of rational yet proven counterproductive efforts on the downside, as well as impressive leadership, organizational and cultural shifts on the upswing. Such research offers valued insights into the 'hows' but leaves open the deeper 'whys'—why were counterproductive efforts intensified up until the point of near bankruptcy? Likewise, why was LEGO able to shift so dramatically and with such reinforcing positive momentum?

It is with these questions in mind that I explore vicious and virtuous cycles of LEGO from a paradox perspective. I begin by reviewing paradox literature and its views on organizational cycles. Next, I apply this lens to analyse cycles at LEGO. Considerable research, my own and others, aids this effort. In particular, I draw on my work with LEGO, with lead researcher, Lotte Lüscher (see Lüscher & Lewis, 2008). I then leverage particularly rich, qualitative studies of the LEGO company (e.g. Rivkin et al., 2013; Rosen, 2013; Robertson, 2014). I conclude by discussing implications for research and practice that might further enrich our understanding of such complex dynamics.

6.1 A Paradox Perspective on Organizational Cycles

According to paradox theory, one's approach to contradictory yet interwoven and persistent tensions can fuel virtuous and vicious cycles (e.g. Lewis, 2000; Schad et al., 2016; Smith & Berg, 1987). Within a vicious cycle, efforts to avoid or combat tensions foster stuckness. Defensive emotional, cognitive, and behavioural responses may prove self-reinforcing and counterproductive. In contrast, the cycle can spiral upward as 'working through paradox' enables movement (Lüscher & Lewis, 2008). Embracing tensions grows both confidence and humility in one's ability and need to continuously learn and change the value of tensions in that process. Paradox scholars draw from diverse literatures to explicate the interplay of cognition, emotions, and behaviours in fuelling organizational cycles. I now examine the self-reinforcing role of each of these factors in turn. Yet I stress that separating these factors is my construction for purposes of clarity. As we shift to LEGO, we will explore their more fluid interplay.

6.1.1 *Self-Reinforcing Role of Cognition*

Cognition may fuel organizational cycles as the cognitive dissonance of paradoxical tensions sparks sense making (Lüscher & Lewis, 2008). Festinger (1957) theorized that cognitive dissonance can trigger change *and* entrenchment of existing mindsets. Faced with paradox, actors sense a disconcerting discrepancy—how can contradictory demands, beliefs, feelings, and 'truths' exist simultaneously? Watzlawick (1993, p. 99) explained: 'Paradox is the Achilles heel of our logical, analytical, rational world view. It is the point at which the seemingly all-embracing division of reality into pairs of opposites, especially the Aristotelian dichotomy of true and false, breaks down and reveals itself as inadequate.'

Cognitively coping with paradoxes requires curiosity and openness to enable higher-order learning. Fuelling a virtuous cycle requires proactively seeking, considering, and valuing contradictory possibilities, and critically reflecting on one's own thinking and underlying assumptions. Argyris (1993) described this as double-loop learning, moving to a different frame of reference to examine interwoven contradictions. Psychologists have long explained that actors cannot break out of reinforcing cognitive cycles by using first-order thinking—slight variations to the logic they have used in the past—because such thinking results in a solution that is polarized and thereby exacerbates the tension (Bartunek, 1988; Smith & Berg, 1987). Accepting paradox allows doubt, fostering consideration of more creative and accommodating both/and alternatives, opening the potential for wisdom (Handy, 1994).

More often, however, cognitive defences trigger biases that narrow, rather than widen their worldview. A vicious cycle ensues as individuals cling to their existing either/or mindsets. Indeed, cognition itself is self-referential (Bartunek, 1988). Formal logic helps actors construct then reinforce polarities between X and non X. As Farson (1996, p. 13) noted: 'Our natural inclination when confronted with paradoxes is to attempt to resolve them, to create the familiar out of the strange, to rationalize them.' While the experience of tensions may surface the need for change, more often individuals interpret events using their existing frame of reference. What slight modifications they make in their thinking, therefore, are more likely to reinforce their existing views. Results reflect a 'double-bind' of learning. Staying within their current frame of reference, individuals choose interpretations that support, rather than challenge, their current mindset.

Smith and Berg's (1987) treatise on group paradoxes examines how varied biases perpetuate existing mindsets to foster stuckness. Faulty attributions, for example, arise when individuals overvalue their existing mindset, attributing success to their current skills and practices, and problems to factors outside of their control. Groups can exacerbate this dynamic by supporting each other's thinking. Likewise, desire for consistency biases our judgement. Experimental psychologists often find that we prefer to use our well-worn criteria and processes in problem solving, regardless of radical contextual changes.

Cognitive entrenchment, rather than double-loop learning, occurs as actors apply their existing mindsets. According to Ford and Ford (1994, p. 758), as we become skilled and comfortable with (and comforted by) our way of thinking, we increasingly take for granted its rules, boundaries, and limitations.

> Logics pose the problems, provide the language for explaining and understanding them, and determine their solutions. Logics give people their 'reality', the truth, the way things are . . . when people are unaware that they are using a logic, or are 'trapped' in only one, this point of view becomes an unwitting limitation to what might be seen or understood, restricting their observations and offering no really new alternatives.

Resulting dynamics of cognition have been described as self-fulfilling. We see what we expect to see. Watzlawick (1993, p. 61) describes self-fulfilling prophecies as having a 'truly magical, "reality"-creating effect . . . If an external event agrees with "prophecy" it is noticed and accepted as further proof. If external event doesn't agree, it is rejected or ignored'. Merton elaborates by explaining the reinforcing link between cognition and behaviour. The cycle begins as an inaccurate definition of the situation evokes behaviours that enable the originally false definition to come true (1996, p. 185). Encouraging managers to remain acutely aware of such processes, Bolman and Deal (2003) reviewed the original, and disconcerting, elementary school experiments that high-lighted this pattern. Labelled the Pygmalion effect, psychologists randomly identified students as 'high achievers' and informed their teachers, who then, arguably unknowingly, altered their expectations for and teaching and praise of those students accordingly. As a result, the 'high achievers' on average substantially surpassed the performance of the other students. Demonstrating similar patterns among managers, Eden (1990) replicated these experiments with the Israeli army. Randomly differentiating high- and low-potential recruits for their supervisors spurred the same pattern of results.

6.1.2 Self-Reinforcing Role of Emotions

Emotions play a powerful, interwoven role in responses to paradox, as the discomfort of coexisting contradictions sparks anxiety. As Freud and subsequent psychologists and psychotherapists stressed, anxiety threatens the ego (Schneider, 1990). Because paradoxes surprise and confuse, they challenge belief in ourselves. As Smith and Berg (1987) explained, anxiety simultaneously triggers a desire to change and to not change. Although critiquing and revising our existing approach would reduce the anxiety, our natural tendency is to protect ourselves. From a psychodynamic perspective, information that threatens self-concept can be ignored, rejected, or reinterpreted to preserve our existing self-concept, as well as debated, considered, and accommodated within an ever expanding self-awareness.

In a virtuous cycle, the discomfort of paradox encourages engagement; movement toward, rather than away from, the experience of tensions. Further such efforts can spark collective adrenaline, as paradox researchers often note that energy rises as groups actively engage tensions (Lüscher & Lewis, 2008). By confronting paradox, participants can come to better understand sources of tension, value competing alternatives, and explore their interconnections. Through repetition, individuals, groups, and organizations build confidence in their ability to work through paradox. As a result, they gain comfort with the discomfort.

Yet the anxiety elicited by tensions also triggers defensiveness that can fuel unintended consequences in a self-reinforcing and vicious cycle. As psychologists explain, defensive efforts to alleviate the anxiety of paradoxes can paradoxically bring about the very outcome they sought to prevent (Watzlawick, 1993, p. 60). Argyris (1993, p. 40) explained that defences include 'any policy or action that prevents someone (or some system) from experiencing embarrassment or threat, and simultaneously prevents anyone from correcting the causes of the embarrassment or threat'. Yet the persistence of paradoxical tensions means that such relief is short-lived. Further, Argyris (1993) stressed that defences can become embedded and taken-for-granted patterns within the organization. Because means of alleviating anxiety are potentially embarrassing, threatening, and anxiety-provoking themselves (i.e. requiring acknowledgement of fallibility, error, and/or ignorance), both the tensions and their potential management become 'undiscussable'. Organizational members too often ignore or cover up the tension, and pretend that they are not doing so. The effect is a double-bind. If not confronted, the tension will intensify, but if confronted the individual as well as the group or organization in which the pattern is embedded risks appearing incompetent.

Studies catalogue varied defences, stressing their temporary relief and counterproductive impact (see Lewis, 2000; Smith & Berg, 1987; Vince & Broussine, 1996). Splitting, for instance, further polarizes the contradictions. Such efforts often appear in the formation or entrenchment of subgroups that intensify we/they distinctions, downplaying links between opposing perspectives, and fostering cliques and turf wars. Projection entails blame and face-saving efforts that transfer frustrations to a scapegoat. Projection can also reinforce splitting as groups blame each other for challenges rather than seek more collaborative and innovative approaches. Repression or denial can help block awareness of tensions. By shifting attention to less perplexing and anxiety-provoking issues, actors can find relief even as tensions mount. Reaction formation entails stressing the favoured, more comfortable, and comforting side of a tension, while ambivalence offers a more subtle defence of 'luke-warm' reactions to tension. Vince and Broussine (1996) found that ambivalence reduces anxiety by suppressing the vitality of the extremes, yet in doing so inhibits open discussion and the potential for collective learning. Further bland compromises might mute opposition initially, but allow strong feelings to fester, often resurfacing in more subtle and destructive ways. Lastly, mixed messages serve as a self-reinforcing defence. As noted previously, Argyris (1993) warns that defences can embed double-binds within the organization. Mixed messages are both clear and ambiguous communications fuelled by related defences. Such messages serve as temporary ego protection for the communicator, but they also intensify the experience of tensions for those receiving the communications. As he explained, these patterns emerge as managers (a) design a message that is inconsistent with reality, (b) act as if there is no inconsistency, and (c) make both (a and b) undiscussable.

6.1.3 *Self-Reinforcing Role of Behaviours*

While cognition and emotions impact behaviour, behaviour also can fuel reinforcing dynamics through habit and routine. Research has described the process of behaviours and their repetition becoming embedded patterns variously as institutionalization, inertia, and path dependency (Dane, 2010). Such patterns may reflect defensive and engaging approaches to paradox, sparking contrasting organizational cycles.

In a virtuous cycle, members come to recognize that past practices likely spurred the initial tension, thereby requiring exploration and change to find an alternative approach. As they experiment with alternatives, they expand their repertoire of options. The result is a growing behavioural complexity within individuals and the organization, as they learn to vary their actions in an ever widening understanding of contextual needs. Rather than seek an artificial stability and consistency, they learn to thrive in a dynamic equilibrium, oscillating between competing practices to suit conflicting and dynamic demands (Smith & Lewis, 2011). Dane (2010) found that practices can embed routines and habits of adaptability as actors come to embrace, even expect doubt, when considering behavioural options. He noted that when an action is followed by an unexpected outcome, openness to surprise can allow doubt to enable greater creativity and learning. By questioning cause–effect relationships, doubt triggers adaptation, helps generate new perspectives, and motivates exploration and creativity.

Vicious cycles, in comparison, reinforce a drive toward the comfort of well-developed routines, fuelling an increasing emphasis on consistency and an inertia that intensifies the persistence of past practice. Leonard-Barton (1992), for instance, found that routinization fuels inertia that may aid innovation efforts in the short run, but impede change in the longer term. She described this as a double-bind between core capabilities and core rigidities. Applying, honing, and enhancing existing skills enables efficient and productive incremental innovation, but distracts actors from exploring new techniques, ideas, and processes vital to radical innovation, also vital for long-term sustainability. Similarly, Miller (1990) likened this vicious cycle to the Icarus Paradox, as success fuels failure. The practices—strategic, tactical, cultural—that enable early organizational success, become unconscious crutches. Through ongoing use, learning enhances but also reinforces their consistent application. Yet as organizations and their contexts become increasingly dynamic and complex, rather than shift to meet changing needs, learning accumulated during times of prosperity simplifies and narrows organizational competencies.

Studies similarly depict the path dependency of behavioural cycles as self-reinforcing processes that narrow the scope of potential behaviours over time. Storey and Salaman (2009), for instance, stressed the path dependency inherent in paradoxes of innovation. Their work depicts how embedded organizational structures, processes, and mindsets influence the direction, and often limit the possibility, of organizational development. Schreyögg and Sydow (2010) examine vicious, self-reinforcing cycles of organizations highly focused on efficiency. Just as Leonard-Barton (1992) identified such cycles among highly innovative firms, their studies demonstrate that excessive focus on efficiency can prove counterproductive by limiting approaches to problem solving. Organizational capabilities become entrenched in those that have proven successful, narrowing over time to those select practices aimed at economizing resources. Yet through that process, organizational members can lose their ability to perceive, seek, and implement alternative ways of selecting and linking, let alone growing resources.

6.2 A Paradox Analysis of LEGO Organizational Cycles

I now apply the paradox perspective to examine LEGO's organizational cycles. The opening vignette highlighted the exceptional nature of this case—as LEGO experienced an intense series of cycles over a relatively short two

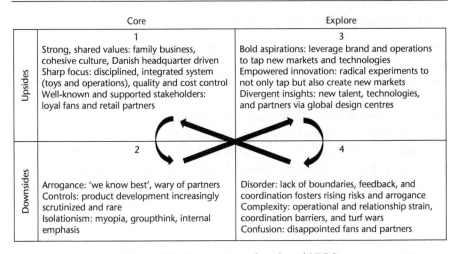

Figure 6.1. Organizational cycles of LEGO
Source: adapted from Johnson (1996)

decades. We now dive more deeply to unpack the fuel for these intense cycles and shifts between cycles.

I adapt Johnson's (1996) polarity map to aid my analysis. Johnson developed the polarity map, shown in Figure 6.1, as a consultation method. I have personally witnessed its use by Johnson to great effect. In such a setting, a group plots the tension they face—e.g. core (traditions and discipline) and explore (radical innovation and creativity)—detailing the upsides and downsides of each pole taken to its extreme, and critically reflecting on their experiences in each of the four quadrants. As a consultation method, the map helps groups learn to engage paradox productively. More specifically, it seeks to foster three insights, fostering learning that helps members: (1) identify when a tension they face is paradoxical—when the poles are interwoven (the downside of one accentuates, defines, and spurs demands for the upsides of the other and vice versa) and thereby will persist (is not a problem to be solved via an either/or tradeoff); (2) accept cyclical swings as natural tendencies—and thereby learn to avoid vicious cycles fuelled by singular emphasis, as one-sided extremes trigger the downsides of that pole and intensify the need for the opposing pole, exacerbating the underlying tension; and (3) embrace paradox—build shared understanding, motivation, and resilience to help groups engage, rather than defend against, paradox.

In contrast to Johnson's original intent for the polarity map, I now use this insightful tool to unpack historical cycles at LEGO. I parse this history into four phases that roughly coincide with each quadrant of the map. Moving through the quadrants, I use existing studies of LEGO to offer examples in that phase and paradox literature to further explicate.

6.2.1 Quadrant 1: Core Foundations

We begin with a view into the early 1990s as LEGO thrived. Company sales, which had risen annually and consistently for over fifty years, continued to increase. Keys to this impressive growth stemmed from a strong focus on its core—the traditions of its family-held values and disciplined control of quality, costs, and brand maintenance. The tightly cohesive culture of LEGO revolved around two mantras of its founder: the development of children through building, and 'only the best is good enough' (Robertson, 2014, pp. 16–17). Top management ensured that all major operational as well as strategic decisions were made at its Danish headquarters in Billund and closely followed those guides. The LEGO 'system of play' represented more than its product of interlocking bricks, it was a mindset that guided their further approach as all decisions in strategy, new products, and manufacturing must be tightly integrated to ensure fit. Further retailers served as trusted partners feeding into decision making and continuous learning, just as loyal fans, particularly children, provided the ultimate litmus test of their success.

Paradox literature proposes that paradoxical tensions remain latent until external factors, namely change, plurality of diversifying stakeholders, and/or scarce resources bring an opposing pole into juxtaposition (Smith & Lewis, 2011). During phase 1, LEGO considered the need to explore a distant secondary priority to their core. Their business model was clear and concise, and learning was purposeful, slow, and methodical. In their case study of LEGO, Rivkin and colleagues (2013) found that because of this core focus, product development could take years. Indeed, adding the colour green to their bricks required a decade of decision making, despite the idea being pushed by the founder's son. Yet during this time the need for exploration remained latent as demand was so high that executives actually debated means to slow sales.

6.2.2 Vicious Cycle toward Quadrant 2

The core-explore tension became increasingly salient, however, in the late 1990s, exposing the downsides of their singular focus. The rate of change was accelerating in the toy industry, thanks to new digital technologies, namely video games, varying competition, most notably Chinese manufacturers as both direct rivals and manufacturing partners of existing rivals, and globally shifting markets, as birth rates declined in their primary markets. Such signals accentuated the need for corresponding changes within LEGO; rising demands to explore more boldly in terms of innovation speed and creativity. Yet LEGO's success had fostered an entrenched focus on core to the neglect of explore. Rather than gain greater balance, efforts within LEGO defended their existing emphasis.

Rising arrogance, controls, and isolationism fuelled a vicious cycle, as discourse and actions during this phase highlight reinforcing cognitive, emotional, and behavioural defences. The more external pressures intensified, the more leaders stressed their past success, strengthened their conservative controls, and focused inward. Given their remarkable history, leaders became overconfident in their ability to predict the future and know their customers. Product development slowed further to a small number of large projects, while leaders looked to each other and their past to support decisions, avoiding critical scrutiny. Indeed, those few major efforts, such as LEGOLAND theme parks, served more as pet projects, proving their innovative capabilities; while energy and focus narrowed to core offerings (Robertson, 2014).

This dangerous mix is arguably best depicted by the lengthy and acrimonious debates over a potential partnership with Lucasfilm Ltd and stories of George Lucas being thrown out of the LEGO boardroom. Yet reviewing discourse in Robertson's (2014) account suggests deep-seated defences at play. As one VP proclaimed during the debate, 'Over my dead body will LEGO ever introduce *Star Wars*' (2014, p. 39). Another top manager described the early reaction as 'one of shock and horror that we would even suggest such a thing. It wasn't the LEGO way . . . LEGO didn't trust outside partners . . . the thinking was always, "We'll do it ourselves. We can do it better"' (2014, p. 40). Tendencies toward myopia and groupthink were only combatted thanks to champion, CEO, and family-owner, Kristiansen. It was the weight of his push as well as his use of market research demonstrating that parents supported this partnership, that persuaded sceptics to enable this unique, experimental partnership for LEGO.

Paradox research suggests that breaking out of vicious cycles is most enabled by a shocking wake-up call and/or the warnings of a respected and 'objective' source (Lewis, 2000; Smith & Berg, 1987). By 1998, both converged as an audit awoke LEGO to its first financial loss in history. Classic of the Icarus Paradox (Miller, 1990), success had fostered stagnation. LEGO leaders stepped back to review their current state, admitting that they had failed to stay attuned to the dramatic changes around them. CEO Kristiansen conceded: 'We were a heavy institution . . . losing our dynamism, and our fun' (Robertson, 2014, p. 27). Changing markets, technologies, and rivals exposed a realization that core traditions and discipline were insufficient without exploration into more radical innovation.

6.2.3 *Swinging the Pendulum Hard: Shift to Quadrant 3*

As Johnson (1996) predicted when mapping experiences of paradox, experiencing the deep downsides of a singular focus can trigger an intense move toward the opposite pole. Such was the case at LEGO. As noted in the opening vignette, shocked leaders asked themselves: do we continue to focus on our core traditions, enhancing our brand and 'the brick', *or* do we boldly explore new markets and technologies to spur radical innovation? They chose the latter, swinging the pendulum hard to achieve the much-needed upsides of exploration and shift focus toward innovation and growth. Viewing the need for radical change, Kristiansen began at the top, hiring a renowned Danish change agent, Poul Plougmann, to take over operations.

Plougmann's push to explore began in earnest by setting bold aspirations. With a team of aggressive strategic planners, they sought to leverage the brand and operational flexibility to tap new markets and technologies. Using market research, he showcased how LEGO was among the world's leading brands with a powerful potential to expand. He then set a new vision: LEGO would become 'the world's strongest brand among families and children' (Robertson, 2014, p. 47). Simultaneously, he sought to ensure that operations, particularly product development and manufacturing, fostered creativity and agility. The radical restructuring was labelled the 'Fitness Program', and included, among other changes, laying off 10 per cent of the staff, nearly 1,000 employees including sixty top executives (Rivkin et al., 2013).

To achieve these aspirations Plougmann sought to build a culture and institutionalize practices that empowered innovation. In his extensive study, Robertson (2014) identified seven 'best practices' for innovation of the era, each implemented in textbook fashion at LEGO. From spurring leaders and employees to 'head for blue-ocean markets' and 'practice disruptive innovation' to 'foster open innovation', the message was clear: 'creativity above all else' (2014, p. 60). Leaders' discourse, operational systems, and rewards were revamped to foster experimentation, speed product development, and motivate radical change.

To fully tap the upsides of explore, however, Plougmann also saw the need for divergent insights via new talent, technologies, and partners. His analysis identified the roots of LEGO's stagnation in homogenized thinking among an isolated and complacent team. In his words, 'Product development was in the hands of people who'd been at LEGO for twenty or thirty years. They were so inward looking, they expected that whatever they created would be right for the market' (Robertson, 2014, p. 47). As Rivken and colleagues (2013) noted, design responsibilities moved rapidly from rural Billund to global centres in London, Milan, and San Francisco. Further to gain direct insights from end consumers, an online shop, and LEGO-owned retail stores; while partners expanded into such areas as Winnie the Pooh and Harry Potter.

6.2.4 *Vicious Cycle toward Quadrant 4*

Although focus on change and creativity were driving innovation to rates never before seen at LEGO, core-explore tensions resurfaced as resources grew increasingly scarce. Top executives, seeing product line growth, had continued to predict greater profitability, but the opposite was occurring. Margins were decreasing as inventories within LEGO and at their primary retailers had sky-rocketed along with other costs. Jørgen Vig Knudstorp, recently hired to lead strategic development, was charged with diagnosing the source of the problem. His findings accentuated the downsides of such an intense focus on explore to the neglect of core strengths.

While the focus on exploration was clear, disorder prevailed. Innovation efforts lacked boundaries, feedback mechanisms, and coordination fuelling escalating risks and arrogance at LEGO. Empowered creatives became increasingly overconfident and unfettered in their efforts. This was most evident in radical projects described by Robertson (2014). For example, in the Galidor project, a sci-fi action line and linked TV series, one designer claimed, 'We had such a belief in ourselves. We thought we could walk on water' (p. 85). Yet as their bravado encouraged rising expectations among the executives, team members grew anxious. This same designer confessed: 'We were very uncomfortable with the (increased forecasts). We talked quite a bit about it (with upper management). But we weren't really heard. Besides, there was really no turning back at that point. The entire portfolio was built around Galidor being the first priority.' Galidor would become the 'worst-selling' LEGO theme in history. Ironically, Plougmann would later say: 'I still don't understand why we didn't burn that project' (p. 86). Likewise, on a different project team (Darwin), a designer explained, 'Whatever we asked for in terms of money and people, we were given . . . (what) we didn't have (was) the proper feedback loops to get that reality check as we went along' (pp. 82–3). The team sought guidance and allies, but disconnected from other project teams and devoid of senior champions, this expensive project also ended in failure.

Rising complexity lines strained operations and relationships within LEGO. According to Robertson (2014), during this period, LEGO tripled its product lines. Rivken and colleagues (2013, pp. 4–5) documented the intensifying challenges. In 2001, reviewing their supply chain, Knudstrop recalled, 'nobody had kept an eye on complexity. Product developers argued that the number of distinct shapes did not matter, as the marginal cost of an extra mold was so low.' Once a firm that took a decade to add a colour to its group of five, the number of components now included 157 colours and over 10,900 elements. Knudstrop illustrated the potential ripple effects: 'You could be out of stock for a product just because you miss one of its 675 pieces, which you did not make when you got the forecast wrong' (2013, p. 5). Yet top management sided with developers and their shared focus on innovation, downplaying potential impacts on manufacturing, retailers, costs, and inventory. Further, complexity pitted disparate groups against each other for attention and resources. Turf wars were particularly evident between groups viewed as innovators (typically located in global centres and focused on innovation, such as the Explore team) versus traditionalists (those based in Billund and focused on core products, such as the DUPLO team). In the case of Explore versus DUPLO, infighting and scapegoating escalated. Given leaders' focus on exploration, the winner was pre-determined. DUPLO was eliminated and resources shifted to Explore—this despite DUPLO being the second-strongest toy brand in Europe. Yet criticisms were deemed dissent and not tolerated. As one designer noted, 'They told us not to come up with any objections. They didn't exactly threaten to fire us, but that was definitely the message' (Robertson, 2014, p. 73).

The vicious cycle intensified as unfettered exploration fostered growing confusion externally. Long-time retail partners and loyal fans questioned their LEGO allegiance. For retailers, the deluge of new products fostered cannibalization, slowed inventory, and reduced margins. Yet Rivken and colleagues (2013, p. 6) found that LEGO managers increasingly blamed declining revenues on factors out of control. For example, in 2004, a Walmart buyer told a LEGO VP, 'Can you please tell me why I shouldn't put dog food on the shelves (instead of LEGO)?' (2013, p. 6). Likewise, removing the DUPLO brand for younger children saddened, even angered parents. One executive recalled, 'Many consumers found the new products did not live up to our promise and missed the LEGO DUPLO brand. A German retailer bluntly asked me, "Have you absolutely lost your mind?" This was only one of several innovation and marketing approaches at the time that customers did not understand' (2013, p. 6).

As occurred in Quadrant 2, shock and respected analysis helped shift this vicious cycle. Yet unlike the previous turnaround, this hole was far deeper. Recounting his presentation to the board (Robertson, 2014, p. 68), Knudstrop explained how he framed a crisis with blunt facts: 2003 would show a 30 per cent drop in sales, a negative cash flow of over $160 million, and likely default on debt of nearly $800 million. And 2004 looked even worse. He stressed, 'we are on a burning platform . . . We need to take action, because the problem is not going away'. In 2003, Kristiansen fired Plougmann, soon after retiring himself to turn over the reins to Knudstorp, who began an intensive rebuild of the LEGO core that could guide future exploration.

6.3 Movement: Toward Continuously Engaging and Thriving with Paradox

The subsequent turnaround at LEGO is particularly impressive, given its sustained and substantial momentum. By 2014, revenues of LEGO tripled with profits soaring to over $1.5 billion (Ashcroft, 2014). Through a retrospective paradox lens, Knudstorp appears an exceptional, paradoxical leader. He recognized that his critical and immediate fixes to disciplined controls had to be balanced, or LEGO would yet again swing the pendulum to an extreme only to eventually resurface the downsides of a single-minded approach.

Paradox theorists stress that thriving with paradox requires continuous engagement with tensions in search of learning (Lewis, 2000). Smith and Lewis (2011) theorized this as a dynamic equilibrium: dedicated efforts to build the strengths of each pole separately, while integrating their benefits through an accommodating higher purpose. The result is fluid. Indeed, as Johnson (1996) stressed in his use of the polarity map, once dynamics are mapped, the pattern appears as an infinity loop (shown in the four arrows of Figure 6.1). The organization continues to oscillate, keeping that loop in the upside quadrants, while remaining vigilant to avoid defensive leanings toward either pole and its looming downsides. LEGO offers examples that illustrate a paradox approach which I analyse now beginning with Knudstrop's paradox mindset, then its influence on actions to rebuild core strengths to enable innovation.

6.3.1 *Paradox Mindset*

Paradox theorists propose that a paradox mindset enables comfort and engagement with paradoxical tensions. Rather than being threatened by interwoven and persistent contradictions, individuals 'shift their expectations from rationality and linearity to accept paradoxes and persistent and unsolvable puzzles' (Smith & Lewis, 2011, p. 385). Analysing Knudstrop's discourse and behaviours, Rosen (2013, pp. 128–30) finds that he is especially comfortable with paradox, valuing tensions for reflecting the intricacies of organizational life and their potential to highlight alternative views and contrasting insights. In Knudstrop's words: 'There's no single answer to anything anymore... What drives me is intellectual curiosity. It's not resolving a trade-off by saying you can get either A or B, but rather resolving it by how we can get A and B.' As an example, he explains:

> Let's be concrete: Walmart wants better delivery service but also lower cost. Supply chain says I can give you low cost, but then I want high predictability. Sales says I want low cost, but more important to me is that I can be flexible... So we can be innovative in our operation setup, may be how we treat an order when it comes in. So planning techniques may be how we develop platforms.

A further signal of Knudstrop's paradox mindset is his blend of confidence and humility, which he further encourages in those around him. In a reinforcing virtuous cycle, his emphasis on learning helps push himself and those at LEGO to not only listen to, but proactively seek contrasting views from customers, retail partners, and LEGO colleagues. Collectively, his approach also fosters trust. Indeed, Rosen (2013, pp. 128–30) found that one of his favourite mantras is 'Take charge and let go.' Once Knudstrop felt confident that operational and financial discipline were solid again at LEGO, he shared power, flattening the organization by expanding top management from six to twenty-two, and empowering executives to explore new areas of potential innovation and efficiencies. As a result, Knudstrop moved to 'take charge of the strategy and then let go like an orchestra conductor'.

6.3.2 Rebuilding Core Strengths to Guide Exploration

Knudstrop's paradox mindset is illustrated in his approach to the LEGO turnaround. Upon assuming leadership, Knudstrop was adamant and dogged in his focus on rebuilding core strengths. Yet he also remained acutely aware of avoiding a return to single-mindedness. In both/and messaging, he stressed that a strong core must guide, not stymie, ongoing exploration.

Reflecting the paradoxical nature of improvisation (Smith & Lewis, 2011), he instituted clear frameworks for innovation. In Knudstorp's view, 'innovation flourishes when the space for it is limited' (Robertson, 2014, p. 116). In this vein, he initiated a series of simple rules, providing boundaries within which others could freely explore and create. For example, on average, at least 70 per cent of a LEGO set would be comprised of standard bricks. And indeed, LEGO found that this rule fostered more creativity as designers could work with a more manageable collection of options. This constraint also ensured that every set would be profitable, while aiding supply-chain planning. Indeed, LEGO's internal research found that the cost of a standard brick, given their scale and continuous production, was so small as to be unquantifiable, while a single specialty brick could rise as high as $1 a piece (Robertson, 2014).

At a higher level of innovation, the new goal was for a portfolio of innovation projects with 90 per cent focused on traditional play experiences and 10 per cent on radical innovation. This mix reflects Handy's (1994) call for paradoxical approaches to innovation, ensuring a manageable set of high-risk, high-return projects, funded by core projects; while those radical projects that succeed build energy and excitement and become future core projects in a never-ending virtuous cycle. Within this constraint, everyone at LEGO could be empowered to explore new possibilities for growth. But their ideas would be rigorously tested against alignment with LEGO expectations for quality and brand recognition (Robertson, 2014, p. 125).

6.3.3 Enabling Integration and Balance through Higher Purpose

From a paradox perspective, higher purpose aids integration of opposing poles at a meta-level (Lewis, 2000). Plougmann's vision of being the top global brand among families offered an aspirational goal, but not a purpose. Brand, like profit, is a means to an end, while purpose serves as an end that can link and balance tensions. Knudstrop returned to LEGO's roots. As shown on their corporate website, the stated purpose is *to inspire and develop the builders of tomorrow*. This overarching mission emphasizes learning through play, as well as the construction emphasis of the core brick.

Knudstrop continues to manage oscillations and the balance of core and explore. In an April 2008 email to corporate managers, for example, he stressed that achieving their purpose would require a 'bifocal perspective' (Robertson, 2014, p. 284). It would demand rigorous focus on cashflow and costs for financial sustainability, as well as riskier projects to create the future. Within the project portfolio, they would seek a mix of 'obviously LEGO' and 'never seen before'. This would entail a never-ending and energizing journey of collaborative learning.

6.4 Implications for Theory and Practice

Applying a paradox perspective, this exploration of organizational cycles at LEGO sought to unpack reinforcing cycles of cognition, emotions, and behaviours spurred by tensions. For practitioners and researchers, the insights should prove sobering as well as encouraging. This analysis was conducted with the power (and limits) of retrospection. In real time, these dynamics were obscured by intricate, likely overwhelming information, pressures, and interactions—social and political, internal and external, known and unknown. Indeed, a snapshot view of popular press and research taken during Quadrants 1 and 3 would suggest that LEGO initiatives at those times represented the rational application of best practice. Hindsight is 20-20.

For practitioners, my hope, however, is that this case motivates double-loop learning. The energy of paradoxical tensions can fuel vicious and virtuous cycles. Managing our and others' defensiveness becomes critical in reducing, if not avoiding, biases, anxiety, and inertia that foster stuckness. In contrast, engaging paradox enables movement. Tensions may serve as signals for critical reflection and open debate, and opportunities to experiment and change.

As researchers we must fight ourselves against our cognitive, emotional, and behavioural defences when studying complex cycles and paradox. Ironically, expertise can intensify the rigidity and entrenchment of existing approaches. Examining extensive experimental and management research, Dane (2010) explains that as professionals deepen their expertise within a particular domain, their flexibility declines in terms of problem solving and creativity. As they accumulate experience and insight, their existing logic stabilizes and inhibits change. Indeed, studies find that highly skilled experts find it particularly difficult to consider others' perspectives, apply alternative approaches, and adapt to new processes or conditions within their domain. In sum, experts become resilient to inconsistencies, such as paradoxical tensions. One of the most frequent findings is that of 'Einstellung' effects. Experts become fixated on a particular problem-solving method, such as applying sophisticated models to develop tradeoffs or contingency models, even when a situation demands a very different approach. It is with Dane's findings in mind that I encourage myself and others to stay confident and humble in our approaches so that we might reflect critically on our preferred lenses and methods, and continuously learn and change. In this vein, I am constantly reminded of the paradox of knowledge: the more we know, the more we know we don't know.

References

Argyris, C. 1993. *Knowledge for Action: A Guide to Overcoming Barriers to Organisational Change.* San Francisco, CA: Jossey-Bass.

Ashcroft, J. 2014. *The LEGO Case Study.* John Ashcroft and Company. http://www.thelegocasestudy.com/.

Bartunek, J.M. 1988. The dynamics of reframing. In K.S. Cameron & R.E. Quinn (eds), *Paradox and Transformation: Toward a Theory of Change in Organizations and Management.* Cambridge, MA: Ballinger.

Bolman, L.G. & Deal, T.E. 2003. *Reframing Organizations.* San Francisco, CA: John Wiley & Sons.

Dane, E. 2010. Reconsidering the trade-off between expertise and flexibility: A cognitive entrenchment perspective. *Academy of Management Review*, 35(4): 579–603.

Eden, D. 1990. Pygmalion without interpersonal contrast effects: Whole groups gain from raising manager expectations. *Journal of Applied Psychology*, 75: 394–8.

Farson, R. 1996. *Management of the Absurd: Paradoxes in Leadership.* New York: Simon and Schuster.

Festinger, L. 1957. *A Theory of Cognitive Dissonance.* Stanford, CA: Stanford University Press.

Ford, J.D. & Ford, L.W. 1994. Logics of identity, contradiction and attraction in change. *Academy of Management Review*, 19(4): 756–85.

Handy, C. 1994. *The Age of Paradox.* Cambridge, MA: Harvard Business School Press.

Johnson, B. 1996. *Polarity Management: Identifying and Managing Unsolvable Problems.* Boston, MA: HRD Press.

Leonard-Barton, D. 1992. Core capabilities and core rigidities: A paradox in managing new product development. *Strategic Management Journal*, 13(S1): 111–25.

Lewis, M.W. 2000. Exploring paradox: Toward a more comprehensive guide. *Academy of Management Review*, 25(4): 760–76.

Lüscher, L.S. & Lewis, M.W. 2008. Organizational change and managerial sensemaking: Working through paradox. *Academy of Management Journal*, 51: 221–40.

Merton, R.K. 1996. *On Social Structure and Science.* Chicago, IL: University of Chicago Press.

Miller, D. 1990. *The Icarus Paradox: How Exceptional Companies Bring about Their Own Downfall*. New York: HarperBusiness.

Rivkin, J.W., Thomke, S.H., & Beyersdorfer, D. 2013. *LEGO (A): The Crises*. HBS Case 9-713-478.

Robertson, D.C. 2014. *Brick by Brick*. New York: Random House.

Rosen, B. 2013. *Grounded: How Leaders Stay Rooted in an Uncertain World*. San Francisco, CA: Jossey-Bass.

Schad, J., Lewis, M., Raisch, S., & Smith W.K. 2016. Paradox research in management science: Looking back to move forward. *Academy of Management Annals*, 10(1): 5–64.

Schneider, K.J. 1990. *The Paradoxical Self: Towards an Understanding of Our Contradictory Nature*. New York: Insight Books.

Schreyögg, G. & Sydow, J. 2010. Organizing for fluidity? Dilemmas of new organizational forms. *Organization Science*, 21(6): 1251–62.

Smith, K.K. & Berg, D.N. 1987. *Paradoxes of Group Life*. San Francisco, CA: Jossey-Bass.

Smith, W.K. & Lewis, M.W. 2011. Toward a theory of paradox: A dynamic equilibrium model of organizing. *Academy of Management Review*, 36: 381–403.

Storey, J. & Salaman, G. 2009. *Managerial Dilemmas: Exploiting Paradox for Strategic Leadership*. Chichester: Wiley.

Sundaramurthy, C. & Lewis, M. 2003. Control and collaboration: Paradoxes of governance. *Academy of Management Review*, 28(3): 397–415.

Tsoukas, H. & Pina e Cunha, M. Forthcoming. On organizational circularity: Vicious and Virtuous cycles of organizing. In W. Smith, M.W. Lewis, P. Jarzkowski, & A. Langley (eds), *Oxford Handbook of Organizational Paradox*. Oxford: Oxford University Press.

Vince, R. & Broussine, M. 1996. Paradox, defense and attachment: Accessing and working with emotions and relations underlying organizational change. *Organization Studies*, 17(1): 1.

Watzlawick, P. 1993. *The Situation Is Hopeless but Not Serious*. New York: Norton.

7

Eternal Today

The Temporality Paradox in Strategy Making

Jenni Myllykoski and Anniina Rantakari

7.1 Introduction

Time and temporality are key issues in process organization research in general (Cunliffe et al., 2004; Huy, 2001; Langley et al., 2013; Tsoukas, 2016) and in strategy process research in particular (Fenton & Langley, 2011; Hydle, 2015; Vaara & Whittington, 2012). In previous strategy process literature, time has been approached from two main perspectives: as an objective dimension of strategy making (Van de Ven, 1992; Sonenshein, 2010) and as a subjective construction (Kaplan & Orlikowski, 2013; Vesa & Franck, 2013). Studies that have adopted an objective view of time have treated it as a linear and divisible dimension for strategy making and contributed to strategy process research by shedding light on the chronological sequencing of events (Burgelman, 1983; Pettigrew, 1990; Sonenshein, 2010). More recent strategy process studies have examined time as a subjective construction and showed how various constructions of temporality (past, present, and future) either enable or constrain collective strategy making (Kaplan & Orlikowski, 2013; Vaara & Pedersen, 2013; Vesa & Franck, 2013). However, both of these views treat time as if it were a passive background for human agency in strategy making. We argue that strategy research needs to go beyond the distinction between objective and subjective time and re-evaluate the relation between time and human agency.

To extend the notion of objective and subjective time, we adopt an 'in-time' view of temporality (Hernes, 2014). In general we conceptualize time as a human attempt to abstract *'the passage of nature'* (Whitehead, 1920, p. 54). Thus, in this chapter, we use time as a concept to describe the ongoing experience of becoming reality. On the other hand, we use temporality to refer to the way periods of time (the ongoing present) connect and relate to other periods in a backward (past) and forward (future) direction (Dawson 2014, p. 286). According to the 'in-time' view, the past and future are immanent in the fluidity of present experience (Chia, 1999; Dawson, 2014; Schultz & Hernes, 2013). We argue that by adopting the 'in-time' view, we can approach temporality in a way that prioritizes the experience of temporal flow over the chronological arrangement of discrete events (Langley & Tsoukas, 2017). This means that we acknowledge that time is a creative force that also works on us (Hernes, 2014).

Adopting the 'in-time' view adds to recent studies of strategy process research that have examined the temporal nature of strategy making (Kaplan & Orlikowski, 2013; Vaara & Pedersen, 2013; Vesa & Franck, 2013). These studies have shown that the subjective articulation, interpretation, and negotiation of the past, present, and future affect managerial strategy making. We extend this notion by examining time as the fluidity of the present. This approach has two main implications. First, it enables us to challenge the overemphasis on intentionality in human agency that is said to prevail in strategy literature (Chia & Holt, 2009; MacKay & Chia, 2013; Rasche & Chia, 2009). In other words, we show how time can also frame human agency. Second, it enables us to examine how the past and future are immanent in the fluidity of present experience (Bakken et al., 2013; Dawson, 2014; Schultz & Hernes, 2013). Hence, we can extend the prevailing 'over-time' perspective on strategy processes (Langley et al., 2013) and better understand the inherent situatedness, complexity, and uncertainty of intentional strategy making (Tsoukas, 2016). Consequently, we are able to re-evaluate the constitutive relation between time and human agency in strategy making.

In this chapter we examine how both the 'over-time' constructions and 'in-time' experiences of managers simultaneously enable, restrain, and constitute strategy making. We use strategy making to mean the open-ended and continuous process of practical coping that results in actual decisions and acts that are defined retrospectively as deliberate and purposeful strategy (Tsoukas, 2010). Empirically, this study builds on two years of participation in strategy-making meetings in a small Finnish software company (Alpha). Since the company was small and manager-owned, even the top management were engaged in practical work. This enabled us to examine both the processes of intentional strategy making and strategy emergence through everyday practical coping (Chia & Holt, 2006).

The rest of the chapter is structured as follows. First, we provide insight into how time and temporality have been considered in previous strategy process research. Second, we present the 'in-time' view of temporality as a lens for examining managerial strategy making. Third, we describe the process of data analysis and our empirical findings. Finally, we discuss the contributions of this study.

7.2 Temporality in Strategy Research

In the following we elaborate on how previous strategy process literature has dealt with the role of time and temporality. In particular, we distinguish two perspectives on temporality in strategy making: the objective and the subjective (Hydle, 2015). The objective perspective on temporality approaches time as a chronological platform for strategy making, while the subjective perspective focuses on the socially constructed nature of temporality in strategy making.

The objective perspective approaches temporality chronologically by presenting it as a timeline that consists of measurable and divisible units. The objective perspective on time can be seen in both the actual practices of strategy making and in the conventions of strategy process research. In the actual practices of strategy making objective time is regarded as an artefact of intentional strategy making (Yakura, 2002; Vaara & Pedersen, 2013) and also as a measure for valuating human labour (Cunliffe et al., 2004; Ingold, 2000; Lee & Liebenau, 1999). Hence time is treated as a scarce commodity for individuals and a resource to be managed (Roe et al., 2009).

In addition to the actual practices of strategy making, the objective perspective resonates with conventional strategy process research (Melin, 1992; Van de Ven, 1992). The central contribution of the process perspective has been to show how organizational strategy making unfolds over time. This has led to a proliferation of longitudinal methods that seek a better understanding of how organizational strategy unfolds dynamically (Burgelman, 1983; Mintzberg, 1978; Pettigrew, 1990). For example, Melin (1992) examined strategy making by describing series of events, short episodes, epochs, and biographical history. On the other hand, time has been treated within the strategy-as-practice field (Vaara & Whittington, 2012) as an objective platform from which practices emerge (Jarzabkowski, 2003). This means that temporality has been expressed retrospectively as a linear succession of immobile, isolated moments and events, or by completely freezing the present moment that analytically separates the past, present, and future as distinct categories. In sum, the objective perspective has treated time as a passive background of strategy making.

The subjective perspective on temporality (Reinecke & Ansari, 2015) differs from conventional strategy process research by highlighting the socially constructed nature of time in strategy making. In particular, these studies have shown how strategies are formed, negotiated, and renewed through subjective experience of temporality, namely the past, present, and future. Consequently, these studies have examined temporality through narratives (Barry & Elmes, 1997; Fenton & Langley, 2011; Vaara & Pedersen, 2013), framing (Kaplan & Orlikowski, 2013), and temporal ordering (Hydle, 2015; Vesa & Franck, 2013).

Especially the narrative perspective on strategy (Barry & Elmes, 1997; Fenton & Langley, 2011) has been pivotal in improving our understanding of the role of time in the processes of strategy making (Vaara & Pedersen, 2013). In their study, Vaara and Pedersen (2013) elucidated the role of narratives as a means to construct temporality in strategy making. In particular, Vaara and Pedersen (2013) highlighted the role of prospective stories in strategy making (Boje, 2008) and showed how time and space are intertwined within strategy narratives. In addition to the narrative approach, Kaplan and Orlikowski (2013) used the notion of temporal work and showed how temporality is embedded in the work of strategists through negotiations between different interpretations of the past, future, and present. They showed that projections of the future are shaped by interpretations of the past and present.

From the perspective of temporal ordering, Vesa and Franck (2013) examined the relationship between strategy work and temporality by observing real-time top-management team meetings. They argued that the core of temporality lies in the experienced time that is negotiated and organized during strategic planning. They found that managers seek to arrange and order the past and the present into a linear and coherent temporal experience. Finally, in a recent study, Hydle (2015) showed how different organizational actors shape strategy through various temporal orientations. Top management was said 'to strategize in the past', project managers were seen as strategists with a present orientation, and professionals, as the company's innovators, presumably formulated future strategy (p. 659).

The studies above have advanced our understanding of how the meaning of the past and future are socially constructed and how these constructions affect present strategy making. However, despite the contributions of these studies, we argue that temporality could be seen more broadly than as a product of either individual or collective sense making. In other words, time as the passage of nature (Whitehead, 1920), also occurs beyond human constructions of it. Hence, we argue that strategy scholars should extend the notions of time and temporality by adopting an 'in-time' view, according to which strategy making takes place in the fluidity of the present. This means that we give primacy to the experience of temporal flow over constructions of the past-present-future that we notice (Langley & Tsoukas, 2017, p. 5). Next we present our conceptualization of the 'in-time' view.

7.3 The 'In-Time' View

Time is a central issue in process organization research (Langley & Tsoukas, 2017; Tsoukas, 2016; Hernes, 2014; Langley et al., 2013). In particular, these studies have followed the metaphysical definition of time as the flow of becoming reality (Whitehead, 1978 [1929]). Hence, process organization studies have challenged both the objective and subjective conceptualizations of time as passive and separate from lived experience and have suggested an 'in-time' view of temporality (Hernes, 2014; Hernes et al., 2013).

In our view we draw on Whitehead's (1920, p. 54) conceptualization of time as the *'passage of nature'* in which he equated the notions of *becoming* and time. We argue that by following Whitehead's (1920, 1925, 1929) notions we can re-elaborate three interrelated issues that are relevant for a better understanding of the temporal nature of strategy making. First, we can take an alternative view on the extensiveness of time and define it in terms of relational events. This means that an individual event does not have an existence apart from any reference to the other events (Mesle, 2008). Central to this notion is the distinction between the conceptualizations of 'over time' and 'in time'. Second, we can treat temporality as an experienced, uninterrupted flow of the becoming of the present in which the past and future are immanent. Third, we can conceptualize time as an active force that enables us to examine temporal processes without reducing them to products of human agency.

The first issue deals with the linearity and extensiveness of time. In particular, we challenge how the 'over-time' view has taken extensiveness for granted by presenting processuality through a chain of discrete, successive events. In other words, the 'over-time' view assumes that an individual event has enduring meaning, without reference to the event from which it is analysed. This means that events can be spread out into simultaneous existence, for example to derive effects from causes. To take another view, Whitehead (1929, p. 35) argued that 'extensiveness becomes, but "becoming" is not itself extensive'. Adopting this notion has two interrelated implications. First, extensiveness can be seen as a retrospective abstraction that is bound to momental experience (Whitehead, 1929). This means that processes cannot be chopped up into stages or categorized into beginnings and ends. Second, by highlighting the indivisibility of the unfolding of events, temporality can be described as a series of relationally constitutive events (Whitehead, 1929; see also Cobb, 2002; Hernes, 2014; Mesle, 2008). This means that events per se do not have enduring meaning.

The second issue deals with temporality as the uninterrupted flow of the present. This issue highlights the difference between the retrospective and prospective view on processuality. Consequently, notions of the past and the future have unique meanings that enable us to understand the fluid nature of the present in its temporal unfolding. More specifically, the meaning of the past and the future in the present can be understood through the concepts of continuity and novelty (Whitehead, 1929). On the one hand, continuity refers to the causal power of the past in the formation of new moments; new moments create themselves out of the previous world. On the other hand, novelty emerges because new moments are subjects in their own creation. In other words, despite the causal power of the past, each new moment creates its own uniquity before turning into a 'resource' for the new becoming moment (Whitehead, 1929). In sum, the 'in-time' view entails the notion of the future as merely the continuous creation of the present, which means that there is no pre-existing, predetermined future out there waiting to be realized (Mesle, 2008).

The third issue is related to an active view of the passing of time, which means that the creative advance of processuality (Langley & Tsoukas, 2017) cannot be explained as emerging from entities. Treating time as an active force has one key implication; it leads us to analytically locate agency in relational events (Hernes, 2014). This deviates from the conventional way of conceptualizing agency as a property of entities (Emirbayer & Mische, 1998). Accordingly, the 'in-time' view continues the relational notion of human agency, which places agency in the flow of time (Emirbayer & Mische, 1998; Kaplan & Orlikowski, 2013). However, distinctive to the 'in-time' view is that it subjugates human agency to relational events. In this approach the notion of agency is not tied to conscious thought or human subjectivity (Whitehead, 1929). This view further stresses that events are not reducible to the individuals that participate in them (Hernes, 2017) just as a whole is not reducible to its constituent parts (Cooper, 2005). Furthermore, the temporal connecting inherent in processes is seen to emerge through the relations between events (Hernes, 2014; Hussenot & Missonier, 2016). Thus, events per se are seen as subjects in processes. Consequently, in accordance with the notion of agentic events, we need to focus on two issues in order to examine processes. First, on how events connect and (re)define each other (Hernes, 2017; Mesle, 2008) and second, on how human beings and materiality evoke their own agency 'in time', through participation in events (Hernes, 2014).

In sum, the 'in-time' view differs from objective and subjective views on time by assigning ontological priority to the unfolding of relational events over individual agency. In this way the 'in-time' view is in resonance with the unowned view of processes, since the unowned view highlights that processuality does not emerge either from individual intention or any linear causality (Chia, 2014; MacKay & Chia, 2013; Rescher, 1996).

7.4 Research Design

7.4.1 Data Collection

In our study we adopt a process relational view according to which both the reality that we try to know and we as knowers are part of a constant process of becoming (Chia & Rasche, 2015; Rescher, 1996). In particular, we stress that knowing comes from direct engagements where the researcher participates in creating the phenomena researched (Cooper, 2005; Shotter, 2006).

The empirical design draws on the ideas of group methods in organizational analysis (Steyaert & Bouwen, 2004). Methodologically, the process of data collection resonates to some extent with participant observation (Alvesson & Deetz, 2000; Laine & Vaara, 2007). The initial reason for choosing participatory methodology was two-fold. First, it offers a way to gain insider insight into everyday organizational life (Vesa & Vaara, 2014). Second, through participatory research we can explain the emergent and fluid nature of the strategy-making process (Cunliffe, 2015; Langley, 2009). In particular, we conducted a real-time, participatory study with a small group of managers of the case company. This permitted us to examine how actors cope in the ongoing present (Hernes, 2014; see also Langley, 2009; Samra-Fredericks, 2003).

The empirical data were collected over a two-year period (2011–13) in a research project focusing on business model development that was part of a large national-level research programme called Cloud Software. The site of data collection was a small Finnish software company seeking international growth (Alpha, pseudonym). The data consist of sixteen face-to-face meetings with two researchers and three managers of the company that were recorded and transcribed (cf. Samra-Fredericks, 2003). The meetings were arranged as part of the research project with the initial purpose of working together to find ways to develop the company's business model. However, after the first meetings it became evident that business model development was only one of the many issues that the managers wanted to discuss. Thus, the discussions ended up consisting of topics that the managers considered important at the time of the meeting. These topics were related to internationalization and growth strategies. Thus, at the time the data had been collected, temporality was not the focus of our study. It was only during the early stage of data analysis that Researcher 2 (R2) started to examine the role of time in strategy making.

Alpha was established in 2006. At the time of data collection, Alpha was run by five owners. Alpha was then offering a software solution to manufacturers and retailers to help its customers visualize physical products during sales events. At the beginning of the data collection, Alpha had twenty-five employees and operated in Europe. However, the majority of the customers were based in Finland where Alpha was the market leader. Although Alpha's explicit strategic objective at this time was rapid growth through increased internationalization, the management group had not yet determined how internationalization and growth would be achieved. This, in fact, was one of the factors motivating participation in the research project.

7.4.2 The Data of the Study

Each meeting started with a discussion about 'what's going on' in the company and proceeded with a more focused discussion of issues that the managers

Table 7.1. The research data

Date of the meeting	Duration	Topics discussed
		FU = frameworks used to structure the conversation
29 August 2011	2h 37min	The managers introduce the company, general discussion about current challenges
29 September 2011	3h 48min	Talking about the product and customer relationships, managers also bring up challenges and new ideas, FU
13 October 2011	3h 14min	Imagining the changes taking place in the future, FU
28 November 2011	3h 9min	Creating future scenarios, FU
15 December 2011	2h 16min	Trying to figure out the implications of cloud technologies for the current business model, FU
27 January 2012	2h 47min	General discussion about contemporary challenges, then talking about two specific customer cases in terms of those challenges and finally trying to devise a new, cloud-based pricing model
16 March 2012	2h 16min	General discussion, then working on a new pricing model
17 April 2012	2h 44min	General discussion, then working on a new pricing model during which the discussion takes up a couple of new business ideas
7 June 2012	1h 53min	General discussion, then working on a new pricing model
10 August 2012	2h 29min	General discussion about what's going on
16 October 2012	2h 26min	General discussion about what's going on
20 December 2012	2h 34min	General discussion about what's going on
22 February 2013	3h 19min	Strategizing related to a new product concept, FU
10 April 2013	2h 14min	Strategizing related to a new product concept, FU
6 May 2013	2h 55min	General discussion (the facilitator-researcher not present)
3 June 2013	1h 38min	General discussion, then strategizing related to a new product concept, FU
2011–13	–	R2's personal notes from the meetings
2011–13	–	Material produced in the meetings (PowerPoint slides)
Data hours:	42.3	

considered relevant. The participants in the meetings were three managers from the company: the CEO/co-founder (CEO), chief operating officer/partner (COO), and sales manager (SM), and two researchers, of which R2 is the first author of this study (R1 = Researcher 1, facilitator of the meetings, not an author of this study, R2 = Researcher 2, a participant observer in the meetings). Table 7.1 describes the data.

In nine meetings the discussion progressed freely and in seven meetings various workshop frameworks were also used at the initiative of the researchers. These frameworks were used both to facilitate discussion around business development and to cover the topics from various viewpoints. As an active participant in the meetings, Researcher 2 asked follow-up questions and commented on the topics discussed in order to create dialogue.

7.4.3 *Data Analysis*

We started our analysis with three separate readings of the transcribed recordings and by grouping the text into themes with NVivo. However, we note that the overall analysis involved ongoing reflection between the data and theoretical work (Kaplan and Orlikowski, 2013). The initial purpose of thematic grouping was to identify central issues from the transcription texts, which consisted of over 800 pages. The following themes were identified: customer relations, decision making and boundary setting, identifying and solving problems, future constructions, stories of events, Alpha's practices and actions, temporal dynamics, strategy, novelty, and practical logic.

In our second phase we used the 'in-time' view as a lens to analyse the themes mentioned above. In particular, we used two guiding research questions. First, 'what are the manifestations of "in-time" processuality?' and second, 'what is the role of time in strategy making?' By using these two questions, we identified instances in which references by managers to events suggested that these events influence their intentions in strategy making.

In our third phase we started to track the unfolding of temporal events where the influence of time was identified. However, this did not mean that we sequenced the events chronologically in a way that would assume that events have an enduring meaning. Instead, our analysis focused on two aspects in the unfolding of events: first on the relations between events and managerial strategy making, and second on the temporal relations between events. In analysing the relations between events we focused on how they emerged 'in time'. This means that we examined how each present event entailed notions of both the past and future. However, in the relational analysis of the unfolding of events we strove to identify how the notions of the events shifted between meetings as the new present events created a novel viewpoint to the past events. In Section 7.5 we present our findings.

7.5 Manifestations of 'In-Time' Processuality

Through our analysis described in Section 7.4 we identified five manifestations of 'in-time' processuality. These manifestations are *black swans, a chameleon past, the uniquity of a lived present, unowned causality*, and *the conditionality of time*. In Table 7.2 we present these manifestations and explain their implication for the process of strategy emergence.

7.5.1 *Black Swans*

'Black swans' as the manifestation of 'in-time' strategy emergence refers to the continuous emergence of *unforeseen events* (cf. MacKay and Chia, 2013). A black swan is characterized by unpredictable novelty, and thus it cannot be anticipated on the basis of past events. However, regardless of how essential this characteristic is to our notion of a black swan, as an event it can be mundane even though its effect can be major.

Table 7.2. Manifestations of 'in-time' processuality

Manifestations of 'in-time' processuality	Explanation and implication for strategy emergence
1. Black swans	Strategy making is characterized by the continuous emergence of unforeseen events. These events introduce radical novelty and disrupt repetition. This manifestation emphasizes the unpredictable, non-linear nature of strategy making.
2. Chameleon past	The emergence of new events changes the meaning of past events. Thus, the meaning of events is defined in the fluid present and emerges through relations between events. This manifestation pinpoints how cause–effect relations are constructed retrospectively, namely as the 'effect' event defines the 'cause' event. Consequently, events significant for strategy emergence cannot necessarily be recognized by strategists when they happen.
3. Uniquity of a lived present	Human agency in the lived present is evoked from within unowned events and is thus tied to them. This means that participating in an emerging situation produces managerial actions from within the situation. Hence, strategic actions can also be immediate responses to uncontrollable present situations that have irreversible, unknown causal power in relation to future events. Analytically, this blurs the boundary between planned activity and practical coping.
4. Unowned causality	Unowned causality is manifest in strategy emergence as the heterogeneity of becoming. This means that we can identify fragments of causality in both relations between different events and between intentions and events. However, this causality is unowned in nature because present events cannot be reduced to any single cause, neither to a single event nor intention, since events and intentions are mutually constitutive.
5. Conditionality of time	The temporal nature of reality defines the relational dynamics of human lives and hence limits human agency to one lived event at a time. This manifestation illustrates how human agency is framed by the temporal nature of reality. We cannot choose the conditions of the time we live in, but we can choose what we do in the events in which we participate.

As an example, one 'black swan' event in particular had perceptible causality in defining Alpha's subsequent strategy. This event was an unexpected contact in 2012 from a notable Australia-based company, Beta (pseudonym). Alpha's sales received an email from representatives of Beta in which they expressed interest in offering Alpha's software solution to the company's customers as part of a new service platform. The prospects of such a relation seemed financially lucrative. This contact eventually led to a business relation that Alpha's managers regarded as radically different from their past relations. Alpha's management had not even considered the possibility of forming such a business relation before this contact was made.

SM: This is very interesting. I couldn't understand X [the same type of company as the Australian company] here in Finland wanting to be our customer. I could not understand it at all. (16 October 2012)

Beta's representatives found Alpha through the internet. Despite Beta's intentional search for a partner, the initial formation of the business relation was based on coincidence. Hence, the black swan event cannot be explained solely by Beta's intentions since Beta's encounter with Alpha on the internet was a coincidence. After the initial contact from Beta, a Japan-based company operating in the same industry as Beta approached Alpha. In addition, other Asian companies in the same industry soon started to perceive of Alpha as a prospective partner. This unfolding of events led Alpha to recognize the possibility of replicating their business concept in geographical locations beyond Australia. Thus, the managers' intentionality emerged as the events unfolded.

> CEO: The situation right now is unbelievable. I would say that after a long time there's finally a kind of new 'vibe' here. There seems to be a new scenario of sorts in all this.   (16 October 2012)

This imagined possibility of replicating the new partner logic made the present situation look even more positive to the managers. Consequently, the imagined possibility described by the manager as an 'unbelievable situation' cannot be reduced to a single source, for example to the intentions of either Beta's or Alpha's representatives. It would seem to indicate that intentions can be seen as embedded in unowned processes.

7.5.2 Chameleon Past

Apart from illustrating the influence of black swans for strategy emergence, the Australian contact from Beta shows how the meaning of past events changes as new events relate to them in becoming the present. This leads to our second manifestation of 'in-time' strategy emergence, namely the *chameleon past*. We use the chameleon past to refer to how the meaning of identifiable events changes continuously as new events emerge. Furthermore, the meaning of any single event is not analytically enduring, since the becoming of new events constitutes the meaning of past events.

This can be seen from the data as follows. While the initial reference from Beta's contact person can be retrospectively defined as a 'black swan' event, it was not immediately clear what it would mean in practice. The subsequent events such as conversations between the people working for Alpha and Beta and trials with 'end customers' continuously redefined the meaning of the black swan event. This cumulative effect of the relations between the events reinforced the managers' conception of a temporal continuity that became 'the Australian case'. Although these relations between events were initiated by the black swan event, the strategic significance of the black swan emerged only retrospectively in relation to later events. Hence the meaning of the case shifted continuously. In sum, this means that human agents define causes from the perspective of the effects.

7.5.3 *The Uniquity of a Lived Present*

We define the third manifestation of 'in-time' strategy emergence as the *uniquity of a lived present*. On the one hand, we use the term 'lived present' to refer to the actual present situation in its eternal becoming. On the other hand, we use 'uniquity' to refer to the immediacy and irreversibility of that present. Accordingly, the uniquity of the lived present helps us to explain the temporally indivisible human experience that creates the necessity of immediate actions within an emerging event. This is shown in the following excerpt from our data. In this excerpt the CEO describes a negotiation with representatives of the potential customer. In the negotiation the CEO had to make an immediate suggestion for the pricing of their solution because he wanted to establish a new pricing model for this new customer relationship. This was because the previous, standard pricing model used for the software solution would have been too low for this new global and larger-than-typical customer.

> CEO: There at the meeting we had to, we had to make up those regions immediately [for pricing] ... this part was really hard-going, luckily we had worked on it ... Of course it would have been easier if we had considered it even further. Then we would have had even more leverage at the meeting. I had to come up with the regions immediately. And then finalize them right there. That these are the regions. Without having time to think whether Asia really is one.   (17 April 2012)

In the excerpt above the uniquity of the lived present becomes visible because the CEO could not postpone the pricing proposition to a more convenient future setting in order to have time to consider the options carefully. Instead, the response within the emerging situation had to be immediate. In the above 'meeting-in-becoming', the CEO also recognized the irreversibility and causal power of the pricing proposition for subsequent events in the customer relation. Hence the momentual uniquity of the meeting becomes explicit through its immediacy and irreversibility. This event also shows how managerial agency was enacted and improvised *from within the unique moment*. The CEO's actions cannot therefore be understood without reference to the meeting event itself. However, in spite of the improvised nature of the pricing proposition, the excerpt shows that modifications for the pricing had been discussed previously. Hence, previous pricing discussion events that took place in both project meetings and internally, within the company, also influenced the pricing proposal given to the customer. This makes it impossible to determine the extent to which the pricing proposition was an immediate improvisation and the extent to which it was the outcome of past work.

7.5.4 *Unowned Causality*

The fourth manifestation of 'in-time' strategy emergence is *unowned causality*. We use 'unowned causality' to refer to a notion of becoming according to which the unfolding of events is heterogeneous in nature (Chia, 1999). This heterogeneity means that even though past events have identifiable causality in relation to the subjective present, we analytically refuse to reduce the unfolding of events to a specific origin, either to a single event or to any human intention. However, this does not mean that it would be pointless to identify fragments of the causality. In other words, both past intentions and events are immanent and hence have causal power in becoming the present. In sum, in terms of strategy making, the present is not reducible to either specific managerial intentions or past events.

One of the key strategic decisions concerning Alpha's internationalization was related to the countries in which the sales and marketing efforts should be focused. As an example, one seemingly rational decision to enter the Japanese market has fragments of unowned causality from both intentions and coincidental events. One of the former workers in Alpha's software development moved to Japan and worked from there for Alpha. This worker approached Alpha's managers and suggested that he could become a reseller in Japan together with a Japanese partner that had suitable contacts with Japanese firms.

> CEO: And we considered this a while and thought that it fits our strategy. That we now try to conquer the market as widely as possible before our competitors catch up...But you asked, why Japan of all countries? It is because we have a foothold there in a way. We have a guy that is inside the culture, but with whom we can nevertheless communicate in Finnish.   (28 November 2011)

The above excerpt illustrates how the past events of hiring a person who later happened to move to Japan can be seen as having causal power in relation to the managers' decision to enter the Japanese market. Thus, these past events, which seemed strategically insignificant at the time of their occurrence, eventually became pivotal for the emergence of the managers' intentions to enter the Japanese market. This notion means that managerial intention per se cannot be seen as something that exists ex ante or originates from a specific or dominant source. Neither could intentions be seen as possessive or enduring. Instead, any intention can be seen as constituted in and through events. In other words, managerial intentions continuously shift *from within* unowned events.

7.5.5 *The Conditionality of Time*

The last manifestation of 'in-time' strategy emergence is the *conditionality of time*. We use this manifestation to mean that each individual can participate only in one emerging event at a time. This means that ongoing organizational processes are conditioned by temporal reality. In particular, temporality creates the conditions under which individuals are able to act. For example, international growth is limited by the number of sales relations in which Alpha's sales people can participate and the development of the software solution is limited by the coder's ability to write code. The temporal constraints of the lived present create the operational frames for strategic plans. In other words, the lived present conditions in which strategic activities are enacted, since the managers would like to do more than is possible. This means that even though multiple future strategic scenarios were created in the meetings, only those strategic plans that were connected to the tangible challenges of the lived present were operationalized. In other words, the present moment and its continuously emerging challenges define the action even though the managers expressed their awareness of the importance of taking purposeful steps toward identified and preferred strategic objectives. This means that in order to be operationalized, strategy plans require temporal continuity in relation to the challenges of the lived present.

> COO: But now we need to understand what the key business issues for supporting this are. Because this is a pressing issue. After that we might for sure have these long-term plans. But if we don't get this basic business running, it will be pretty difficult to build these different paths.   (27 January 2012)

7.6 The Temporality Paradox

In Section 7.5 we focused on the manifestations of 'in-time' strategy emergence. In this section we elaborate on how managers live and operate in two temporalities simultaneously: 'over time' as the constructed linearity and 'in time' as the experienced present. Even though both 'over time' and 'in time' seem logical when considered in isolation, they seem contradictory when juxtaposed (see Lewis, 2000). From the perspective of strategy making, this means that managers seem to live and operate in a temporality paradox because conceptually, both 'over time' and 'in time' can be construed as contradictory while at the same time they are interrelated elements of strategy making (cf. Smith & Lewis, 2011). In other words, strategy making can be characterized by the coexistence of both of these temporal conceptualizations.

From the data, the 'over-time' temporality became explicit when managers expressed a sense of over-time linearity. This can be shown for example in how they reflected upon organizational development issues. In particular, managers talked about their organizational actions in these 'development mode' talks as a sequential, cumulative process extended over time. This meant that they divided their actions into a linear continuum of the past, present, and future. In this process, past actions had formed a platform enabling present actions, which in turn were seen to enable future actions. In that setting, future actions could be described as a list of chronological actions not yet taken. On the basis of the above notions, we describe 'over-time' strategy making as the establishment of constructed linearity. In other words, the 'over-time' linear platform is used in organizing actions.

This 'over-time' strategy making implicitly uses objective, linear time as a platform that provides a temporal extension to the present that supports repetition and the cumulative development of actions.

> CEO: This is what we have done. We have put two virtual servers [on the cloud]... They are on Azure, so artificially we are now in the cloud. We are waiting to get the licenses running with the customer and then we'll establish a new development project with them, where the system is put on the cloud. And then, when we have a paying customer, we'll do the work and by that time we'll have already investigated the technicalities and solved the problems.
>
> (20 December 2012)

The above excerpt illustrates how constructed linearity is used in implementing a new technology for the software solution. Thus, implementation is described as steps, the first of which has already been taken. The others will only be planned in the future.

However, the construction of over-time linearity can be seen as a result of practical coping with the conditionality of time. Dividing complex acts into cumulating subactivities may be considered necessary for strategic planning and operationalization. However, relying on constructed linearity caused problems for the managers since they continuously faced new events that conflicted with the constructed linearity. In other words, acting in accordance with constructed linearity narrowed managers' scope for action when emerging events required a response. This became explicit when commitments to constructed linearity bound the managers to stick with pre-organized actions and thus their ability to manoeuvre in emerging situations was restricted.

> CEO: There is the picture where the American Indians attack the fort. And in the fort they have barrel-loaded guns. Then a salesman comes there with a machine gun and says: 'hey, look what I have'. And they just tell him 'sorry, we're too busy right now'. This is what it's all about.   (16 October 2012)

In addition, the example below shows that reliance on constructed linearity is not always sustainable because strategy making also necessitates immediate responses to the unfolding of everyday mundane challenges.

CEO: In this customer case, we have three problems. There is the geographical problem, because so far we've had our servers in Finland. And then, there is the problem related to content production. And there is the scalability problem in our pricing model. This is an urgent issue that needs resolving now.   (27 January 2012)

Another example of the temporality paradox has to do with software development.

CEO: So lately, the AR-based applications have been popping up in the App Store like mushrooms in the rain . . . This is what has been happening among the competition now. And, maybe we haven't been that agile in this issue, because our effort has been put into [tackling] issues other than AR this year. And now, we have added something called markerless AR to the roadmap.   (22 February 2013)

As the above quote illustrates, the roadmap manifests a linear ordering of intentional actions whenever they involve making modifications to the software. In this way, the roadmap can be seen as a constructed linearity in the continuous, cumulative development of a software solution. This roadmap is constantly modified in response to evolving events. However, in the above example it took a while before the emergence of new competition was addressed intentionally, as the managers were tied to their earlier developmental commitments. In other words, these pre-organized development activities prevented immediate responses to the emerging competition. Hence, 'overtime' organizing of the software development activities affected the ability of managers to respond to the emerging competition 'in time'. Linearity constructed 'over time' and present experienced 'in time' coexist and are interrelated, and thus neither of them completely determines intentional actions. In sum, the temporality paradox becomes explicit through tension between linearity constructed 'over time' and the emergence of new events 'in time'.

7.7 Discussion and Conclusions

Temporal work is now acknowledged as one of the key issues in strategy process and practice research (Kaplan & Orlikowski, 2013). However, recent developments in process organization research (Helin et al., 2014; Hernes, 2014; Langley & Tsoukas, 2017) have opened up new avenues to broaden our understanding of temporality in strategy making by conceptualizing it as an inherent characteristic of processuality rather than as an outcome of human sense making. Thus, we have argued that we need to extend the analysis of the various temporal orientations of organizational actors (e.g.

Kaplan & Orlikowski, 2013; Reinecke & Ansari, 2015) by examining how the relational becoming of events creates lived temporality for human agents. This allowed us to approach temporality without reducing it to a product of human actors (Rescher, 1996). In our empirical analysis, we first identified five manifestations of 'in-time' processuality in managerial strategy making: *black swans, a chameleon past, the uniquity of a lived present, unowned causality,* and *the conditionality of time.* Second, we examined how these manifestations related to the forms of temporal strategy work. As a result, we showed how managers operate in a temporality paradox.

Our study suggests interrelated contributions to two streams of literature. First, we add to the process perspective on organizational research (Tsoukas & Chia, 2002; Hernes, 2014; Langley & Tsoukas, 2017) by elaborating the relation between time as the passage of nature and human agency. Second, we add to the process perspective on strategy research in two ways. First, we re-examine the nature of intentions in strategy making (Chia & Holt, 2006; Mintzberg & Waters, 1985). Second, we extend the notion of temporality in strategy making (Kaplan and Orlikowski, 2013).

In terms of process organization studies, by showing how human intentions emerge from within relational events, we contribute to the understanding of events and human agency as mutually constitutive (Chia, 1999). This approach enables us to show that human intentions are embedded in events rather than in a causal relationship with them. However, this does not mean that we are of the opinion that events determine human agency. Subsequently, the 'in-time' view enables us to overcome the dualism between events and human agency. More specifically, it allows us to engage with prehensive processuality (Langley & Tsoukas, 2017) and hence to understand the temporal nature of human agency without falling into methodological individualism (Ingold, 2000). Thus, we argue that to better understand the temporal unfolding of events, we should not reduce processes to either a single event or to the intentions of human agents, but instead examine them relationally. Consequently, the 'in-time' view opens up the possibility to approach the agentual nature of relational events (Hernes, 2017). This means that while we recognize the agency of human actors, the 'in-time' view enables us to take into account that time also works on us through the unowned becoming of events (Hernes, 2014).

Approaching the nature of individual intention from the 'in-time' perspective also impacts how we understand strategy making. This is particularly relevant for studies of strategy emergence (Mintzberg & Waters, 1985; Mirabeau & Maguire, 2013), because our view challenges the assumption that intentionality and emergence are opposites of each other in a continuum (Mintzberg & Waters, 1985). By placing explicit emphasis on the fluidity of the experienced present, we show how strategic intentions are constituted in and through unowned events. In other words, we re-examine the nature of intention in the Mintzbergian view on strategy process (intended, deliberate, and emergent strategies) according to which realized strategies can be evaluated in terms of the degree of intentionality and emergence. Instead, we extend this notion by showing that intentions are fluid by nature and thus should not be treated as ex ante.

In addition, by adopting the notion of 'in time', our study continues the recent strategy research that has examined the role of temporality in strategy making (Kaplan and Orlikowski, 2013; Vesa and Franck, 2013; Vaara and Pedersen, 2013). In spite of recent developments with respect to strategy as temporal work, previous strategy literature is still strongly characterized by practices of intentional decision making and over-time planning. In other words, previous studies have mainly focused on the various forms of constructed linear 'over time' in strategy making. Thus, by empirically identifying the temporality paradox, our study shows how managers simultaneously engage with two contradictory conceptualizations of time, namely constructed linear 'over time' and the experienced present becoming 'in time'. Hence we argue that the temporality paradox emerges as *the lived present makes managers rely on linearity constructed 'over time' when organizing action; they are at the same time bound by this constructed linearity, which makes it challenging to relate to continuously emerging new events 'in time'*. In sum, this study builds theoretical bridges between two views on strategy processes, namely between subjectively constructed linear temporalities (Kaplan & Orlikowski, 2013) and unowned everyday practical coping (Chia & Holt, 2006; MacKay & Chia, 2013).

Last, this study has its limitations. First, while in our empirical analysis we have mostly focused on manifestations of 'in-time' processuality, at the same time we acknowledge that this can lead to downplaying of 'over-time' strategy making. Second, even though participating in the strategy-making conversations enabled us to gain in-depth, real-time data on strategy making, we acknowledge that involvement in the daily operations of the examined company would have enabled even more profound elaboration of some of the aspects of the temporal dynamics. Moreover, we note that this study has limitations related to our focus on the managerial perspective in strategy making. Thus further research that would focus on the non-managerial viewpoint in strategy emergence could complement the findings of this study. Last, we acknowledge the impact of the interpretation of the observer in data collection.

Acknowledgements

This work was carried out as a part of the Cloud Software and Need for Speed research programmes by Digile.

References

Alvesson, M. & Deetz, S. 2000. *Doing Critical Management Research*. London: Sage.

Bakken, T., Holt, R., & Zundel, M. 2013. Time and play in management practice: An investigation through the philosophies of McTaggart and Heidegger. *Scandinavian Journal of Management*, 29: 13–22.

Barry, D. & Elmes, M. 1997. Strategy retold: Towards a narrative view of strategic discourse. *Academy of Management Review*, 22(2): 429–52.

Boje, D.M. 2008. *Storytelling Organizations*. London: Sage.

Burgelman, R.A. 1983. A model of the interaction of strategic behaviour, corporate context, and the context of strategy. *Academy of the Management Review*, 8(1): 61–70.

Chia, R. 1999. A 'Rhitzomic' model of organizational change and transformation: Perspectives from a metaphysics of change. *British Journal of Management*, 10(3): 209–27.

Chia, R. 2014. The praise for silent transformation: Allowing change through 'letting happen'. *Journal of Change Management*, 14(1): 8–27.

Chia, R. & Holt, R. 2006. Strategy as practical coping: A Heideggerian perspective. *Organization Studies*, 27: 635.

Chia, R. & Holt, R. 2009. *Strategy without Design: The Silent Efficacy of Indirect Action*. Cambridge: Cambridge University Press.

Chia, R. & Rasche, A. 2015. Epistemological alternatives for researching strategy as practice: Building and dwelling worldviews. In D. Golsorkhi, L. Rouleau, D. Seidl, & E. Vaara (eds), *Cambridge Handbook of Strategy as Practice*, 2nd edition. Cambridge: Cambridge University Press.

Cobb, J.B. 1993. Alfred North Whitehead. In D.R. Griffin, 2002, (ed.), *Founders of Constructive Postmodern Philosophy: Peirce, James, Bergson, Whitehead, and Harshorne*. New York: State University of New York Press.

Cooper, R. 2005. Peripheral vision: Relationality. *Organization Studies*, 26(11): 1689–710.

Cunliffe, A. 2015. Using ethnography in strategy-as-practice research. In D. Golsorkhi, L. Rouleau, D. Seidl, & E. Vaara (eds), *Cambridge Handbook of Strategy as Practice*, 2nd edition. Cambridge: Cambridge University Press.

Cunliffe, A., Luhman, J.T., & Boje, D.M. 2004. Narrative temporality: Implications for organizational research. *Organization Studies*, 25: 261–86.

Dawson, P. 2014. Reflections: On time, temporality and change in organizations. *Journal of Change Management*, 14(3): 285–308.

Emirbayer, M. & Mische, A. 1998. What is agency? *American Journal of Sociology*, 103(4): 962–1023.

Fenton, C. & Langley, A. 2011. Strategy as practice and the narrative turn. *Organization Studies*, 32(9): 1171–96.

Helin, J., Hernes, T., Hjorth, D., & Holt, R. 2014. *The Oxford Handbook of Process Philosophy and Organization Studies*. Oxford: Oxford University Press.

Hernes, T. 2014. *A Process Theory of Organization*. Oxford: Oxford University Press.

Hernes, T. 2017. Process as the becoming of temporal trajectory. In A. Langley & H. Tsoukas (eds), *The Sage Handbook of Process Organization Studies* (pp. 601–6). London: Sage.

Hernes, T., Simpson, B., & Söderlund, J. 2013. Managing and temporality. *Scandinavian Journal of Management*, 29: 1–6.

Hussenot, A. & Missonier, S. 2016. Encompassing stability and novelty in organization studies: An events-based approach. *Organization Studies*, 37(4): 523–46.

Huy, Q.N. 2001. Time, temporal capability, and planned change. *Academy of Management Review*, 26(4): 601–23.

Hydle, K.M. 2015. Temporal and spatial dimensions of strategizing. *Organization Studies*, 36(5): 643–63.

Ingold, T. 2000. *The Perception of the Environment: Essays on Livelihood, Dwelling and Skill*. London: Routledge.

Jarzabkowski, P. 2003. Strategic practices: An activity theory perspective on continuity and change. *Journal of Management Studies*, 40(1): 23–55.

Kaplan, S. & Orlikowski, W.J. 2013. Temporal work in strategy-making. *Organization Science*, 24(4): 965–95.

Laine, P. & Vaara, E. 2007. Struggling over subjectivity: A discursive analysis of strategic development in an engineering group. *Human Relations*, 60(1): 29–58.

Langley, A. 2009. Studying processes in and around organizations. In D. Buchanan & A. Bryman (eds), *Sage Handbook of Organizational Research Methods*. London: Sage.

Langley, A. & Tsoukas, H. (eds). 2017. *The Sage Handbook of Process Organization Studies*. London: Sage.

Langley, A., Smallman, C., Tsoukas, H., & Van de Ven, A.H. 2013. Process studies of change in organization and management: Unveiling temporality, activity, and flow. *Academy of Management Journal*, 56(1): 1–13.

Lee, H. & Liebenau, J. 1999. Time in organization studies: Towards a new research direction. *Organization Studies*, 20(6): 1035–58.

Lewis, M. 2000. Exploring paradox: Toward a more comprehensive guide. *Academy of Management Review*, 25(4): 760–76.

MacKay, R.B. & Chia, R. 2013. Choice, change, and unintended consequences in strategic change: A process understanding of the rise and fall of Northco Automotive. *Academy of Management Journal*, 56(1): 208–30.

Melin, L. 1992. Internationalization as strategy process. *Strategic Management Journal*, 13: 99–118.

Mesle, C.R. 2008. *Process-Relational Philosophy: An Introduction to Alfred North Whitehead*. West Conshohocken, PA: Templeton Foundation Press.

Mintzberg, H. 1978. Patterns in strategy formation. *Management Science*, 24(9): 934–48.

Mintzberg, H. & Waters, J.A. 1985. Of strategies, deliberate and emergent. *Strategic Management Journal*, 6(3): 257–72.

Mirabeau, L. & Maguire, S. 2013. From autonomous strategic behavior to emergent strategy. *Strategic Management Journal*, 35(8): 1202–29.

Pettigrew, A.M. 1990. Longitudinal field research on change: Theory and practice. *Organization Science*, 1(3): 267–92.

Rasche, A. & Chia, R. 2009. Researching strategy practices: A genealogical social theory perspective. *Organization Studies*, 30: 713–34.

Reinecke, J. & Ansari, S. 2015. When times collide: Temporal brokerage at the intersection of markets and developments. *Academy of Management Journal*, 58(2): 618–48.

Rescher, N. 1996. *Process Metaphysics*. New York: State University of New York Press.

Roe, R.A., Waller, M.J., & Clegg, S.R. 2009. Introduction. In R.A. Roe, M.J. Waller, & S.R. Clegg (eds), *Time in Organization Research*. Oxon: Routledge.

Samra-Fredericks, D. 2003. Strategizing as lived experience and strategists everyday efforts to shape strategic direction. *Journal of Management Studies*, 40(1): 141–74.

Schultz, M. & Hernes, T. 2013. A temporal perspective on organizational identity. *Organization Science*, 24(1): 1–21.

Shotter, J. 2006. Understanding process from within: An argument for 'Withness'-Thinking. *Organization Studies*, 27(4): 585–604.

Smith, W.K. & Lewis, M.W. 2011. Toward a theory of paradox: A dynamic equilibrium model of organizing. *Academy of Management Review*, 36(2): 381–403.

Sonenshein, S. 2010. We're changing—Or are we? Untangling the role of progressive, regressive, and stability narratives during strategic change implementation. *Academy of Management Journal*, 53(3): 477–512.

Steyaert, C. & Bouwen, R. 2004. Group methods of organizational analysis. In C. Cassell & G. Symon (eds), *Essential Guide to Qualitative Methods in Organizational Research*. London: Sage.

Tsoukas, H. 2010. Practice, strategy-making and intentionality: A Heideggerian onto-epistemology for strategy-as-practice. *Cambridge Handbook of Strategy as Practice*, 3: 47–62.

Tsoukas, H. 2016. Don't simplify, complexify: From disjunctive to conjunctive theorizing in organization and management studies. *Journal of Management Studies*. DOI: 10.1111/joms.12219.

Tsoukas, H. & Chia, R. 2002. On organizational becoming: Rethinking organizational change. *Organization Science*, 13: 567–604.

Vaara, E. & Reff Pedersen, A. 2013. Strategy and chronotopes: A Bakhtinian perspective on the construction of strategy narratives. *M@n@gement*, 16(5): 593–604.

Vaara, E. & Whittington, R. 2012. Strategy-as-practice: Taking social practices seriously. *Academy of Management Annals*, 6(1): 285–336.

Van de Ven, A. 1992. Suggestions for studying strategy process: A research note. *Strategic Management Journal*, 13: 169–88.

Vesa, M. & Franck, H. 2013. Bringing strategy to time, studying strategy as experiential vectors. *Scandinavian Journal of Management*, 29: 23–34.

Vesa, M. & Vaara, E. 2014. Strategic ethnography 2.0: Four methods for advancing strategy process and practice research. *Strategic Organization*, 12(4): 288–98.

Whitehead, A.N. 1920. *The Concept of Nature*. London: Cambridge University Press.

Whitehead, A.N. 1967 [1925]. *Science and the Modern World*. New York: Free Press.

Whitehead, A.N. 1978 [1929]. *Process and Reality*, edited by D.R. Griffin & D.W. Sherburne. New York: Free Press.

Yakura, E.K. 2002. Charting time: Timelines as temporal boundary objects. *Academy of Management Journal*, 45(5): 956–70.

8

Paradox and Dialectic in Cultural Knowledge Systems

From Cosmological Science to South Indian Kinship

Charles W. Nuckolls

This chapter is about knowledge systems, their internal paradoxes, and the dialectics these paradoxes create. Religious systems, for example, usually link theodicy, or a theory of suffering, to a plan of salvation that depends on the will of God. If bad things did not happen to good people, and for apparently no reason, the link could not be made. Religious systems would then lose one of their supporting doctrines. Unexpected events are useful precisely to the extent that they are explainable, and thus convertible into non-events at a higher level of explanatory adequacy where the causally omniscient deity resides. Of course, believers have always struggled with the observation that the deity, thus conceived, could not preside over an accident-filled universe without limiting or giving up his causal omniscience. That is the paradox that exists at the heart of the knowledge system that identifies itself as Christianity. What is important is not that such internal paradoxes are ever solved—they almost never are—but that they continue to serve as points of departure for continuing inquiry, scientific discovery, even mystical revelation. The very fact that they are paradoxes—and thus insoluble—assures development of the belief system, as the system strives for a resolution that its inner structure always and invariably prevents.

For example, orthodox Christian apologists admit no limitation on God's power or knowledge. How, then, is it possible for human beings to make real (not merely imaginary) choices, and for those choices to affect ultimate destiny? The question comes up repeatedly, and each major figure in the history of Christian theology, from Augustine to Kierkegaard, has offered a solution—or, rather, in the absence of a permanent solution, a compromise that identifies the great contradiction as a sign or token of the *mysterium tremendum*. As a religious system, Christianity would lack a hermeneutics as well as a history if it were not for this fact, and it is no less true of modern Christian history than it was at the first Council of Nicaea in the fourth century. Heterodox movements emerge and develop when the accepted compromises break down or no longer seem serviceable. The underlying paradox then reasserts itself, and a new structure (but with the old opposition at its core) comes into being.

An interesting case in point is the uniquely American solution to the Christian causal paradox: Mormonism. In the 1830s and 1840s, a new religion—or, in its own terms, the restoration of an ancient one—began to attract hundreds, then thousands of members. Several years earlier, an impoverished New York farmer, Joseph Smith, had announced a 'new dispensation' through which God's word would be known on earth again. The movement he created became known as Mormonism, or officially, the Church of Jesus Christ of Latter-Day Saints. Among its several significant claims is that God is an exalted man, finite in knowledge and limited in his ability to govern events. Human beings are possessed of 'intelligences' that are co-eternal with God, and therefore capable of agency. They can make choices over which God, in principle, can have no certain advance knowledge. By making choices, human beings develop, and so, perhaps, does God, as he responds to the choices his children make. Thus, Mormon theology endeavours to solve the problem of free will and determinism by limiting God's capacity for knowledge, and relating human and divine wills so that they depend on each other. Does that 'solve' any sort of paradox? Not really.

Like most long-lasting dialectical systems, Mormonism ends up retaining its central paradox. It thereby elaborates its internal contradiction through the dialectical development of its associated knowledge systems (Murphy, 1971; Nuckolls, 1996, 1998). It is easy to see how. A finite God of limited knowledge prompts questions of the infinite regression variety: if God was once a man, who was God's father? And if a finite God is subject to this qualification, why is he worthy of respect or adoration? By attempting to solve one problem—that of determinism and free will—Mormon theology creates others, which it then answers by continuing to refine its theory of Godhood. Thus the knowledge system develops. That is precisely what is happening (and probably will happen) as long as the underlying paradox remains. But instead of defining intractable dilemma as a weakness, we could, as Kant recommends, recognize the dynamic quality of paradox as a source of motivational power and direction. Paradox is what powers the dialectic of the system. Without paradox the belief system would be flat, with only limited powers to attract attention or endure through time. Paradox is what keeps it going by guaranteeing, in advance, that the fundamental problem (or problems) at the core of the knowledge system can never be solved.

It is one thing to try to solve deep and troubling paradoxes. Many religions change, grow, and develop by repeatedly attempting resolution. The other option is to hold paradoxical alternatives in suspension, and deliberately avoid trying to bring them into resolution. In a larger sense, paradox can then be seen as a manifestation of the divine, as evidence of the limitations of human reason, or proof that the universe is absurd. Certainly various forms of Christian thought have played with these options, from Athanasius, Tertulian, and Meister Eckert to Kant. Such is the power of the value of rational consistency, however, that these doctrines only occasionally (and, for the most part, briefly) become the basis of a religious movement in the West. The same cannot be said of other knowledge systems, including cosmology and particle physics, whose form and development have been determined by the play of unresolvable oppositions and contradictions.

8.1 The Antinomies of Cosmology and Particle Physics

In Kant's first critique, the 'antinomies' are understood as logical contradictions that develop as natural and inevitable consequences of reason's overextension of itself (Kant, 1965). By antinomy Kant means a pair of equally defensible but mutually opposed explanatory accounts. The word 'antinomy' appears to have come from jurisprudence, where it referred to a conflict between laws, or from biblical exegesis, where it referred to a conflict between scriptural passages. Kant himself considered Zeno the inventor of the antinomic mode

> of watching, or rather provoking, a conflict of assertions, not for the purpose of deciding in favor of one or the other side, but of investigating whether the object of the controversy is not perhaps a deceptive appearance which each vainly tries to grasp, and in regard to which, even if there were no opposition to overcome, neither can arrive at any result. (Kant, 1965, p. 395)

In the *Critique of Pure Reason*, Kant describes four antinomies, as follows:

Thesis 1: The world has, as to time and space, a beginning.
Thesis 2: Everything in the world consists of elements which are simple.
Thesis 3: There are in the world causes through freedom (spontaneous causes).

Thesis 4:   In the series of causes in the world, there is some necessary being.

Antithesis 1:   The world is as to time and space infinite.

Antithesis 2:   There is nothing simple, but everything is composite.

Antithesis 3:   There is no freedom, but all is nature (a complex of causes in space and time).

Antithesis 4:   There is nothing necessary in the world, but all is contingent.

The theses, Kant says, constitute the claims of 'dogmatic philosophy' about what cannot be experienced; he calls them 'rationalistic' and 'Platonic', and they are, in fact, the teachings of the Leibniz-Wolffian rational cosmology. The antitheses are described as the teachings of 'empiricism', 'naturalism', and 'Epicureanism' and represent the claims of empirical science when extended into metaphysics. The moral interests of mankind, Kant holds, are invested in the theses, while the speculative (i.e. theoretical) interests favour the antitheses, which forbid any 'break in the thread of physical inquiries' and urge 'moderation in our pretensions, modesty in our assertions, and the greatest possible extension of our understanding... through experience' (Kant 1965, p. 498).

Recognition of the antinomies as artefacts of reason has an interesting effect, since it effectively destroys dogmatic metaphysics of both the rationalistic and naturalistic schools. But that is not the point of interest for us. The point is that opposing propositions—stripped of their metaphysical trappings—become what Kant called 'regulative principles' or maxims for the conduct of inquiry. The totality of conditions is not given (*gegeben*) but the search for the totality of conditions (the unconditioned) is assigned (*aufgegeben*) to us as a task which must be performed without end.

This turns out to be important, because it functions as the epistemological justification for much of the scientific enterprise as a process both constrained and facilitated by the principles of reason.

Take, as a quick example, the third antinomy. It describes the opposing programmes of the ethical and the anthropological inquiries: one sees man as free (thesis) and the other sees him as product of nature and thus governed by deterministic natural laws (antithesis). While neither principle is ultimately true (because both are products of reason and therefore not given in the nature of things) they nevertheless shape and constrain inquiry about the human condition, leading sometimes to useful results. In other words, we learn important things about ourselves when we consider the object of our analysis from both free-will and deterministic perspectives. Theory in cultural anthropology is partly (perhaps even largely) the result. Anthropology, however, is not the only discipline whose theoretical development has been shaped by the play of logically irreconcilable oppositions, as we see below.

8.2 The Four Kantian Antinomies: What They Are and What They Do

8.2.1 *The First Antinomy*

This antinomy is made up of the following counterclaims:

> *Thesis*: The world has a beginning in time, and is also limited in space.
> *Antithesis*: The world has no beginning, and no limits in space; it is infinite as regards both time and space.

The thesis is 'proved' by the logical inference that if the world has no beginning in time, then up to every time an eternity has elapsed, and there has passed away an infinite series of successive states of things. This is absurd. Therefore, the world must have a beginning in time. On the other hand, the equally logical inference is possible: if we assume that the world has a 'beginning', then it must have been preceded in time by something, and so on in infinite regress. Therefore, the world cannot have had a beginning, nor can it be limited in space. The antinomy constituted by these two logically opposed positions reveals that it is possible to develop two valid arguments for incompatible conclusions based simply on the logical extension of their different premises. Is the question of the world's origin and size therefore a non-question, the result of faulty reasoning, or does it represent a valid inquiry into the nature of things? According to Kant, the trick is not to view this question as ultimately decidable, but to use its opposed alternatives 'regulatively' as a framework for inquiry. Is the universe infinite and forever expanding? Or is it specially and temporally limited, with real boundaries? Much of Western philosophy unwittingly reproduces answers to these (logically undecidable) questions, as we can see from considering the following:

(1) *The universe is eternal, and may have no beginning.* This perspective is associated with Aristotle, Averroes, Wilhelm Ockham, Thomas Aquinas, Boethius of Dacia, Giles of Rome, Godfrey of Fontaines, Henry of Harclay, Thomas Wilton, Thomas of Strassburg, Giordano Bruno, and Baruch de Spinoza.

(2) *The universe is eternal but emanates from the deity*: Plotinus, Proclus, Origen, and Avicenna.

(3) *The universe is timeless*: Johannes Scotus Eurigena and Meister Eckhart.

(4) *The universe is continuously maintained and recreated (creation continua)*: Anaximenes, Augustine, Gregor the Great, and Rene Descartes.

(5) *The universe has an absolute beginning out of nothing (creation ex nihilo)*: Johannes Philoponos, Moses Maimonides, Albertus Magnus, Wilhelm of Auvergne, Roger Bacon, Bonaventure, and Marsilius of Inghen.

(6) *The universe has a beginning, but no end*: Philo of Alexandria.

(7) *The universe as transcendental appearance*: Immanuel Kant

Not all of these possibilities are necessarily in contradiction in every respect. A *creatio ex nihilo* and a *creatio continua*, for instance, could both be true. What is interesting is the extent to which modern scientific inquiry is shaped by the same paradigms of contradictoriness—paradigms that ensure inquiry into their properties can never achieve final resolution. Later, after examining a few Western scientific paradigms and their antinomies, we will consider the contradictions embedded in the explanatory systems of Hindu south Asia: a drama by the famous Sanskrit dramatist Kalidasa and the kinship system of an Indian coastal population known as Jalaris.

Let us first consider the science of cosmology. Cosmological science remains divided on the question of the universe's age and shape and, given its antinomian structure, perhaps always will be (Bartels, 1996; Kanitscheider, 1991; Kragh, 2011). The controversy between the 'big bang' and 'steady state' models, for example, or the current attempt to explain the big bang within a quantum cosmological framework, both take shape as responses to the Kantian first antinomy (Kragh, 1996, 2007). One side assumes as its starting place a unique cosmological beginning whereas the other posits a timeless universe of dynamic fluctuations. There is no resolution to this paradox. Perhaps, then, this should be taken as grounds for abandoning cosmological inquiry altogether. But if we did (or had) done that, then certain interesting observations would not have been made. Without an interest in the question of the universe's size or age, for example, would Eddington have discovered the 'red shift'? The finding that galaxies are all moving away from each other with velocities that are roughly proportional to their distance from us completely changed the discussion of origins, and led directly to the conclusion that there must have been a primordial originating event (the 'big bang'). The problem, of course, is that the nature of the originating event may not be determinable, if, as some physicists assert, the laws of normal space and time do not apply to a singularity. (Kant himself never had any reason to assume that non-Newtonian principles might be at work.) A 'singularity' means an ultimate edge or boundary, a state of infinite density where space and time have ceased. In any case, even if the originating event has a nature that can be investigated, it does not preclude (but actually demands) inquiry into the cause that preceded it, and so on in infinite regress. This is the nature of the investigation: to pursue contradictory alternative causal accounts which nevertheless function regulatively to stimulate and condition lines of inquiry. 'For when the arguments of reason are allowed to oppose one another in unrestricted freedom, something advantageous, and likely to aid in the correction of our judgments, will always accrue, though it may not be what we set out to find' (Kant, 1965, p. 449). In other words, the fact that they are artefacts of reason does not render the antinomies of no use when investigating the properties of the sensible universe.

Long after Kant, Stephen Hawking acknowledged the relevance of paradox in stimulating his own work. In his 1988 speech, 'Origin of the Universe', he pointed to the relevance of contradictory alternatives to the history of his discipline:

> The problem of the origin of the universe is a bit like the old question: Which came first, the chicken or the egg? In other words, what agency created the universe? And what created that agency? Or perhaps the universe, or the agency that created it, existed forever, and didn't need to be created . . . The debate about whether, and how, the universe began, has been going on throughout recorded history.
>
> (Hawking, 1988, p. 1)

Hawking then goes on to consider the arguments for and against the universe's eternality, and not surprisingly, he is drawn to frame the issue in completely Kantian terms—without, however, ever acknowledging the intellectual history, or (apparently) even being aware of it. What he says, in essence, is that arguments for the thesis and antithesis of the first antinomy of time are effectively the same, even though they are really based on different principles. The argument for the thesis—that the universe has a beginning—is based on the impossibility of constructing an infinite series, while the argument for the antithesis—that the universe is infinite in time and space—is an argument from the principle of 'sufficient reason', a kind of argument first used by Parmenides. (One recalls Parmenides' famous saying, *nihil fit ex nihil*, 'out of nothing comes nothing'). Although Hawking says that both arguments are based on an 'unspoken assumption' of infinite time, he actually agrees with the argument of the thesis that time is not infinite. This leads Hawking to conclude (unlike most astrophysicists) that cosmological theory is not incompatible with—and may even require—the existence of an outside force or being to get the whole process started.

It is interesting the extent to which contemporary theory in astrophysics is dominated by the paradox described by Kant in the first antimony. Hawking is not unique. Earlier I presented a table of the philosophers whose work dealt in whole or in part with the question of the universe, its spatial extent, and eternality. In modern cosmological science, the same thing is true, and interesting how various paradigms constitute themselves out of dialectic of the first antinomy (see Appendix).

Basically, all of the various theories on the size and age of the universe—and there are more than the twenty or so listed in the Appendix—boil down to the question of whether or not the universe has an initial state or is eternal. Eternal cosmologies do not have to posit a first cause or accident; they simply shift the burden of explanation to the infinite past. Unfortunately, eternal cosmologies cannot address why a temporally infinite cosmos exists or why it is the way it is. This renders them vulnerable to the critique that they are internally contradictory and therefore unsuitable as a basis for constructing causal laws. What cosmologists call 'initial' theories, on the other hand, posit the existence of an initiating cause, but this, too, runs into problems. How can something come out of nothing? Why is there something rather than nothing at all? To be sure, one can assert that creation *ex nihilo* still depends on physical laws that were (in some strange sense) 'there' even before the first thing existed. But this makes cosmological theory a simple variant of Platonism. As Hawking points out,

> even if there is only one possible unified theory, it is just a set of rules and equations. What is it that breathes fire into the equations and makes the universe for them to describe? The usual approach of science of constructing a mathematical model cannot answer the question of why there should be a universe for the model to describe. Why does the universe go to all the bother of existing?
>
> (1988, p. 174)

8.2.2 The Second Antinomy

The second antimony of the Kantian system is framed as follows: does everything divide up into discrete units that are indivisible or is matter infinitely divisible into smaller and smaller discrete units? Once again proofs allow one to draw either conclusion. The thesis is essentially a statement of atomism: if there were no basic units then matter would be infinitely divisible, and infinitely divisible matter must end up being matter of no size at all. Matter cannot be made up out of a collection of nothings, consequently, matter must consist of basic constituent units of some kind. The antithesis, on the other hand, states that matter is infinitely divisible because all matter exists in space and space is necessarily divisible into smaller and smaller segments. Once again we confront diametrically opposed but equally logical demonstrations of contradictory alternatives. Both cannot be true, yet both appear to be correct in their account of matter.

As Kant pointed out, the effect of the second antinomy is to frame or regulate the search for a solution to the question of whether or not there is a fundamental unit of all matter. It does not matter that all possible explanations are subject to logical disqualification. The history of particle physics (broadly conceived) reveals the productivity of a search premised on antinomian alternatives. Democritus in the fifth century BC is usually credited with introducing the search for elementary non-divisible particles, or 'atoms', and until little more than a century ago the view was that atoms of each element (like hydrogen or gold) were the basic constituents of all matter. However, the existence of what seems to be a fundamental particle only provokes the question from the opposite side of the antinomy: what makes up an atom? By the 1930s, it seemed that particle physics had the answer. Atoms were made up of protons, neutrons, and electrons—the so-called 'elementary particles'. This remained the dominant view until the early 1960s, by which time evidence had accumulated (mainly through high-energy experiments using colliders) that there were even more fundamental particles. Murray Gell-Man named these particles 'quarks', from a word coined by James Joyce in *Finnegan's Wake* (which Gell-Man, apparently, was reading at the time). One of the consequences of the search for the most elementary particle was the world-wide-web—a thing that is decidedly useful despite being the product of irresolvable paradox with reference to the fundamental unit of matter. Again, it does not necessarily make a difference to the productive consequences of science that one of its constituent paradigms—the divisibility or indivisibility of matter—ends up in a state of permanent contradiction.

8.2.3 *The Third Antinomy: Fate and Free Will*

The third antinomy represents the opposition between fate and free will. The thesis states that there are uncaused causes, such as acts of free will, while the antithesis maintains that there can be no free will. If all acts and events can be explained in terms of their antecedents, Kant said, causal sequences disappear in an infinite regress. However, since an infinite regress is impossible there must be some ultimate initiating action that was determined by the exercise of free agency. There must be at least one active cause, in other words, to initiate the series, and thus at least one cause that is not determined by anything else. The antithesis maintains that every event depends on an earlier event that is its antecedent. If that were not the case, then it would mean that something new had been introduced into the order of things, thus violating the principle of sufficient reason. There must be a reason for every event—otherwise we confront a violation of the principle of sufficient reason—and thus there can be no action that is utterly free of determining causes (Allison, 1983).

Like the other antinomies, this one, too, is due to 'mere misunderstanding' (Kant, 1965, p. 423), by which Kant means that it is an artefact or product of reason itself and does not necessarily inhere in the natural order of things. But the result, for Kant, is not the abandonment of free will. On the contrary, freedom is preserved because freedom is a pure transcendental idea, 'which, in the first place, contains nothing borrowed from experience, and which, secondly, refers to an object that cannot be determined or given in any experience' (p. 464). If it were in experience, then it would be understood according to the principles of reason, one of which, as we have seen, is the infinite causal regress when we contemplate causes. There can be no freedom of agency in a universe thus conceived, and hence we must dispense with the attempt to formulate a totality of causes. According to Kant: 'But since in this way no absolute totality of conditions determining causal relation can be obtained, reason creates for itself the idea of a spontaneity which can begin to act of itself, without requiring to be determined to action by an antecedent cause in accordance with the law of causality' (p. 465). For freedom to exist, in other words, it must exist in the realm of transcendental cognition, not in the realm of appearances as grasped through the senses and categorized according to the regulative principles of pure reason.

Does this explain how freedom of the will is preserved against what would seem to be the corrosive pressures of the third antinomy? Not really. In effect, freedom becomes ineffable and unexplainable, but at the same time necessary: we could not think unless we were free. In other words, we know that we are free in a transcendental sense, but we cannot explain how. Freedom exists, but remains forever unknowable, putting it in the same domain as religion and mystical experience. One recalls the passage from Kant's *Religion within the Limits of Reason Alone* in which he writes:

> Freedom of the power of choice (*Willkur*) has the characteristic, entirely peculiar to it, that it cannot be determined to action through any incentive except so far as the human being has incorporated it into his maxim (has made it into a universal rule for himself, according to which he wills to conduct himself); only in this way can an incentive, whatever it may be, coexist with the absolute spontaneity of the power of choice (of freedom). (Kant, 1960, p. 19)

The force of the argument appears to be more normative than descriptive. Kant believes that the principle of action embedded in the commitment to free will leads (or should lead) to actions that are morally correct. The method of transcendental idealism can produce no other result. Notice that we only reach this conclusion via the frustration the third antinomy sets up; its very insolubility requires recourse to another mode of analysis, from transcendental realism to transcendental idealism (Allison, 1983). There it remains pretty much at the level of the Cartesian extrapolation of the *cogito*: I cannot coherently doubt that I am a thinker since even the act of doubting is a form of thinking.

8.2.4 *The Fourth Antinomy*

The thesis of the fourth antinomy states that some form of absolutely necessary existence belongs to the world, whether as its part or as its cause. As proof Kant points out that phenomenal existence is mutable and consistent, and therefore every event is contingent on a preceding condition. The conditioned presupposes the existence of the unconditioned. Therefore, the whole of past time, as the whole of past conditions, must necessarily contain the unconditioned or absolutely necessary. Reason moves from what is conditioned in experience to the postulation of an ultimate, unconditioned ground of being. As soon as this ground is treated as an object and personified as 'God', we have the object of transcendental theology. The antithesis to this line of reasoning states that there is no absolutely necessary existence, in this world or outside of it, as its cause. Kant shows that the assumption of a first unconditioned link in the chain of cosmological conditions is self-contradictory, for such a link would have to be subject to the law of all temporal existence, and so be determined—contrary to the original assumption—by another link or cause before it. In other words, the postulation of an absolutely necessary cause of the world, existing outside the world, ends up destroying itself. If it is outside the world, it is not in time; but for it to act as a cause, it must be in time. The supposition is therefore absurd.

The fourth antinomy is important because of its frequent appearance as either justification or rejection of the idea of God's necessity to creation and the process of causality. It was (and is) one of the most frequently cited popular proofs of the existence of God, since it must surely be the case—so the argument goes—that a universe that exists as a series of causal moments must itself have a cause. But is the cause within or outside the series itself? Kant refers to this as the 'rational' argument for God's existence, but points out (as above) that systematic assertion of its underlying principles must lead to contradiction and paradox. It therefore demonstrates the limits of reason when applied to transcendental questions of the kind of most interest to theology. Speculative reason does not disclose the existence of a creator. Still, the power of such arguments, however flawed, cannot be doubted, nor can we dismiss the relevance of the fourth antinomy to the development of popular notions of divinity and its denial.

The argument for the existence of God based on a decision to adopt the thesis of the fourth antinomy appears in a variety of forms, both classically and in the present day. One is reasoning by simple analogy: since the world is similar to the most intricate artefacts produced by human beings, we can infer the existence of an intelligent designer who created the world. Just as the watch has a watchmaker, then, the universe has a universe maker. Reduced to formal simplicity, the argument consists of four steps in logical relation to each other: (1) the material universe resembles the intelligent productions of human beings in that it exhibits design; (2) the design in any human artefact is the effect of having been made by an intelligent being; (3) like effects have like causes; (4) therefore, the design in the material universe is the effect of having been made by an intelligent creator. This is the kind of explanation by design argument that undergirds most of the ontological arguments for God's existence, including today's most popular incarnation, 'intelligent design'.

Another argument, similar to the argument by analogy but more sophisticated, is associated with the nineteenth-century theologian William Paley and his watchmaker analysis:

> [S]uppose I found a watch upon the ground, and it should be inquired how the watch happened to be in that place, I should hardly think...that, for anything I knew, the watch might have always been there. Yet why should not this answer serve for the watch as well as for [a] stone [that happened to be lying on the ground]?...For this reason, and for no other; viz., that, if the different parts had been differently shaped from what they are, if a different size from what they are, or placed after any other manner, or in any order than that in which they are placed, either no motion at all would have been carried on in the machine, or none which would have answered the use that is now served by it. (1802, p. 1)

What Paley suggests is that the watch performs functions that an intelligent agent would regard as valuable. The useful function of the watch, that is, attests to the intelligent design that informed its construction. Second, the watch could not perform this function if its mechanisms were differently arranged. The fact that the ability of a watch to keep time depends on the precise arrangement of its parts suggests that the watch has these characteristics because an intelligent agency designed it to these specifications. The watch therefore possesses a functional complexity that distinguishes objects that have intelligent designers from objects that do not.

Evolutionary theory develops as an argument against intelligent design, and therefore becomes (incidentally if not deliberately) an argument for the counterthesis proposed by Kant in the Fourth Antinomy. In *The Origin of Species*, Darwin argued that more complex biological organisms evolved gradually over millions of years from simpler ones through a process of natural selection. Julian Huxley describes the logic of this process:

> The evolutionary process results immediately and automatically from the basic property of living matter—that of self-copying, but with occasional errors. Self-copying leads to multiplication and competition; the errors in self-copying are what we call mutations, and mutations will inevitably confer different degrees of biological advantage or disadvantage on their possessors. The consequence will be differential reproduction down the generations—in other words, natural selection.
> (Huxley, 1953, p. 4)

But the existence of complex elements in organized relationship to each other does not require a grand design or intelligent agent. Evolutionary theory simply states that the replication of genetic material in an organism results in mutations that give rise to new traits in the organism's offspring. Sometimes these new traits are so unfavourable to a being's survival prospects in particular environmental circumstances that beings with the traits die off. But sometimes new traits enable the possessors to survive such circumstances.

If the trait is sufficiently favourable, only members of the species with the trait will survive. Through this natural process, complex organisms evolve over millions of years from simple organisms.

Antinomies being what they are—non-resolvable contradictions that sometimes create dialectical knowledge systems—there is no such thing as a final resolution, and consequently the contemporary response to evolutionary theory from intelligent design returns the argument to Kant's original thesis. One example will suffice to see how this is working at present. Dembski (2002; Dembski & Ruse, 2004) has argued that there are two kinds of complexity, one cumulative and the other irreducible. A city is an example of cumulative complexity, since one can successively remove people, services, building, and administrative structures without rendering the city unable to perform its functions. A cigarette lighter, by contrast, is an example of irreducible complexity, since to remove any one of its working parts renders the entire contraption unserviceable. Design proponents find various biochemical processes to be irreducibly complex, and therefore necessarily the products of design, not random mutation and natural selection. A cilium, for example, cannot perform its function unless its microtubules, nexin linkers, and motor proteins are all arranged and structured in precisely the manner in which they are structured. Similarly, the blood-clotting function cannot perform its function if either of its key ingredients, vitamin K and antihemophilic factor, are missing. Both systems are thus irreducibly complex. Behe draws the following conclusion:

> An irreducibly complex system cannot be produced . . . by slight, successive modifications of a precursor system, because any precursor to an irreducibly complex system that is missing a part is by definition nonfunctional . . . Since natural selection can only choose systems that are already working, if a biological system cannot be produced gradually it would have to arise as an integrated unit, in one fell swoop, for natural selection to have anything to act on.   (Behe, 1996, p. 39)

So to return to Behe's example of the cilia: a cilium precursor (i.e. one that lacks at least one of a cilium's parts) cannot perform the function that endows a cilium with adaptive value, and consequently, organisms that have the cilium precursor are no 'fitter for survival' than they would have been without it. Since chance-driven evolutionary processes would not select organisms with the precursor, intelligent design is a better explanation for the existence of organisms with fully functional cilia (Behe, 2007).

The point here is not to argue claims and counterclaims for intelligent design, but to suggest that arguments on both sides are intractable and unresolvable. In that sense (and in that sense only) they are logically equivalent. They emerge from the paradox that is at the heart of Kant's fourth antinomy. To be sure, there are a variety of sophisticated analytical tools for getting rid of Kant's antinomies, or showing how they are misconceived or misunderstood or simply irrelevant. But that does not matter—not as long as the dialectic established by the antinomy drives the arguments (as well as scientific discovery processes) on both sides of the intellectual divide. In other words, the antinomy remains productive *no matter what* is done to eliminate it, and this, I will argue, is the nature of cultural contradictions in general—at least for as long as they exist. The circumstances in which contradictions become extinct—that is to say, no longer interesting or motivating—do arise, but this lies beyond the scope of the present discussion.

Now, having established something of the power of the Kantian antinomies to condition the development of formal knowledge systems, both scientific and religious, it is time to consider the circumstances in everyday life in which antinomian dialectics shape experience. I will argue that the appearance of 'the accidental' points to one primary locus in which the dialectics of cultural paradox realizes itself—that is, in the midst of uncertainty when events fail to conform to our expectations. The unforeseen event forces us to explain, and in doing so, we may confront the opposed alternatives a paradox presents. Observational and experimental science—from cosmology to the biophysics of respiration—are deliberately 'accident-prone', by which I mean they look for the unexpected, and when they find it, the unexpected observation or result forces revision of the governing theory. This makes scientific observations and experimental results a bit like 'accidents', and makes science comparable to other kinds of events in everyday life that are unexpected. What they share in common, moreover, is their capacity to reveal the dynamics of their relevant knowledge systems—systems, many of which, at least, are internally contradictory (antinomian, specifically) at their cores.

Soon we will consider in more detail the meaning of the term 'accident' and its most important distinguishing features. Then we will examine a couple of events that ended up exposing the hidden background assumptions that made the events difficult to explain. Explanatory difficulties often signal the existence of cultural paradox and the dialectical knowledge systems such paradoxes create. Elsewhere (Nuckolls, 1998), I make the radical claim that much of culture consists of problematics of this sort. But here my objective is different, and it is sufficient to describe some events that are seen as 'accidents' and which therefore call attention to the dialectics that constitute the inner scaffolding of their formal explanatory structures.

8.3 Incident, Accident, and Cultural Antinomies

The term 'accident' does not by itself signal the existence of underlying antinomian thinking. Rather, it typically applies simply to events we deem unanticipated (that is, they happen 'by chance') and undesirable. Yet there are obviously problems with this definition. The so-called 'act of God', such as being hit by lightning, is generally considered to be the most unanticipated category of events. At the opposite end of the scale, the 'act of man' would refer to events that are due to some human intervention. However, there are plenty of cases in which making a distinction between the two is essentially arbitrary, especially since science constantly enlarges the domain of human causation to include things that were once thought beyond human ability to influence or anticipate. Undesirability is even more problematic as an attribute of the accidental, since clearly, to say that an event is not desired depends on the value orientation of the individual. No unitary definition of 'accident' is possible, and therefore, we might do better to consider the attributes of causation that make it more likely the term will be employed.

First, there should be a degree of unexpectedness. The less the event in question could have been anticipated the better if it is to be considered accidental. Second, there should be a degree of avoidability. The less an event could have been avoided the more likely it is to be considered an accident. Third, there should be a degree of intentionality. The less an event is the result of a deliberate action the more likely it is to be defined as an accident. Thus an accident could be defined as that category of events which involves a low level of expectedness, avoidability, and intention. Notice that the definition eliminates desirability—in fact, all consequences, material and emotional—from the list of criteria.

This definition, unfortunately, still casts the net too broadly to be suitable in framing our understanding of the term 'accident' in everyday use. For example, if the event in question happened with little or no warning, is it more or less likely to be considered 'accidental'? If so, then the degree of warning should be included as a criterion in the assessment. The less warning there is, the more likely the event will be considered an accident. What about recklessness or carelessness? If something happens that is perceived to be the result of recklessness, then we assume the event was avoidable and therefore not accidental. What about the duration of the event? The more quickly it happens, the more it seems to be an accident, since the speed of accident confirms that we who experience it could not have been in control. Finally, what about misjudgement? The more we acknowledge mistakes in our judgement the less likely we are to attribute the causes of events to accidents.

Apparently, a number of probabilistic criteria are used when we attribute accidental qualities to an event. The history of philosophical attention to these criteria is extensive, and beyond the scope of the present discussion. My purpose is to propose one more criterion, possibly the most important one, at least when it comes to explanations of causality. I refer to a set of background assumptions whose internally paradoxical structure is exposed by certain kinds of unforeseen events, results, or incidents. These events are often 'accidental', that is, they appear unexpectedly, but only against certain background assumptions. This background already exists, of course, having been constructed either intentionally, as in the case of experimental science, or unintentionally, as in the case of traditional knowledge systems, like the Hindu divinatory system described below. In this analysis, we use accidents in the broad sense to expose underlying paradoxes in explanatory knowledge systems.

As an example, take the case of a tidal wave that hit the southeastern coast of India in 1977. In the aftermath villagers in the affected area explained the cause of their misfortune in two ways. One way attributed the event to fate over which one could have no control. The other way located the cause of the event in the misdeeds of the villagers themselves. Both explanations were equally cogent and 'made sense' in terms of the relevant background assumptions. The point, however, is that they were contradictory, and the magnitude of the event—a tidal wave that killed more than 20,000 people—highlighted this fact and made it a subject of debate. Obviously the same opposed explanatory accounts had confronted each other before, probably many times, in the everyday lives of the villagers. Normally the contradiction was ignored, since it is easy, barring unusual circumstances, for people to compartmentalize alternative contradictory causal explanations. Confronted with the horror of mass death, however, people whose lives had been decimated by the tidal wave sought satisfactory explanations in the two perspectives described earlier—the one based on fate and the other on human control. What was interesting was that they acknowledged the contradiction and sought a resolution through a culturally innovative explanatory model. Perhaps it is the case that many, or most explanatory innovations begin this way, in a head-on collision between traditionally opposed causal frameworks. In this case, several of the villagers began to say that fate had indeed caused the cyclone. But 'fate', they said, requires power or energy to affect events. The cyclone had temporarily depleted this power, and therefore, in the interval, human beings could exercise complete control over their destinies. In this way, fate as a causal framework was retained, but free will was allowed to win out—for a short time, at least—as the villagers began the arduous task of putting their lives back together. The point is that the new model only developed in response to an event whose causal properties—'accidental' or 'deliberate'—were deeply troubling and called attention to themselves.

The type of contradictions that call attention to themselves when 'accidents' occur are what interests us here. Some accidents provoke a response in the knowledge system deemed relevant to their explanation because the accident calls attention to contradictions, or antinomies, internal to the causal frameworks that constitute the system. Not all accidents are like that. In the case above, people were forced to confront opposed explanatory frameworks in circumstances of extreme duress, and did so, with the result that they revised the frameworks and produced a novel interpretation of fate that allowed for the exercise of free will. For the most part, however, villagers felt no need to reconcile and eliminate opposed alternatives. Everyday life is usually like that. The situation is different when we consider formal knowledge systems in the West. Like physics and cosmology, these systems reveal a peculiar tendency to develop in the direction of consistency and generalizability—the features of what Kant called the 'architectonic' of pure reason. They are therefore sensitive, in some (but not all) circumstances, to events that reveal this objective to be inherently non-achievable. In other words, the contradictions at the core of the knowledge system, like cosmology, prevent the realization of a fully consistent and generalizable system, and this is recognized as problematic when events considered unexpected suddenly confront the system. Of course experimental science is meant to generate precisely this kind of result. The search for an absolute origin of the universe turns up evidence that cannot be considered consistent with this view. How should one react? One way is to do nothing, but simply to define such events as peculiar or weird. One often sees this kind of response in imaginative literature. Another response is to seek the reconciliation or elimination of contradictory alternatives, and thus render the system more consistent in its own terms. This is usually taken to be desirable in the natural sciences. But it is not unique to it. One sometimes sees this in the law, when, for example, we confront contradictory but equally appealing alternative explanations of crime. Can someone who is mentally ill be guilty of attempted murder? Until the mid-1980s, American juries generally had to decide between these two alternatives and select only one: *either* innocent by reason of insanity *or* guilty. But this changed abruptly after the trial of John W. Hinckley, Jr., Ronald Reagan's would-be assassin, who was found innocent by reason of insanity. Many Americans found this verdict unacceptable. It contradicted their notion of agency and free will, and made it necessary to choose the opposite notion when certain circumstances (such as mental illness) were in play. Unlike the cyclone-ravaged Indian villagers, people demanded a permanent solution to the antinomy. Accordingly, the legal code in most states was revised to allow for guilty verdicts even when the defendant is found to be mentally ill—the so-called GBMI, or 'Guilty But Mentally Ill' verdict. This, then, fundamentally altered the system, and removed the need to decide between equally tenable and attractive causal alternatives. It is only in the most extraordinary circumstances—such as the attempted assassination of a president—that a major revision in the explanatory system results.

Another reaction is to hold contradictory alternatives 'in suspension', allowing them to serve as indications that the system itself is beyond human reason, and thus ineffable. This could also be the 'mystical' response, since the ineffable and the divine are often viewed as related. It has been claimed that mystical experience is beyond or above the grasp of reason. The famous colonial civil servant-turned-philosopher, Walter Stace (1960), for example, identified paradox as an essential characteristic of mystical experience, and in this sense confirmed the long-standing tradition within 'negative theology' of denying positive attributes to God because God cannot be named. But the statement 'God cannot be named' is itself problematic because it names God as the one who cannot be named—thus naming God. If we then reply that God cannot be named we are still naming God, and so on, in infinite regress. The 'solution' to this problem, in some conceptual systems, is to define the problem *itself* as proof of ineffability, and of the need to dispense with language altogether in favour of mystical experience. St John of the Cross comes readily to mind as someone who adopted this approach, as does Thomas Merton, especially in his later writings on contemplative prayer.

Obviously, not all accidents call into question the internal dynamics of the system, and my interest is not with them. To make this point clear it will be necessary to reconstruct the concept of accident and to link it (as I will below) to other notions. What we seek is the nature of the cultural 'event horizon', the point at which events, recognized as aberrant or unusual, fall into the dynamic constituted by the play of opposed or contradictory forces. It is at this point that interesting things begin to happen in the world of causal explanation.

8.4 The Case of the Missing Ring: Accidents and Causal Contradictions in a Classical Sanskrit Drama

The story of Shakuntala is one of the best known of the ancient Sanskrit dramatic canon, composed some time before the sixth century AD. Known and beloved throughout India, the text was one of the first to be translated into a European language, in the late eighteenth century. Goethe is said to have been utterly charmed by it. *Shakuntala* tells the story of its eponymous heroine, her love for a king, and how a lost ring almost led to their permanent estrangement.

The story goes like this: when King Dushyanta met Shakuntala, daughter of the sage Vishvamitra, he fell in love with her, and they eloped. Kingly duties in the capital then forced Dushyanta to leave her, but before going, he gave Shakuntala a royal ring as a sign of their love, promising her that he would return. When Dushyanta returned to his capital, he became absorbed in affairs of state. Shakuntala waited in despair.

One day, a sage visited the hermitage, but Shakuntala, who was preoccupied by her devotion to Dushyanta, forgot to serve him food. In a fit of indignation, the sage cursed her, saying that the person she was thinking about would forget her. A shocked Shakuntala begged for forgiveness and the sage, now somewhat mollified, promised that the other person would remember her again when she showed him some proof of their acquaintance. So Shakuntala set off to the capital to remind Dushyanta of their past love.

But then an 'accident' took place. A fish swallowed the royal ring, leaving Shakuntala with no convincing evidence of her relationship to the king. Dushyanta did not remember Shakuntala when she arrived, but his memory and love were rekindled when a sage (not the one who cursed Shakuntala) recovered the ring and brought it to the court. Dushyanta then formally wed Shakuntala, who became his queen and mother of his son, Bharata.

Shakuntala's appeal can be understood on a number of levels. It is, of course, a love story, and develops a theme familiar elsewhere in Indian literature—the theme of the noble woman whose virtues are ultimately acknowledged after various challenges. While the play depends on the understanding of love and virtue, its action develops in response to the characters' struggle to come to terms with fate and free will. Do Shakuntala and her forgetful husband exercise agency, and if so, over what? If Shakuntala had not failed to observe the proprieties in welcoming the sage to the hermitage, would she have lost the ring? The play suggests that we have a choice in these matters, and that our failure to choose rightly results in unpleasant future effects. But the play also purports to accept the fact that some events are fated to occur, and therefore no act of choice can alter or interrupt them. Does the play celebrate choice and agency, and therefore function as an advocate of correct action, or does it accept the rule of fate over our lives and recommend no more than a passive acceptance of what is bound to occur no matter what we do or think?

Despite the continuing popularity (even in India) of the notion that Hinduism is a 'fatalistic' religion, there are no cut-and-dried answers to these questions—a conundrum that *Shakuntala*, far from avoiding, deliberately highlights. From texts as various as Upanishadic treatises and popular narratives, the same issue crops up repeatedly and receives different responses. Tracing the philosophical and literary lineages of these responses has occupied scholarly attention for decades. We are interested in the power of events we call 'accidents' to illuminate causal frameworks and their internal contradictions. Such contradictions, to use a wildly out of place metaphor, are like black holes at the centres of galaxies. We know they are there; the size and rotation of galactic stars are governed by their presence; and yet we cannot see them. In *Shakuntala*, the opposing perspectives of fate and free will constitute the black hole around which the play gravitates. The accidental loss of the ring, and the consequent struggle for truth, allow Kalidasa (the author) to explore the difficulties that arise in contemplation of karma. One view holds that current events are caused by the residues (good or bad) of past deeds, and cannot be otherwise. According to the other view, events are determined by karma, but the balance (good or bad) can be shifted through voluntary action. Here, in other words, we see the literary attempt to grapple with unseen yet powerful concepts of causality, the one defining action as determined and the other as subject to free will.

Any event, of course, can be examined for the degree to which it exposes the conundrum of fate and free will. There is nothing uniquely Indian in this. To take one example: I tripped over my dog this morning. Was it destined to occur given the chain of events leading up to it? Or, if I had been more careful (that is, more awake) would I have avoided the peril at my feet? The fact is the question gave me very little pause for reflection. But other events more readily provoke interrogation of their causal dynamics, because their status as 'accidents' is problematic and attention-getting. The loss of the ring in *Shakuntala* is a case in point. A lot of things probably happened to Shakuntala in her life that she could not, nor ever be bothered to, explain. The loss of the ring took on special prominence, not only because it threatened to transform Shakuntala from wife to whore, but also because it called attention to two causal frameworks in contradiction with each other. The frameworks in question are causation according to 'merit' (*punya*) and causation according to fate (*vidhi*).

The *punya* perspective is based on a moral calculation of right acts, and says that ill effects result from poor moral choices at some point in the past— perhaps in this life, perhaps in a previous one. There is no discussion in *Shakuntala* of the transmigration of souls, nor of the view that acts in a previous life govern effects in this one. The moral calculus at work, therefore, is entirely this-worldly, and relates effects in the present to misdeeds we commit in our own immediate past. The *vidhi* framework, on the other hand, is explicitly oriented to the view that some effects are fated to occur. There is nothing one can do about them, and therefore no moral opprobrium attaches to their occurrence. At different points in the play, Kalidasa seems to prefer one or the other, but significantly, there is no attempt to reconcile or eliminate contradictory alternatives. In fact, the playwright does not seem especially concerned with this issue, being content to acknowledge the difficulty and then permit the characters to act as they see fit in a world of paradoxical alternatives.

It is interesting how often the epics and stories of India use gambling as a device for setting in motion the conflicts of causality. One might think of gambling in such contexts as a kind of 'arranged accident'. That is, instead of waiting for an unanticipated occurrence to take place, one deliberately creates a situation of heightened uncertainty that must give rise to events whose occurrence could not have been anticipated. The principle Greek narratives, from the epics to the tragedies, display a contrasting lack of interest in gaming. One could imagine the Oedipus stories activated by a game of dice, I suppose, but Sophocles (like most of the tragedians) preferred a different approach. Oedipus suffers 'accidents' (killing his father, sleeping with his mother) which later turn out to confirm the will of the gods represented in the words of their oracles. There is no need to play dice in the Sophoclean worldview because the oracles already perform this function, and for a reason: to reveal the insufficiency or incompleteness of everyday causal frameworks, of justice and right conduct, to explain why things happen.

Hindu worldviews are different, and in the principal Hindu texts, such as the *Mahabharata*, gaming ultimately proves the relevance of moral frameworks and not their insufficiency in explaining the nature of events. In the *Mahabharata*, two cousins play dice to determine the rightful heir to the throne. The initial loser, Yudishthira, is the son of Dharma, identified as the god of universal law (and therefore of cause and effect). Yudhishthira undergoes a thirteen-year sojourn in the forest, during which he learns a vast amount of spiritual principles which the text describes in great detail. Only after he passes certain tests presented by deities can he return to take his rightful place as ruler. Without the 'accident' of a gambling result, such a progression would not have been possible. The fact that nothing is truly accidental in a world governed by the rules of *karma* is beside the point. In other words, the realization of the accident, and its power to govern a progression of ideas, is like a Hegelian *aufhebung* in that the moment it appears it begins to undergo decomposition into its constituent oppositions.

My point is that paradoxes (and their associated dialectics) tend to cluster around events seen as unexpected or accidental. These events never just happen; they only appear noticeable against a causal background of some kind, one that is shot through with contradictions. These contradictions are historically and culturally contingent, or might be, as Kant saw them, inherent in the nature of reason. To go back to cosmology for a moment: the discovery of radioactive decay rates in the 1930s led to the hypothesis that the earth, and therefore the universe, were much older than scientists had thought. Theoretical models put the age of the earth at 2 to 3 billion years, and the age of the universe at about twice that. Decay rate analysis indicated that the earth is more than 4 billion years old. And as for the universe, the age is now estimated at 18 billion years (Kragh, 2007). The intellectual process of comprehending these results was conditioned by two factors. The first was the relevant causal background—in this case, the background conundrum posed by the opposing perspectives of Kant's first antinomy. How can we determine the age of the universe if we cannot ask about its beginning? The second was experiential, based on the data obtained by examining the decay rates of unstable atomic nuclei. Discovery of the latter, with more and more refined analysis of the results, made it necessary to push back the age of the universe. To be sure, experimentally discovered 'facts', like decay rates, are not accidents in the conventional sense of the term. They do, however, constitute incidents of the unexpected, and therefore function—like any accident—as events that can, in some circumstances, serve to point up the existence of underlying paradox. After all, no matter what the age of the universe, one can still ask the question, what happened before the beginning? In this way, scientific inquiry proceeds, not by achieving a fully systematic and generalizable theory, but by continuing to push against its foundation.

8.5 Paradox Embedded in a Kinship System

Here I wish to give one final example, a case study in the paradox embedded in a kinship system. The ethnographic focus is the Jalaris, a Telugu-speaking fishing caste that resides in villages on the southeastern coast of India. The village where I work, Jalaripet, is close to the large port city of Visakhapatnam, and has a population of about 10,000. The Jalaris, like most south Indians, are organized patrilineally into clans and lineages and live in patrilineally extended families. They practise a form of marriage known as cross-cousin. When misfortunes occur, the Jalaris consult diviners to find out why, and inevitably their inquiry leads them to discover that a social dispute is to blame.

The paradox of the Jalari social system is detectable in the course of arguments or disputes between family members. Jalari culture recognizes two prototypic sources of dispute: (1) the patrilineal group, defined prototypically as men related to each other as 'brothers'; and (2) the affinal group, defined as members of families related to the patrilineal group by real or potential alliance through cross-cousin marriage. Prototypically, the patrilineal group is coterminous with a three-generation family and consists of the paternal grandfather, his married sons, and their sons. Affinal groups are the families of married sisters, mother's brothers, and father's sisters with whom the patriline has traditional alliance relationships.

Disputes are predictable outcomes of situations that arise within and between relations of these two groups—the patrilineal group (brothers) and the affinal group (brothers and sisters). In the patrilineal group, a crisis first develops when younger men marry and again later when their children approach adulthood. Because each crisis intensifies, in different ways, each man's desire to create his own, independent patrilineal group, disputes arise precisely at those points when joint action and collection endeavour are essential—in fishing and household goddess worship, to mention just two. Among affinal groups—families, that is, related by cross-cousin marriage— similar crises arise when joint responsibilities are most intense—in the exchange of money and goods, and in the making of cross-cousin marriage alliances. We find that divinations cluster at these crisis moments in the development of same-sex and cross-sex sibling relationships.

To be more specific: in patrilineal households a crisis develops when an individual—usually an adult brother—expresses interests that diverge from the patrilineal group that consists of adult brothers. Until then the family is 'joint' and brothers live and work together. There are two crisis 'moments'. In the first, male patriline members marry and set up independent (but adjacent) dwellings; at this point they are still a joint family because they still cook and eat in the father's (or, if he is dead, the elder brother's) house. This house is known as the 'big house' (*peddillu*) and it is there where family members worship the household goddesses. This turns out to be very important, since the failure of brothers to agree on offerings to the household goddesses is the primary instigator of the sequence of events culminating either in illness or poor fishing. The second crisis moment arises when adult brothers—usually in their thirties—press to create their own 'big houses' and thus constitute their own families as the nuclei of new patrilineal sublineages. This, then, starts the cycle all over again, when their sons grow up and eventually split off and found their own extended households.

Before patrilineal crisis moments produce division, a state of relations exists which sociologists would term 'breach' but which the Jalaris themselves describe in more colourful language, referring to 'birds that have flown away, each to a separate tree'. 'Birds' are male patriline members and 'trees' are their separate houses. What happens is that brothers (typically) find coordination on any of the affairs they still share in common increasingly irksome. For example, fulfilling their joint ritual obligations requires each to contribute a set portion of his income to a common fund kept in the elder brother's house, the *peddillu* ('big house'). But some brothers are reluctant to contribute, either on time or in full measure, or, having contributed, to refrain from asking the elder for loans from the common fund. In either case, sufficient money for the offerings to the household goddesses (*ammavallu*)—the main object of the collective fund—may not be received, with the result that a state of offertory neglect ensues. The household goddesses respond, 'beating' their victims and inflicting mild forms of illness or loss of livelihood on household members.

The crises that lead to disturbed relations between adult brothers and sisters are different. Brothers and sisters have two sets of obligations to each other. The first is the obligation to take and receive material goods from each other. In principle, transactions are of goods and clothing, and take place without the exchange of money. But in practice, simple transaction becomes the basis for important business exchange, with the result that a man's sister is often his most reliable trading partner, buying fish (usually on credit) and selling them at market. The brother receives a sure market for his catch in return for extending favourable terms to his sister. The brother–sister relationship is probably the most important traditional financial relationship in the village.

The second obligation brothers and sisters have to each other is to make and maintain marriage alliances between their children. In Jalari culture, the preferred forms of alliance (from the male ego's perspective) are marriage to the father's sister's daughter or marriage to the mother's brother's daughter. Usually the children of married brothers and sisters are promised to each other at birth. Other rituals, performed at the time of the girls' first menses, reconfirm these alliances prior to marriage. In the Jalari wedding ceremony—a simple affair, usually, without the pomp usually associated with Hindu nuptials—the most important ritual moment takes place as they promise their unborn children in marriage alliance to their cross-cousins. 'Alliance' means the traditional matrimonial connection between two patrilineal clans. The process continues, generation after generation, each confirming the alliance relationships of its predecessors.

When the unexpected occurs, people consult a diviner, who communicates with goddesses to find out which one has attacked. In one form of divination, called 'seeing the pulse', the diviner holds the wrist of the afflicted individual, and carefully monitors the pulse. Each goddess has her own distinctive 'beat', somewhat like Morse code, and when the diviner calls out the relevant goddess' name, she causes the patient's pulse to take on this beat. Another form of diagnosis—indeed, the one considered most precise and reliable—involves dropping handfuls of rice into a vessel filled with water. The diviner asks a series of questions, and the goddess responds by making the rice float (meaning 'yes') or sink (meaning 'no'). A long and complicated argument structure is thus constructed that relates the unexpected event to an attacking goddess, and the goddess to the patrilineal family of the afflicted person or to his/her affinally related families. The ultimate cause of distress, in other words, is a dispute, either among brothers (a patrilineal issue) or between brothers and sisters (an affinal issue).

In short, the problems that result in divination are problems that arise, inevitably and predictably, in the dynamics of sibling relations. These relations constitute the core paradox of the Jalari kinship system. The patrilineal joint family depends on fraternal solidarity for its structure and continuity across generations. It is true that the group must eventually divide, since there is no such thing as a patrilineal group (or sublineage) of unlimited genealogical depth and collateral extension. The family also depends on cross-cousin marriage to maintain the traditional alliances between itself and other families. (The family that is wife-giver in one generation becomes the wife-taker in the next, and so on, sustaining the alliance system). Both sets of relationships conflict, both internally and with each other, a fact that

Jalaris—like many south Indians (Trawick, 1990)—do sometimes recognize. However, they do not blame the system itself or seek changes that would address the underlying contradictions. What they blame is the institution of marriage itself. How does that work?

When fraternal disharmony leads to divination, it is because brothers are quarrelling with each other and are unable to agree on contributions to their common fund. This is what amounts to the 'official' reason—the only one that can be remedied in divination when brothers promise to return, 'as birds of single nest', to their joint household. Unofficially, however, brothers usually point to the relationship with their wives as the true point of origin in the sequence of events that led to the current crisis. Wives bicker with each other, and, in a scenario familiar from throughout India, embroil husbands in an endless series of tit-for-tat arguments that usually boil down to some question of fairness in the distribution of the brothers' communal assets. Eventually, or so husbands say, they have no choice but to divide their families and create the nuclei of independent sublineages, a process we already know must happen anyway, given the structural imperatives of the patrilineal system. The point is that wives become the unofficial scapegoat for problems that must arise in the relationship between brothers.

When we turn to the relationship between brothers and sisters, we see a similar issue in play. In everyday life, cross-sex obligations of the traditional kinds (economic exchange and marriage alliance) are transgressed. Jalaris recognize that brothers and sisters' continuing material transactions—often in the form of market exchange—may undermine the unity of the patrilineal joint family made up of married brothers and their households. It is easy to see how. Instead of concentrating their resources in the family, brothers tend to invest their funds separately, in maintaining outside transactions with their sisters. Wives resent these relations and press their husbands to break them off. Tension arises as brothers attempt to satisfy the conflicting moral demands of their sisters and their wives, of their duties to their own nuclear families and to their married sisters' families.

In the same way, sisters undermine the solidarity of their husbands' families by devoting more time and attention to their brothers. They do this, of course, because they must: the economic exchange between brothers and sisters (fish for money) is the cornerstone of the economy. Nevertheless, husbands resent this arrangement. They even consider it tantamount to accepting a centre of power outside their families. And many say they dislike the appearance of financial reliance on their affines (married kin) since it calls into question their own earning capacities. Does it matter that they themselves rely on their own sisters for business? After all, the same men who depend on their own sisters resent their wives for acting in the role of sisters to their own brothers. The answer is that it does not. The fact that the kinship system sets up mutually opposed, and logically irreconcilable, alternatives is not recognized for what it is—an intractable paradox. But cultures everywhere abound in paradoxes; indeed, some have argued that paradox is at the heart of many cultural knowledge systems (Murphy, 1971).

8.6 Conclusions

From cosmological science to south Indian divination, the case studies discussed here disclose the power of the unexpected to illuminate the context of its occurrence and the relationship between peculiar or unforeseen occurrences and the paradoxical causal frameworks that define them. An event challenges the expected order when it fails to conform to the constraints of normative intentionality. This does not exhaust the meaning of the term 'accident', but it does suggest what kind of accidents will most likely provoke rich explanatory dynamics. I have argued that there is a connection between cultural paradoxes—intractable contradictions—and concepts of the unexpected. Paradoxes pit opposing but equally compelling causal accounts against each other by offering equally plausible, but incommensurable, causal frameworks. Sometimes an event defined as an accident will occur and the explanation offered will conform to one pole or the other of the relevant paradox. In that case, we might say that the paradox has been resolved (at least temporarily) in favour of a single position. Other times explanations are offered that satisfy equally well both poles, and in such cases we might say that the event to be explained (the *explanandum*) remains causally 'trapped'. It cannot move, or rather, the explanatory complex exists for a while in a kind of holding pattern where it can incite doubt or confusion, even mystical delight. This is a description of 'accident' as I have used the term here. It is an immobilized explanation suspended in uncertainty. It exists for some period of time. Any attempt to explain the event further, in terms of one explanatory framework, results in the paradoxical strengthening of the opposing framework, and thus, in some cases, to the dialectical development of whole systems of causal frameworks.

Explanations do not have to remain forever in this condition; in fact, most probably do not. They are resolved in some fashion, forgotten or superseded by other events demanding other kinds of explanation. But while they are there, in the limbo-land of explanatory paralysis, they illuminate the causal orders that predispose them to this condition. That is why it makes sense to look at them: when they happen, they light up the internal dynamics of the systems which constitute them. At the very least, unexpected results interrupt the flow of the expected, and cause the system to reassert its explanatory adequacy. This is probably the usual outcome. At such moments the outlines of the system become more visible. Feelings of surprise and delight, or apprehension and horror, accompany such moments and characterize the brief period between apparent system failure and actual recovery in the system of explanation. Such moments can surprise or horrify us. Art would probably be impossible without them.

Yet there is one respect in which unexpected happenings, in Western scientific cosmology and Jalari kinship, are very different. Both are founded on paradox, it is true, but in the one case (cosmology) this is realized as such, whereas in the other (Jalari kinship) it is not. Cosmologists talk about the paradoxical positionings of their theories, but the Jalaris do not talk about the internal dynamics of their kinship system or discuss the paradoxical nature of the relationship between agnatic and affinal solidarity. So what is the difference? An example will help. Einstein (1931) in 1917 knew that the theory of general relativity predicts either that the universe is expanding forever or that it is contracting. For whatever reason—aesthetic, perhaps—Einstein resisted both of these, in essence rejecting the dialectic born, not of general relativity, but of Kant's first antinomy. He preferred the idea of a static universe. So he introduced a value into his equations—the so-called 'cosmological constant'—that functioned mathematically to suspend the implications of gravity for an expanding or contracting universe. He abandoned the cosmological constant only after Hubble demonstrated through observation that galaxies are all moving away from each other. Now, gravity should still slow expansion, even if total contraction is not observed. The problem is that toward the end of the twentieth century cosmologists discovered that intergalactic expansion is actually speeding up, meaning that there must be something other than gravity, or at least 'normal' gravity, at work. This led physicists to postulate the existence of 'dark energy' and 'dark matter', which, it turns out, must constitute a majority of energy and matter in the universe, and act as a kind of anti-gravity on the movement of galaxies away from each other. Now, no one has seen dark matter, and no one knows what it is (Kragh, 2007). Notice, in all of this, that progress in the development of cosmological theory is motivated—at least in part—by the degree of discomfort scientists, like Einstein, experience in the presence of difficult and possibly insoluble paradox.

The Jalaris do not lack in terms of their ability to abstract or generalize, but in the case of the kinship system, they prefer not to, which means that the paradoxes of solidarity (affinal versus agnatic) do not a require solution. It is not a problem of that type. The antinomies of kinship do not consciously 'bother' anyone, and therefore no effort is made to reconcile or eliminate opposed perspectives. Divination is the language into which the oppositions are projected, and it is in this form that the Jalaris deal with the matter. What causes paradoxes to be abstracted—and therefore to be realized as such, as they are in Kant's first critique? It is a critical question, but beyond the scope of this discussion.

Appendix

(1) *The universe has a beginning and an end*:
   A. Classical big bang/big crunch: Alexander Friedmann (1922), Stephen Hawking and Roger Penrose (1965).
   B. Quantum tunnel effect: Alexander Vilenkin (1982).
   C. No boundary instanton: James Hartle and Stephen Hawking (1983).

(2) *The universe has a beginning but no end*:
   A. Classical big bang/big whimper: Alexander Friedmann (1922), Georges Lemaitre (1927).
   B. Phoenix universe: Alexander Vilenkin (1982).
   C. Cosmic Darwinism: Lee Smolin (1992).
   D. No boundary instanton: Stephen Hawking and Neil Turok (1998).

(3) *The universe has no beginning and no end (static versus evolutionary versus revolutionary)*:
   A. Static universe: Albert Einstein (1931).
   B. Empty expanding universe: Willem de Sitter (1917).
   C. Eternal expansion out of a static universe: Arthur Eddington (1930).
   D. Steady state: Hermann Bondi and Thomas Gold (1948).
   E. Quasi-steady state: Fred Hoyle (1948), Fred Hoyle, Geoffrey Burbidge, and Jayant Narlikar (2000).
   F. Chaotic inflation: Andrei Linde (1983).
   G. Planckian cosmic egg: Mark Israelit (1989).
   H. Big bounce: Hans-Joachim Blome and Wolfgang Priester (1991).
   I. Ekpyrotic and cyclic universe: Paul Steinhardt and Neil Turok (2002).

(4) *The universe has no beginning, but an end*:
   A. Oscillating universe: Mark Israelit (1989).
   B. Cyclic universe: Paul Steinhardt and Neil Turok (2002).
   C. Circular time in a rotating universe: Kurt Godel (1949).
   D. Big brunch/time-reversal: Claus Kiefer (2007), Claus Kiefer and H. Dieter Zeh (1995).

(5) *The universe is in a time loop with and without an end*:
   Self-creating universe: John Richard Gott and Li-Xin Li (1998).

(6) *The universe has a pseudo-beginning with/without a local end*:
   A. Soft bang/emergent universe: Eckard Rebhan (2000).
   B. Quantum fluctuation: Edward Tyron (1973), Alexai Starobinsky (1979), David Atkatz and Heinz Pagels (1982), Mark Israelit (1999).
   C. Pre-big bang: Gabriele Veneziano (2004).
   D. Pregeometry: John Wheeler (1993), Peter Atkins (1994), Stephen Wolfram (2002).
   E. Loop quantum cosmology: Abhay Ashtekar and Martin Bojowald, and Jerzy Lewandowski (2003).

References

Allison, H. 1983. *Kant's Transcendental Idealism*. New Haven, CT: Yale University Press.

Ashtekar, A., Bojowald, M., & Lewandowski, J. 2003. Mathematical structure of loop quantum cosmology. *Advances in Theoretical and Mathematical Physics*, 7: 233–68.

Atkatz, D. & Pagels, H. 1982. Origin of the universe as a quantum tunneling effect. *Physical Review*, 25: 2065–73.

Atkins, P. 1994. *Creation Revisited: The Origin of Space, Time, and the Universe*. New York: Penguin.

Bartels, A. 1996. *Grundprobleme der modernen Naturphilosophie*. Paderborn: Schöningh.

Behe, M. 1996. *Darwin's Black Box: The Biochemical Challenge to Evolution*. New York: Free Press.

Behe, M. 2007. *The Edge of Evolution: The Search for the Limits of Darwinism*. New York: Free Press.

Blome, H. & Priester, W. 1991. Big bounce in the very early universe. *Astronomy and Astrophysics*, 250: 43–9.

Bondi, H. & Gold, T. 1948. The steady-state theory of the expanding universe. *Monthly Notices of the Royal Astronomical Society*, 108: 252–70.

De Sitter, W. 1917. On Einstein's theory of gravitation, and its astronomical consequences. *Monthly Notices of the Royal Astronomical Society*, 78: 3–28.

Dembski, W. 2002. *No Free Lunch*. Lanham, MD: Rowman and Littlefield.

Dembski, W. & Ruse, M. 2004. *Debating Design: From Darwin to DNA*. Cambridge: Cambridge University Press.

Eddington, A. 1930. On the instability of Einstein's spherical world. *Monthly Notices of the Royal Astronomical Society*, 90: 668–78.

Einstein, A. 1931. Kosmologische betrachtungen zur algemeinen relativitatstheorie. *Sitzungsberichte der Preussischen Akademie der Wissenschaften*: 235–7.

Friedmann, A. 1922. Uber die krummung des raumes. *Zeitschrift der Physik*, 10: 377–86.

Godel, K. 1949. An example of a new type of cosmological solutions of Einstein's field equations of gravitation. *Reviews of Modern Physics*, 21: 447–50.

Gott, J. & Li, L.-X. 1998. Can the universe create itself? *Physical Review D*, 58.

Hartle, J. & Hawking, S. 1983. Wave function of the universe. *Physical Review*, 28D: 2960–75.

Hawking, S. 1988. Origin of the universe. Speech. http://www.ralentz.com/old/astro/hawking-1.html.

Hawking, S. & Penrose, R. 1965. *Nature of Space and Time*. Princeton, NJ: Princeton University Press.

Hawking, S. & Turok, N. 1998. Open inflation without false vacua. *Physics Letters*, B425: 25.

Hoyle, F. 1948. A new model for the expanding universe. *Monthly Notices of the Royal Astronomical Society*, 108: 372–82.

Hoyle, F., Burbridge, G., & Narlikar, J. 2000. *A Different Approach to Cosmology: From a Static Universe to the Big Bang towards Reality*. Cambridge: Cambridge University Press.

Huxley, J. 1953. *Evolution in Action*. New York: Harper.

Israelit, M. 1989. A gauge-covariant bimetric tetrad theory of gravitation and electromagnetism. *Foundations of Physics*, 19: 33–55.

Israelit, M. 1999. *The Weyl-Dirac Theory and Our Universe*. New York: Nova Science.

Kanitscheider, B. 1991. The anthropic principle and its epistemological status in modern physical cosmology. In E. Agazzi, E. & A. Cordero (eds), *Philosophy and the Origin and Evolution of the Universe* (pp. 361–97). Amsterdam: Kluwer Academic.

Kant, I. 1960. *Religion within the Limits of Reason Alone*. New York: Harper.

Kant, I. 1965. *Critique of Pure Reason*, translated by Norman Kemp Smith. New York: St Martin's Press.

Kiefer, C. 2007. *Quantum Gravity*, 2nd edition. Oxford: Clarendon Press.

Kiefer, C. & Zeh, H. 1995. Arrow of time in a recollapsing quantum universe. *Physics Review*, D 51: 4145–53.

Kragh, H. 1996. *Cosmology and Controversy: The Historical Development of Two Theories of the Universe*. Princeton, NJ: Princeton University Press.

Kragh, H. 2007. *Conceptions of Cosmos: From Myths to the Accelerating Universe: A History of Cosmology*. Oxford: Oxford University Press.

Kragh, H. 2011. *Higher Speculations: Grand Theories and Failed Revolutions in Physics and Cosmology*. Oxford: Oxford University Press.

Lemaitre, G. 1927. Un univers homogene de masse constrante et de rayon croissant rendant compte de la vitesse radiale des nebuleuses extra-galactiques. *Annales de Societes Scientfique de Bruxelles*, 47: 49–56.

Linde, A. 1983. The new inflationary universe scenario. In G. Gibbon, S. Hawking, and S. Siklos (eds), *The Very Early Universe*. Cambridge: Cambridge University Press.

Murphy, R. 1971. *The Dialectics of Social Life: Alarms and Excursions in Anthropological Theory*. New York: Basic Books.

Nuckolls, C. 1996. *The Cultural Dialectics of Knowledge and Desire*. Madison, WI: University of Wisconsin Press.

Nuckolls, C. 1998. *Culture: A problem that Cannot Be Solved*. Madison, WI: University of Wisconsin Press.

Paley, W. 1802. *Natural Theology, or, Evidences of the Existence and Attributes of the Deity. Collected from the Appearances of Nature*. Philadelphia, PA: John Morgan.

Rebhan, E. 2000. 'Soft bang' instead of 'big bang': Model of an inflationary universe without singularities and with eternal physical past time. *Astronomy and Astrophysics*, 353: 1–9.

Smolin, L. 1992. 'Did the universe evolve?' *Classical and Quantum Gravity*, 9: 173–91.

Stace, W. 1960. *The Teachings of the Mystics*. New York: New American Library.

Starobinsky, A. 1979. Spektr reliktovogo gravitatsionnogo izlucheniya i nachal'noe sostoyanie vselennoi. *Pis'ma v ZhETF*, 30(11): 719–23.

Steinhardt, P. & Turok, N. 2002. A cyclic model of the universe. *Science*, 296: 1436–9.

Trawick, M. 1990. *Notes on Love in a Tamil Family*. Berkeley, CA: University of California Press.

Tyron, E. 1973. Is the universe a quantum fluctuation? *Nature*, 246: 396–7.

Vilenkin, A. 1982. Creation of universes from nothing. *Physics Letters*, 117B: 25–8.

Veneziano, G. 2004. The myth of the beginning of time. *Scientific American*, 290: 54–65.

Wheeler, J. 1993. On recognizing law without law. *American Journal of Physics*, 51: 398–404.

Wolfram, S. 2002. *A New Kind of Science*. Champaign, IL: Wolfram Media.

9

Studying Paradox as Process and Practice

Identifying and Following Moments of Salience and Latency

Paula Jarzabkowski, Rebecca Bednarek, and Jane K. Lê

9.1 Introduction

In this chapter, we take a strong process (Rescher, 1996) and practice (Schatzki, 2002) approach to studying paradox. Paradoxes are persistent, contradictory yet interdependent elements of social life (Lewis, 2000; Putnam et al., 2016; Smith et al., 2017). Such paradoxes, while persistent, may go through periods of salience, in which they are more evident and so can readily be studied, and latency in which they are not in an active state of contradiction and less easy to observe (Smith & Lewis, 2011; Werner & Baxter, 1994). Our aim is to show that a strong process and practice approach can illuminate the study of paradox during both its salient and latent periods and how this can be done methodologically. While other methods may render salience observable, our approach provides particular tools for eliciting how such moments of salience are constructed, and also has unique insights for studying latent paradoxes, which, being harder to observe, have been less studied. As much has been written about the strong process (e.g. Hernes, 2014; Jarzabkowski et al., 2016; Langley et al., 2013) and the practice approaches (e.g. Feldman & Orlikowski, 2011; Nicolini, 2013), we provide only a brief overview of them here, sufficient to set the theoretical background for our methodological approach to paradox. The chapter then addresses the key issues this approach raises for identifying empirically paradox salience and latency.

A strong process approach is grounded in an ontological understanding of social life as continuously under construction (Langley et al., 2013) or in a process of becoming (Tsoukas & Chia, 2002). This perspective assumes that the world, rather than being made up of things such as organizations, strategies, or paradoxes, is made of processes of organizing (Bate et al., 2000; Cooren, 2013; Pye & Pettigrew, 2006), strategizing (Balogun et al., 2014; Whittington, 2006), and constructing paradox (Abdallah et al., 2011; Jarzabkowski & Lê, 2017; Lê & Bednarek, 2017). Such studies direct us to examining how such processes are constructed moment by moment (Spee & Jarzabkowski, 2017) within actors' not necessarily intentional or goal-directed activities (Chia & Holt, 2009; MacKay & Chia, 2013). The strong process approach is within the same family of theorizing as a practice approach (Whittington, 2007), directing attention to those practices within which the collective social order is continuously constructed and reconstructed (Feldman & Orlikowski, 2011; Nicolini, 2013; Schatzki, 2002). From this perspective, we need to go beyond seeing collective social orders as entities that exist separately to these practices of their construction. For example, the notion of a financial market cannot be considered separately from the multiple, nested practices of pricing and trading in financial deals (Beunza et al., 2006; Jarzabkowski & Bednarek, 2018; Jarzabkowski et al., 2015b) and the legal profession cannot exist except within the negotiating and contracting practices of lawyers (Smets et al., 2012). For the purposes of this chapter, the strong process and practice approaches provide a focus on social phenomena as continuously under construction within the moment-by-moment activities and practices of the actors engaged in those phenomena.

These approaches provide two key insights into how we should study paradox. First, that paradox is not some reified 'thing' that exists outside the practices of the actors who are constructing it. That is, paradox does not exist in some external state that demands a response: actors construct paradox and any associated responses within their own moment-by-moment activities and practices (Jarzabkowski & Lê, 2017; Lê & Bednarek, 2017). Second, while paradoxes may indeed be experienced as more salient or latent, these experiences are not inevitable but are constructed within actors' activities and practices. This approach thus directs us, methodologically, to look at what these activities and practices are and how we may identify their role in the construction of paradox salience and latency. The focus of this chapter is to provide guidance for researchers about how they might effectively study salience and latency. We begin with salience, which is more commonly studied, and then turn our attention to the much less studied, but as we will show equally important, latency. The notions of salience and latency, and their core implications, are summarized in Table 9.1.

Table 9.1. Studying salient and latent paradoxes

		Description	Suggested indicators	Data requirement	Examples
Salience	Language	The way actors speak, the words they choose	• Word choice • Word co-location • Discursive practices (e.g. rhetoric)	In-depth, real-time data, ideally featuring interaction and reflection; focused on *organizational actors* and their experience.	Bednarek et al., 2017; Jarzabkowski & Sillince, 2007; Sillince & Golant, 2017
	Emotion	Emotional reactions, either focused on tension or complementarity	• Word choice • Tone of voice • Gestures and facial expressions	Observation-based data; diaries; reflective interviews	Hatch & Erhlich, 1993; Jarzabkowski and Lê, 2017; Vince & Broussine, 1996
	Action	The things organizational actors do and the practices in which they engage	• Resource allocations • Situation-specific doings, such as auditing, selling, sparring • Enacting role assignments		Jay, 2013; Lê & Jarzabkowski, 2015; Lüscher & Lewis, 2008; Smith, 2014
Latency	Everyday	How paradox unfolds in a taken-for-granted way as part of everyday practices	• Attention to what is potentially being silenced and marginalized • What is absurd or surprising to the researcher but taken-for-granted by participants? • Embodied and material manifestations of contradiction	Observational methods and deep interviewing as part of ethnographic embeddedness in the field	Ashcraft, 2001; Pratt & Rafaeli, 1997; Smets et al., 2015
	Juxtapose time	Studying transitions between salience and latency over time to understand when, why, and how paradoxes become latent	• Switches in action and practice in the moment and over time • 'Disappearance' or 'appearance' of a paradox within long-standing practices and processes	Longitudinal data is required and may be retrospective and/or real time	An emerging area of paradox research; can draw from studies such as Abdallah et al., 2011 and institutional approaches (e.g. Tracey & Creed, 2017)
	Juxtapose place	Explore multiple interconnected spaces where a paradox manifests (e.g. similar cases within the same macro-context or interconnected practices that are followed across space).	• Differences in action and practice in different places that have a common overarching paradoxical context • Differences in the experience of paradox at the systemic/network level and the organizational or individual level	Comparative cases (Eisenhardt, 1989); data about specific organizations and macro-context; multi-site ethnographies (Jarzabkowski et al., 2015a)	Limited studies of latency specifically; but examples of multi-case studies within paradox theory (Andriopoulos & Lewis, 2009; Bednarek et al. 2017)

9.2 Identifying Salience

9.2.1 *Definition of Salience*

Salient paradoxes are those paradoxes that are consciously observed, articulated, and experienced by organizational actors (Smith & Lewis, 2011; Lewis, 2000). Salience has often been a feature of paradox studies with authors using salience (e.g. Smith, 2014) or 'critical tension' (Jarzabkowski et al., 2013) as evidence for the existence of paradox. Indeed, recent studies have started to theorize and investigate the mechanisms that make paradoxes salient (e.g. Knight & Paroutis, 2017; Smith & Lewis, 2011). This focus is not surprising, given that 'salience' by definition means that paradoxes are prominent and noticeable and thus likely to 'jump out' at the researcher, so enabling their study.

Paradoxes may be experienced as salient to organizational members during periods of particular disruption or change in the organization or its environment when actors might experience shifts in power, resource allocation, and resource scarcity (Smith & Lewis, 2011) that they construct as paradoxical. Salient paradoxes can be experienced as either tensions (Jarzabkowski et al., 2013; Lewis, 2000; Smith & Lewis, 2011) or complementarities (Abdallah et al., 2011; Bednarek et al., 2017). For example, when key financial or human resources are diverted from exploitation efforts to develop exploration, actors may experience these shifting resource allocations as tension between the existing exploitation-focused product division and the new exploration-focused research and development division (Andriopoulos & Lewis, 2009; Smith, 2014). Alternatively, actors may construct paradoxical goals, for instance those of commercial/social and science excellence/impact in science organizations, as necessary and complementary (Bednarek et al., 2017). Of course, the experience of these distinctions as either tensions or as complementary is socially constructed, leading us to consider indicators of their salience.

9.2.2 *Indicators of Salience*

Salient paradoxes can be identified using three powerful indicators that are central to our strong process/practice approach: language, emotion, and action. There are two things to note with regard to these indicators. First, they privilege the experience of organizational actors. That means that, while contextualization and interpretation remain relevant in terms of why actors may be experiencing a situation as paradoxical, the researcher does not impose an assumption of paradox. Rather, the cues for paradox must come from the participants themselves. Second, each indicator can point to paradox constructed either as a difficult and unnecessary feature (generally exhibiting as a tension) or as a valuable and useful characteristic (generally exhibiting as complementarity).

Thus, we must seek evidence of both tension and complementarity, without emphasizing one over the other (Lewis, 2000; Smith & Lewis, 2011).

LANGUAGE

Language is a useful indicator of salience, as it draws on organizational members' own words to seek evidence of paradox. It has been the most frequently used indicator of salience, with scholars often adopting discursive or linguistic approaches to the study of paradox (e.g. Abdallah et al., 2011; Bednarek et al., 2017; Jarzabkowski & Sillince, 2007). Researchers often use specific focal words, sentences, or phrases that indicate contradiction and interdependence to identify paradox. For instance, Smith (2014, pp. 1597–8) talks about salient issues being described 'using words such as "difficult", "very hard", "uncertain", "unclear", "challenging", "tensions", or "problem"' and describes participants' language as including 'words that indicated paradoxical tensions, such as "tensions", "yet", "but", "balance", and "on one hand/on the other hand" … "tradeoffs", "choice", "resolve", and "either/or"'. We may also look for *conflict-laden language*—including terms like 'outrageous', 'ridiculous', 'scary', 'threat'—or *language of transcendence*—including terms like 'synergy', 'additive', 'exciting', 'opportunity' as potential signals of paradox.

One example of using language as an indicator of paradox is Abdallah et al.'s (2011) exploration of discourses of transcendence, whereby members of a cultural organization are observed explicitly talking about the complementarity between interdependent commercial and social goals: 'aggressive commercial targets … would contribute to the "oiling" of the machine, providing the funds needed to fulfil cultural and social goals' (p. 341; see also Bednarek et al., 2017). A second example is Jarzabkowski & Sillince's (2007) study which demonstrates how actors rhetorically construct different teaching, research, and income-generation goals within a university as complementary or contradictory, for example: 'there is a real contradiction here. Research funding brings the prestige, they bring the articles but they don't bring the overheads for the University'. Such language constructs the paradox as salient, in so much as actors articulate it in either contradictory or complementary terms. Indeed, Sillince & Golant (2017) show how rhetorical practices of irony and metaphor can construct paradoxical tensions as both differentiated and integrated within the same process of organizational change, so enabling it to unfold within the participants' experiences of change as both comprising continuity and also constituting disruption.

EMOTION

Another important indicator of salience is emotion, which can alert us to the centrality of contradiction within a particular setting. Moments of salience are often associated with and brought into being through an emotional expression, such as anger (Smets et al., 2015), frustration, or laughter (Hatch & Erhlich, 1993; Jarzabkowski & Lê, 2017). While emotional expressions vary in organizations (e.g. Huy, 2011; Huy et al., 2014; Liu & Maitlis, 2014), these studies suggest that we look for indicators of frustration, dissatisfaction, or anger by observing when actors allow exasperation into their voice, slamming their fist on the table, or raising their voice, thereby signalling tension and conflict (Jarzabkowski & Lê, 2017; Vince & Broussine, 1996). Similarly, excitement (Bednarek et al., 2017) or happiness (Abdallah et al., 2011), as expressed via tone or tenor of voice, may signal complementarity or transcendence. Other emotionally laden practices, such as humour, may be used to express either of these (Jarzabkowski & Lê, 2017). Indeed, Collinson (1988) showed how shop-floor workers used humour to distinguish themselves as working class and so distinct from managers, even as this humour also revealed contradictions in their roles and identities.

Vince and Broussine (1996) offer one prominent example of studying emotions in the context of paradox. In this study, drawings created as part of team workshops in public service organizations were explicitly used to 'express feelings'; these drawings were then reflected on and feelings put into words and phrases by individual managers; the group reflected on the drawings and constructions; these reflections were collated and further discussed; and, finally, managers synthesized and made sense of the collective data, reflecting on their individual experience. This process surfaced emotions such as 'hatred' and 'hope' (p. 13) through which actors constructed an experience of paradox that may be, respectively, more contradictory or complementary. Another example of studying emotion comes from Lê & Jarzabkowski (2015: 445), who use a coding scheme that included changes in inflection (broken or high-pitch speech), emotive word usage (using mean, crass, or emotion-invoking words), volume (raised voices or yelling), and physical gestures (such as banging a fist on the table) to show how actors constructed particular tasks as conflictual.

ACTION

The third indicator of salience is action: the things that people in organizations do as they live paradox. The actions that people take in such contexts are powerful indicators of how actors construct both their experience of, and their response to paradox (Jarzabkowski & Lê, 2017). Indeed, we propose that those concepts that others have identified as responses to paradox, such as confrontation, acceptance, regression, or transcendence (Jarzabkowski et al., 2013; Lewis, 2000; Smith & Lewis, 2011), are actually those actions within which actors are constructing paradox and making it salient. For example, Lüscher and Lewis (2008) show how managers at LEGO engaged in different sparring actions, through which they constructed the change they were undergoing as more or less paradoxical and which, in turn, shaped the way they constructed their own responses to the change.

Another powerful example of studying actions comes from Smith's (2014, p. 1592) study of paradoxical leadership practices, which documents a 'consistently inconsistent pattern of addressing tensions' across multiple organizations. She demonstrates that managers who are aware of and articulate paradox often engage in the competing practices of differentiating and integrating. Differentiating practices include the assignment of domain-specific roles and highlighting differences between domains, while integrating practices include the emphasis on overarching goals and joint problem solving. Another example of studying actions comes from Jay's (2013) study of a public–private partnership. In this study, actors, through their practices, define organizational success in different ways, either oscillating between different institutional logics or synthesizing them in a new way to better understand the paradox. Practices explored included actions such as framing, financial transactions, sense making, personnel changes, but also smaller actions, such as documenting what is important, conducting audits, and trying to sell services to clients (p. 145).

9.3 Identifying Latency

9.3.1 *Definition of Latent Paradox*

Latent paradoxes are at the heart of Lewis and Smith's (2011) dynamic equilibrium model; a model which depicts the movement between latent and salient paradoxes as explanatory of persistent contradiction. Namely, paradoxical contradictions may persist but remain 'dormant, unperceived, or ignored' (p. 388) at different times or in different parts of an organization or system. Research has shown how paradoxes can be made salient by leaders (Knight & Paroutis, 2017), but has remained silent on the experience of paradoxes during periods where they are latent. This is in large part because it is difficult methodologically to study something that is defined by virtue of its hidden or unobserved nature, even to those involved (Adler et al., 2007). We therefore address how paradox scholars can study latent paradoxes to expand our understanding of persistent contradiction. We suggest that a strong process and practice approach, with its focus on both the taken-for-granted everyday practices through which people both shape and are shaped by their wider social order (Nicolini, 2013; Schatzki, 2002) and the ongoing becoming and continuous flux of this social order over time (Tsoukas & Chia, 2002), constitute useful methodological resources for identifying latent paradox. At the same time, we emphasize that it is important that the identification of paradox should not simply be imposed by the researcher. Therefore, below we offer three possible methodological resources, studying mundane everyday practices and juxtaposing across space and time, for uncovering and understanding latent paradoxes.

9.3.2 Studying Latent Paradoxes (Methods and Indicators)

We do not privilege the particular means through which latency has arisen. One can imagine that a latent paradox could arise as the contradiction and interdependences become taken for granted and forgotten as part of, for instance, transcendence and a corresponding 'feeling' of resolution, however temporary (Abdallah et al., 2011; Bednarek et al., 2017). For instance, the dynamics of exploration and exploitation might work so seamlessly within a high-performing research organization that thinking about them as contradictory, rather than simply interrelated, becomes absurd to those involved. One can equally imagine that latency can arise when an organization is able to ignore, again at least temporarily, a paradox by suppressing one element of the paradox or constructing the elements as not interrelated. For instance, firms experiencing a cash-flow crisis could have an overwhelming focus on short-term survival in which long-term goals are simply not applicable for those involved, such that no paradox between current exploitation and longer-term exploration is constructed, not because it is unimportant but because it is not the focus of actors within the firm. Alternatively, the taken-for-granted privileging of one group of actors over another, or some tasks over others, may be assumed benign or non-paradoxical, even as such socially constructed inequalities suppress inherent contradictions within social order (Ashcraft, 2001; Fairhurst et al., 2016; Putnam et al., 2016; Van Bommell & Spicer, 2017). Hence, we do not focus on why actors do not experience or construct distinctions as paradoxical, but rather focus on methods for uncovering such latent paradoxes.

MUNDANE EVERYDAY PRACTICES

If we view much of lived everyday experience as a flow of practice rather than necessarily consciously articulable (Chia & Holt, 2006; Heidegger, 1962; MacKay & Chia, 2013), then understanding the construction of paradox as a taken-for-granted component of the flow of everyday organizational life is important (Lê & Bednarek, 2017). For example, Smets et al.'s (2015) study of Lloyd's of London illustrates how an underlying contradiction but also interdependence between market and community logics plays out in the everyday practices of reinsurance underwriters. This underlying contradiction was not articulated by participants directly as a tension but it nonetheless emerged as defining their every practice. For instance, when underwriters put on a tie as they switched from one context to another they were not necessarily conscious that this everyday practice was part of segmenting the market and community elements of their work and certainly did not articulate it as such (or as a problem). This switching between logics was simply what they did. In this sense, when studying latent paradoxes we can understand them as taken-for-granted elements of practice, as part of the flow of actions, rather than articulable experiences of tension or a cognitive frame or sense-making process about conflicts. Accessing latent paradoxes, instead, means ascertaining whether contradiction may explain the unarticulated and often unconscious everyday flow of practices of the context being studied (Chia & Holt, 2009; MacKay & Chia, 2013).

To study latent paradoxes in this way requires a reliance on *observational methods* and *deep immersion* in the field. That which cannot be articulated must be observed within the flow of day-to-day practice as it unfolds in situ (Suchman, 1987). This is important given that, by definition, latent paradox is not necessarily something participants are even aware of (Chia & Holt, 2009). Rather it is embedded in what they do, including their embodied and material ways of working such as the putting on of ties and movement between spaces observed by Smets et al. (2015) or the wearing of either street clothes or medical 'scrubs' as a way of layering multiple contradictory identities for nurses within a hospital (Pratt & Rafaeli, 1997). It also involves a degree of immersion in the field that is decidedly ethnographic in spirit (Van Maanen, 1988; Watson, 2011). For instance, to understand that 'putting on a tie' was part of managing the contradiction between market and community forces, or that nurses' dress codes were a way of negotiating politicized work identities, rather than something else, demands deep embeddedness in the field (Geertz, 1973). Insights about what is latent yet integral to a particular setting will not 'jump out' at you on day 1 . . . or maybe even day 30. Indeed, the afore-mentioned examples involved, respectively, a year's immersion in Lloyd's of London (Smets et al., 2015) and participant observation including being members of a dress task force in a rehabilitation hospital (Pratt & Rafaeli, 1997).

Beyond immersion, there are particular things to look for as potential indicators of latent paradox. We suggest a, still preliminary, list here as the basis for future research. First, researchers can become attuned to what is being silenced within the field. For instance, there might be particular marginalized stakeholders, because the taken-for-granted social structure overlooks, silences, or discounts their needs (Adler et al., 2007). Paying attention to that which is absent may provide a means to understanding a context where a paradox has become latent; with debate and discussion around both of its poles silenced. Second, instances that strike the researcher, as an outsider, as absurd or surprising, such as Pratt & Rafaeli's (1997) surprise that nurses would want to have less autonomy over their dress codes, but which are experienced as effortless, 'normal', or unsurprising by field participants may similarly provide a clue that this could be investigated further as an underlying latent paradox. For instance, being told by industry participants that a particular type of risk is incalculable and then watching those same individuals 'effortlessly' calculate and trade on that very risk in their everyday practice (Jarzabkowski et al., 2015b), could be the beginning of teasing apart the notion of calculating the incalculable as a latent paradox. Third, latent paradoxes can often be embodied rather than consciously articulated. For instance, Michel (2011) shows how the tension of working in a context in which habitual overwork was constructed by bankers as self-chosen, rather than as embedded in corporate values, meant that the contradiction emerged between bankers and their bodies, as their bodies quite literally 'broke down'. Latent paradoxes might similarly be uncovered and understood through paying attention to their embodied nature; whether that is switching between embodied performances (Pratt & Rafaeli, 1997; Smets et al., 2015), bodily breakdowns that are experienced personally rather than attributed to the navigation of contradictions, or other, potentially unarticulated, signs of tension or stress (Whiting et al., 2016). There is, thus, much scope for video-ethnography (Gylfe et al., 2016; Smets et al., 2014) within paradox research as part of ethnographic immersion, to join more traditional textual-based methods.

JUXTAPOSITION WITH SALIENCE ACROSS TIME AND SPACE

Another way to study paradox is to identify latency in relation to its juxta-position with salience. This can be done through (a) studying paradoxes either as they unfold across time (e.g. process studies of paradox); or (b) space (e.g. multisite studies where paradoxes emerge as salient in one space and latent in another). While these are slightly different methods, involving longitudinal methods that need not be comparative across sites, or comparative sites that need not be longitudinal, the two are not mutually exclusive; for example, it is possible to follow multiple sites over time in order to further identify how, when, where, and why salience and latency flux. Hence, we treat the two—time and space—within the same methodological heading.

First, we know that studying the ebb and flow of paradox is important (Lê and Bednarek, 2017; Werner & Baxter, 1994). For example, scholars have studied response pathways to show how initially positive organizational responses can become self-defeating (Abdallah et al., 2011) and how responses can transition from defensive to active responses to paradox (Cuganesan, 2017). Knight and Paroutis (2017) highlight the movement from a period of latency to salience but their focus is on the shift itself and what happens once the paradox becomes salient. Paradox scholars can use these methods that follow paradox over time to explore the contradiction within the period of latency itself rather than using this as a largely unexplored starting point after which the real 'action' of interest to paradox theory begins. This could be similar to how longitudinal studies of change increased our understanding of this phenomena through juxtaposing it with periods of stability (Pettigrew, 1985). Indeed, longitudinal studies of the waxing and waning of change over time often identify the underlying tensions and contradictory objectives that shape the unfolding process (e.g. Denis et al., 2001; Jay, 2013). Similarly, paradox scholars could use the existing indicators of salient paradox, as described above, to identify paradox but continue their investigation to follow the contradiction and interdependencies within a particular site either before those indicators became explicit or following their 'disappearance'.

The existing literature provides an array of applicable methodologies. These range from ethnographies that span periods of change, perhaps interspersed with other data-collection methods between the observational episodes (Grodal & O'Mahony, 2017; Jarzabkowski et al., 2013); to phased interviews (Cuganesan, 2017; Huq et al., 2017); and archival data and retrospective interviews to cover multiple time periods (Knight & Paroutis, 2017). To follow such processes in real time would mean that such analysis would only develop inductively if a shift between explicit and latent paradoxes—or vice versa—emerge as part of the unfolding longitudinal cases that a scholar is following. Nonetheless, a mix of retrospective and real-time methods could be used, drawing on archives to establish prior patterns that may continue to furnish paradoxical elements of salience and latency in the present. For example, Tracey and Creed (2017) discuss the institutionalization of social class within dining rituals at the University of Cambridge (Dacin et al., 2010), explaining such institutions as long-duration paradoxes that continue to shape ongoing contradictions between meritocracy, social mobility, and elitism, and which are experienced as more or less latent/salient by different university students. Thus, current practices that appear to indicate a paradox in real-time observation may also be traced retrospectively to uncover how patterns of salience and latency emerged and, indeed, may have been experienced simultaneously by different actors.

Second, scholars can follow contradiction across space (Marcus, 1995; Nicolini, 2013; Seidl & Whittington, 2014) as a means to capture latent paradoxes. One way this could be done is via a multiple case study methodology (Eisenhardt, 1989), a research method already used in much paradox literature (Andriopoulos & Lewis, 2009; Bednarek et al., 2017). Scholars might find they encounter similar organizations experiencing similar conditions within their wider environment but constructing that experience in very different ways. These distinctions, where some sites appear to experience contradictions that are salient to them, while others do not, could then be the basis for understanding and studying latent paradoxes in those sites that do not express the same contradictions. For instance, the work in an NHS general practitioner clinic within a particular UK city might be identifiable as defined by a particular tension—for instance, between market and public-good demands—and this might alert the scholar to paradox as an applicable lens in their study of this type of organization. However, in another clinic explored in the same study paradox might not be explicit despite the same paradoxical conditions within the environment remaining constant. This could be a cue to explore whether and how the contradiction is latent within one particular organizational site, and how and why different experiences of paradox arise across sites, using the comparative case method (Eisenhardt, 1989; Yin, 2009).

Alternatively, scholars can contextualize their studies of particular local sites within a broader context: zooming out (Nicolini, 2013) to illuminate the existence of persistent contradictions observable at the system level that are then latent within a particular organizational site (Smith & Lewis, 2011). One way this could be done is to situate a study of an organization within broader contradictory-laden discourses at the extra-organizational or 'field' level in order to explore whether this is constructed as a contradiction at the organizational level. For example, Lounsbury (2007) shows how competing trustee and performance logics at the field level for mutual funds did not result in consistent practice within organizations but rather displayed practice variation in how and with whom these funds contracted. Such findings are insightful for paradox scholars, suggesting that zooming out to similar contradictory conditions, and zooming in to different organizational constructions of those contradictions can shed light on differences in salience and latency between organizations experiencing similar environmental conditions.

Such wider discourses could be accessed through interviewing stakeholders external to the organization itself, combined with a study of secondary data, such as media accounts, at the intraorganizational level (e.g. Vaara et al., 2004). Other methods include following the same global processes and practices across different sites so as to situate specific instances of latency and salience in particular settings within a broader view of a particular paradox as an interconnected nexus of practices that span multiple sites (Jarzabkowski et al., 2015a; Marcus, 1995; Nicolini, 2013). Such a study would likely incorporate insight regarding where in a particular system, network, or nexus of practices paradoxes are latent and salient. For instance, a study of a science system following neoliberal economic reform might illuminate a central contradiction between immediate impact and long-term science excellence as defining science work (e.g. Bednarek et al., 2017) but also find places where this tension is experienced as latent rather than salient.

9.4 Verifying Salient and Latent Paradox

The indicators and methodologies outlined above are helpful in showing where we might look for, and how we might provide evidence of, paradox. However, it is important to remember that any one indicator in and of itself does not substantiate the presence of a paradox. In the case of *salient paradoxes*, language, emotion, and action may be symptoms; and symptoms can be misleading, stemming from a host of other possible conditions, such as dialectics or conflict (Putnam et al., 2016). For instance, observing a participant in the field slamming down the phone in a burst of anger can reflect a conflict rather than a persistent contradiction in the way their work is constructed. Thus, the analyst also has the responsibility of ensuring that the indicators identified are indeed manifestations of paradox rather than something else. A critical aspect of using these indicators of language, emotion, and action that we highlighted is to ensure that each is socially constructing an underlying condition of paradox: contradictory yet interrelated, and persisting over time.

This methodological task of careful definition and identification of paradox—as a specific form of tension—is particularly pertinent to the study of *latent paradoxes*. As Professor Ann Langley noted in her 2016 presentation on paradox at the European Group for Organization Studies and Academy of Management Meeting, we as scholars have to be careful not to impose paradox onto the field and our participants because of our own theoretical leanings. With latent paradoxes in particular, therefore, the methodological question arises: if no one in the field can tell you that a paradox exists, does one exist (even as a social construct), and if it does, how can it be important? It is no small challenge to identify something which is dormant, unperceived, or ignored and justify it as being central to your study. This tension between 'projecting' (paradoxes as seen by scholars) versus 'eliciting' (paradoxes as articulated by actors in organizations) is well recognized by paradox scholars (Andriopoulos & Gotsi, 2017). However, we believe it is a challenge worth wrestling with. Identifying latent paradoxes through our suggested indicators is, ultimately, a *hermeneutical* exercise that brings together the different horizons of the field experience and the interpretive toolkit of the researcher (Gadamer, 1989). The researcher builds from a deep immersion in the field and the experience and practices of those within it to follow their hunches (Locke et al., 2008) about latent paradox and make interpretive leaps (Wolcott, 1994) that reflect their own immersion within a particular setting (Ybema et al., 2009). In particular, identification of latent paradoxes that participants themselves do not articulate may arise from the sort of deep immersion and analytic reflexivity that allows us as scholars to go beyond a strict emic-only treatment of our field participants' experiences, unreflexively parroting their own interpretations as theory, to going to the heart of those aspects we regard as explanatory of their experience. Hence, our potential indicators of latent paradox are but tools in the service of the scholar's own interpretive process, which they must be able to explain as a central task of paradox scholarship and analysis. If we do not demand it of ourselves, our reviewers certainly do and will!

9.5 Implications and Conclusions

The aim of this chapter is to help people study the construction of paradox by participants and, through the interpretations of the researcher, to demonstrate both salient and also the much less studied latent paradox. Drawing on an underlying strong process/practice approach, we have shown how researchers may study salience by focusing on language, emotions, or actions, and how researchers may study latency by focusing on everyday practices, and by juxtaposing salient and latent paradox across different times and in different places. Studying paradox in this way has important methodological implications.

First, we reassert the case for qualitative methods and *studying paradox by being embedded in the field*. Researchers must be embedded in the organization to access the social construction of paradox within the methodological indicators we have suggested. Furthermore, as we have suggested, since the identification of paradox, particularly latent paradox, is ultimately a hermeneutical process, if we as scholars are to trust our interpretations and also convince others to trust them, we need the deep understanding of context that arises from those qualitative methods typically associated with a strong process/practice view (Feldman & Orlikowski, 2011; Jarzabkowski et al., 2014, 2016; Langley et al., 2013). Smith et al. (2017) point out that much existing paradox scholarship is qualitative in nature and call for more quantitative testing of insights surfaced thus far by qualitative scholars. One recent example has been efforts to develop measures of cognitive 'paradoxical mindsets' at the individual level (Miron-Spektor et al., 2017). Alongside this agenda we would argue that qualitative methods have only begun to scratch the surface regarding the full breadth and depth of constructing and working through paradox. Our study has called for, amongst other things, a focus on embodied paradoxes and those that manifest materially, which may be best accessed through deep field immersion and longitudinal methods.

As we have argued, *paradox is processual*, such that latency and salience may fluctuate over time (Werner & Baxter, 1994) and, indeed, the distinction between them is likely stronger in our theorization than in practice. It is thus important to methodologically trace the flows of salience and latency, finding ways not only to study contradictions, but also interdependence, showing how field participants may both cope with (Jarzabkowski & Lê, 2017) and even value the persistent nature of paradox (e.g. Smets et al., 2015). Indeed, a strong process and practice approach to paradox enables this focus on the construction of paradox as salient or latent, contradictory or interdependent, problematic or valued, both as they occur within the moment and also as they unfold over time (Jarzabkowski et al., 2016; Lê & Bednarek, 2017). This focus on the moment-by-moment construction of paradox is critical to our approach, as it is important not to simply think of processes as a form of punctuated equilibrium: characterized by large shifts and periods of salience followed by the comparative calm of latency. For instance, Bednarek et al. (2017) show how transcendence is defined by rhetoric that slips between 'moments' of articulating tension followed by moments of rhetorically transcending that tension, which in turn leads to another moment of articulation of a different element or aspect of paradox… and so on in an ongoing process of becoming (Langley et al., 2013; Tsoukas & Chia, 2002).

The demands of studying latent paradox go *beyond response, cognition, and discourse*. Certain elements of our current ways of studying paradox are challenged when exploring latent paradox. In particular, a majority of paradox studies have explored explicit tensions and how organizations and individuals respond to those tensions (e.g. Andriopoulos & Lewis, 2009; Bednarek et al., 2017; Jarzabkowski & Lê, 2017; Smith, 2014). Alongside this, paradox research has been long focused on paradoxical *frames* and thinking paradoxically (Lewis, 2000; Miron-Spektor et al., 2017), as well as methodologically on the rhetorical or discursive ways that responses to paradox are articulated (Bednarek et al., 2017; Dameron & Torset, 2014; Sillince & Golant, 2017). Yet the notion of strategically *responding* to something assumes active recognition of paradox: recognition which does not occur in periods or places of latency. We suggest that at times studying paradox as simply part of the flow of everyday practice rather than as something being *responded* to via an active strategic response is illuminating (Lê & Bednarek, 2017). Recent discussions of the construction and response of paradox as entangled have already begun to move us beyond the distinction between paradox and response (Jarzabkowski & Lê, 2017). However, there is more we can do to further shift our language around paradox as well as our standard methodological approach to paradox as a process of identifying paradox via tensions and critical incidents and the associated organizational or individual responses (e.g. Andriopoulos & Lewis, 2009; Bednarek et al., 2017; Jarzabkowski et al., 2013; Smith, 2014) to one that is more evocative of living with, around, and alongside paradox as part of everyday life. In this regard, we have suggested that, alongside the specific methodological techniques discussed, a strong process and practice approach to paradox is particularly helpful in uncovering latent paradox. It focuses us not only on what people think or say but what they do, including those practical coping, material, and embodied elements of doing that are unarticulated (and unarticulable).

We hope that scholars will be as inspired as we are by the rich array of avenues and potential within paradox theory. We have in this chapter sought to provide some methodological reflections that both make the *doing* of paradox research more transparent as well as enabling ongoing theoretical leaps in our field. Ongoing robust and innovative qualitative methods will go hand in hand with investigating the full complexity of organizational paradox. As one example, our brief foray into and mentions in this chapter of video-ethnography, embodied paradoxes, materiality, and more generally latent paradoxes shows, we have still only begun to scratch the surface.

References

Abdallah, C., Denis, J.-L., & Langley, A. 2011. Having your cake and eating it too: Discourses of transcendence and their role in organizational change dynamics. *Journal of Organizational Change Management*, 24(3): 333–48.

Adler, P.S., Forbes, L.C., & Willmott, H. 2007. Critical management studies. *Academy of Management Annals*, 1(1): 119–79.

Andriopoulos, C. & Gotsi, M. 2017. Methods of paradox. In M. Lewis, W.K. Smith, P. Jarzabkowski, & A. Langley (eds), *Oxford Handbook on Organizational Paradox*. Oxford: Oxford University Press.

Andriopoulos, C. & Lewis, M.W. 2009. Exploitation-exploration tensions and organizational ambidexterity: Managing paradoxes of innovation. *Organization Science*, 20(4): 696–717.

Ashcraft, K.L. 2001. Organized dissonance: Feminist bureaucracy as hybrid form. *Academy of Management Journal*, 44(6): 1301–22.

Balogun, J., Jacobs, C., Jarzabkowski, P., Mantere, S., & Vaara, E. 2014. Placing strategy discourse in context: Sociomateriality, sensemaking, and power. *Journal of Management Studies*, 51(2): 175–201.

Bate, P., Khan, R., & Pye, A. 2000. Towards a culturally sensitive approach to organization structuring: Where organization design meets organization development. *Organization Science*, 11(2): 197–211.

Bednarek, R., Paroutis, S., & Sillince, J. 2017. Transcendence through rhetorical practices: Responding to paradox in the science sector. *Organization Studies*, 38(1): 77–101.

Beunza, D., Hardie, I., & MacKenzie, D. 2006. A price is a social thing: Towards a material sociology of arbitrage. *Organization Studies*, 27(5): 721–45.

Chia, R.C.H. & Holt, R. 2006. Strategy as practical coping: A Heideggerian perspective. *Organization Studies*, 27(5): 635–55.

Chia, R.C.H. & Holt, R. 2009. *Strategy without Design: The Silent Efficacy of Indirect Action*. Cambridge: Cambridge University Press.

Collinson, D.L. 1988. 'Engineering humour': Masculinity, joking and conflict in shop-floor relations. *Organization Studies*, 9(2): 181–99.

Cooren, F. 2013. *Communication as Organizing: Empirical and Theoretical Explorations in the Dynamic of Text and Conversation*. London: Routledge.

Cuganesan, S. 2017. Identity paradoxes: How senior managers and employees negotiate similarity and distinctiveness tensions over time. *Organization Studies*, 38(304): 489–511.

Dacin, M.T., Munir, K., & Tracey, P. 2010. Formal dining at Cambridge colleges: Linking ritual performance and institutional maintenance. *Academy of Management Journal*, 53(6): 1393–418.

Dameron, S. & Torset, C. 2014. The discursive construction of strategists' subjectivities: Towards a paradox lens on strategy. *Journal of Management Studies*, 51(2): 291–319.

Denis, J.-L., Lamothe, L., & Langley, A. 2001. The dynamics of collective leadership and strategic change in pluralistic organizations. *Academy of Management Journal*, 44(4): 809–37.

Eisenhardt, K.M. 1989. Building theories from case study research. *Academy of Management Review*, 14(4): 532–50.

Fairhurst, G.T., Smith, W.K., Banghart, S.G., Lewis, M.W., Putnam, L.L., Raisch, S., & Schad, J. 2016. Diverging and converging: Integrative insights on a paradox meta-perspective. *Academy of Management Annals*, 10(1): 173–82.

Feldman, M.S. & Orlikowski, W.J. 2011. Theorizing practice and practicing theory. *Organization Science*, 22(5): 1240–53.

Gadamer, H.G. 1989. *Truth and Method*. London: Sheed and Ward.

Geertz, C. 1973. Thick description: Toward an interpretive theory of culture. *Culture: Critical Concepts in Sociology*, 36(6): 1465–514.

Grodal, S. & O'Mahony, S. 2017. How does a grand challenge become displaced? Explaining the duality of field mobilization. *Academy of Management Journal*, 60(5): 1801–27.

Gylfe, P., Franck, H., Lebaron, C., & Mantere, S. 2016. Video methods in strategy research: Focusing on embodied cognition. *Strategic Management Journal*, 37(1): 133–48.

Hatch, M.J. & Erhlich, S.B. 1993. Spontaneous humour as an indicator of paradox and ambiguity in organizations. *Organization Studies*, 14(4): 505–26.

Heidegger, M. 1962. *Being and Time*. Oxford: Blackwell.

Hernes, T. 2014. *A Process Theory of Organization*. Oxford: Oxford University Press.

Huq, J.-L., Reay, T., & Chreim, S. 2017. Protecting the paradox of interprofessional collaboration. *Organization Studies*, 38(3–4): 513–38.

Huy, Q.N. 2011. How middle managers' group-focus emotions and social identities influence strategy implementation. *Strategic Management Journal*, 32(13): 1387–410.

Huy, Q.N., Corley, K.G., & Kraatz, M.S. 2014. From support to mutiny: Shifting legitimacy judgments and emotional reactions impacting the implementation of radical change. *Academy of Management Journal*, 57(6): 1650–80.

Jarzabkowski, P. & Lê, J. 2017. We have to do this *and* that? You must be joking: Constructing and responding to paradox through humor. *Organization Studies*, 38(3–4): 433–62.

Jarzabkowski, P. & Sillince, J. 2007. A rhetoric-in-context approach to building commitment to multiple strategic goals. *Organization Studies*, 28(11): 1639–65. DOI: 10.1177/0170840607075266.

Jarzabkowski, P., Lê, J., & Van de Ven, A.H. 2013. Responding to competing strategic demands: How organizing, belonging, and performing paradoxes coevolve. *Strategic Organization, 11*: 245–80.

Jarzabkowski, P.A. & Bednarek, R. (2018). Toward a social practice theory of relational competing. *Strategic Management Journal*, 39(3): 794–829.

Jarzabkowski, P., Bednarek, R., & Lê, J.K. 2014. Producing persuasive findings: Demystifying ethnographic textwork in strategy and organization research. *Strategic Organization*, 12(4): 274–87.

Jarzabkowski, P., Bednarek, R., & Cabantous, L. 2015a. Conducting global team-based ethnography: Methodological challenges and practical methods. *Human Relations*, 68(1).

Jarzabkowski, P., Bednarek, R., & Spee, A.P. 2015b. *Making a Market for Acts of God: The Practice of Risk Trading in the Global Reinsurance Industry*. Oxford: Oxford University Press.

Jarzabkowski, P., Lê, J., & Spee, P. 2016. Taking a strong process approach to analyzing qualitative process data. In A. Langley & H. Tsoukas (eds), *The Sage Handbook of Process Organization Studies* (pp. 237–53). London: Sage.

Jay, J. 2013. Navigating paradox as a mechanism of change and innovation in hybrid organizations. *Academy of Management Journal*, 56(1): 137–59.

Knight, E. & Paroutis, S. 2017. Becoming salient: The TMT leader's role in shaping the interpretive context of paradoxical tensions. *Organization Studies*, 38(3–4): 403–32.

Langley, A., Smallman, C., Tsoukas, H., & Van de Ven, A.H. 2013. Process studies of change in organization and management: Unveiling temporality, activity, and flow. *Academy of Management Journal*, 56(1): 1–13. DOI: 10.5465/amj.2013.4001.

Lê, J. & Bednarek, R. 2017. Paradox in everyday practice: Applying practice-theoretical principles to paradox. In M. Lewis, W.K. Smith, P. Jarzabkowski, & A. Langley (eds), *Oxford Handbook on Organizational Paradox* (pp. 490–509). Oxford: Oxford University Press.

Lê, J.K. & Jarzabkowski, P. 2015. Conflict as a micro-process shaping the relationship between strategy process and content. *British Journal of Management*, 26(3): 439–62.

Lewis, M.W. 2000. Exploring paradox: Toward a more comprehensive guide. *Academy of Management Review*, 25(4): 760–76.

Liu, F. & Maitlis, S. 2014. Emotional dynamics and strategizing processes: A study of strategic conversations in top team meetings. *Journal of Management Studies*, 51(2): 202–34.

Locke, K., Golden-Biddle, K., & Feldman, M.S. 2008. Perspective—making doubt generative: Rethinking the role of doubt in the research process. *Organization Science*, 19(6): 907–18.

Lounsbury, M. 2007. A tale of two cities: Competing logics and practice variation in the professionalizing of mutual funds. *Academy of Management Journal*, 50(2): 289–307.

Lüscher, L.S. & Lewis, M.W. 2008. Organizational change and managerial sensemaking: Working through paradox. *Academy of Management Journal*, 51(2): 221–40. DOI: 10.5465/amj.2008.31767217.

MacKay, R.B. & Chia, R. 2013. Choice, chance, and unintended consequences in strategic change: A process understanding of the rise and fall of NorthCo Automotive. *Academy of Management Journal*, 56(1): 208–30.

Marcus, G.E. 1995. Ethnography in/of the world system: The emergence of multi-sited ethnography. *Annual Review of Anthropology*, 24: 95–117.

Miron-Spektor, E., Ingram, A., Keller, J., Smith, W., & Lewis, M. 2017. Microfoundations of organizational paradox: The problem is how we think about the problem. *Academy of Management Journal*, 61(1): 26–45.

Michel, A. 2011. Transcending socialization: A nine-year ethnography of the body's role in organizational control and knowledge workers' transformation. *Administrative Science Quarterly*, 56(3): 325–68.

Nicolini, D. 2013. *Practice Theory, Work and Organization*. Oxford: Oxford University Press.

Pettigrew, A.M. 1985. *The Awakening Giant: Continuity and Change in Imperial Chemical Industries*. Oxford: Blackwell.

Pratt, M.G. & Rafaeli, A. 1997. Organizational dress as a symbol of multilayered social identities. *Academy of Management Journal*, 40: 862–98.

Putnam, L.L., Fairhurst, G.T., & Banghart, S. 2016. Contradictions, dialectics, and paradoxes in organizations: A constitutive approach. *Academy of Management Annals*, 10(1): 65–171.

Pye, A. & Pettigrew, A. 2006. Strategizing and organizing: Change as a political learning process, enabled by leadership. *Long Range Planning*, 39(6): 583–90.

Rescher, N. 1996. *Process Metaphysics: An Introduction to Process Philosophy*. New York: SUNY Press.

Schatzki, T. 2002. *The Site of the Social: A Philosophical Account of the Constitution of Social Life and Change*. Pennsylvania, PA: Penn State University Press.

Seidl, D. & Whittington, R. 2014. Enlarging the strategy-as-practice research agenda: Towards taller and flatter ontologies. *Organization Studies*, 35(10): 1407–21. DOI: 10.1177/0170840614541886.

Sillince, J. & Golant, B. 2017. The role of irony and metaphor in working through paradox during organizational change. In M. Lewis, W.K. Smith, P. Jarzabkowski, & A. Langley (eds), *Oxford Handbook on Organizational Paradox*. Oxford: Oxford University Press.

Smets, M., Morris, T., & Greenwood, R. 2012. From practice to field: A multi-level model of practice-driven institutional change. *Academy of Management Journal*, 55(4): 877–904.

Smets, M., Burke, G., Jarzabkowski, P., & Spee, P. 2014. Charting new territory for organizational ethnography: Insights from a team-based video ethnography. *Journal of Organizational Ethnography*, 3(1): 10–26.

Smets, M., Jarzabkowski, P., Spee, A.P., & Burke, G. 2015. Reinsurance trading in Lloyd's of London: Balancing conflicting-yet-complementary logics in practice. *Academy of Management Journal*, 58(3): 932–70.

Smith, W., Erez, M., Jarvenpaa, S., Lewis, M., & Tracey, P. 2017. Adding complexity to theories of paradox, tensions, and dualities of innovation and change: Introduction to *Organization Studies* special issue on paradox, tensions and dualities of innovation and change. *Organization Studies*, 38(3–4): 303–18.

Smith, W.K. 2014. Dynamic decision making: A model of senior leaders managing strategic paradoxes. *Academy of Management Journal*, 57(6): 1592–623.

Smith, W.K. & Lewis, M.W. 2011. Toward a theory of paradox: A dynamic equilibrium model of organizing. *Academy of Management Review*, 36(2): 381–403.

Spee, P. & Jarzabkowski, P. 2017. Agreeing on what? Creating joint accounts of strategic change. *Organization Science*, 28(1): 152–76.

Suchman, L.A. 1987. *Plans and Situated Actions: The Problem of Human-Machine Communication*. Cambridge: Cambridge University Press.

Tracey, P. & Creed, D. 2017. Beyond managerial dilemmas: The study of institutional paradoxes in organization theory. In M. Lewis, W.K. Smith, P. Jarzabkowski, & A. Langley (eds), *Oxford Handbook on Organizational Paradox* (pp. 490–509). Oxford: Oxford University Press.

Tsoukas, H. & Chia, R. 2002. On organizational becoming: Rethinking organizational change. *Organization Science*, 13(5): 567–82.

Vaara, E., Kleymann, B., & Seristö, H. 2004. Strategies as discursive constructions: The case of airline alliances. *Journal of Management Studies*, 41(1): 1–35.

Van Bommell, K. & Spicer, A. 2017. Critical management studies and paradox. In M. Lewis, W.K. Smith, P. Jarzabkowski, & A. Langley (eds), *Oxford Handbook of Organizational Paradox*. Oxford: Oxford University Press.

Van Maanen, J. 1988. *Tales of the Field: On Writing Ethnography*. Chicago, IL: University of Chicago Press.

Vince, R. & Broussine, M. 1996. Paradox, defense and attachment: Accessing and working with emotions and relations underlying organizational change. *Organization Studies*, 17(1): 1–21.

Watson, T.J. 2011. Ethnography, reality, and truth: The vital need for studies of 'how things work' in organizations and management. *Journal of Management Studies*, 48(1): 202–17.

Werner, C.M. & Baxter, L.A. 1994. Temporal qualities of relationships: Organismic, transactional, and dialectical views. In M. Knapp & G. Miller (eds), *Handbook of Interpersonal Communication*. Thousand Oaks, CA: Sage.

Whiting, R., Symon, G., Roby, H., & Chamakiotis, P. 2016. Who's behind the lens? A reflexive analysis of roles in participatory video research. *Organizational Research Methods*. DOI: 1094428116669818.

Whittington, R. 2006. Completing the practice turn in strategy research. *Organization Studies*, 27(5): 613–34.

Whittington, R. 2007. Strategy practice and strategy process: Family differences and the sociological eye. *Organization Studies*, 28(10): 1575–86.

Wolcott, H.F. 1994. *Transforming Qualitative Data: Description, Analysis and Interpretation*. Thousand Oaks, CA: Sage.

Ybema, S., Yanow, D., Wels, H., & Kamsteeg, F. 2009. Studying everyday organizational life. In S. Ybema, D. Yanow, H. Wels, & F.H. Kamsteeg (eds), *Organizational Ethnography: Studying the Complexities of Everyday Life* (pp. 1–20). London: Sage.

Yin, R.K. 2009. *Case Study Research: Design and Methods*, 4th edition. Thousand Oaks, CA: Sage.

10

Artefacts and the Dynamics of Truces in Organizational Routines

Nicolás J.B. Wiedemann, Leona Wiegmann, and Juergen Weber

10.1 Introduction

Research regarding organizational routines and their interrelated artefacts as a central unit of analysis has become increasingly important (Becker, 2004; Parmigiani & Howard-Grenville, 2011) as a means of examining and illustrating how organizations accomplish their work (Cyert & March, 1963; March & Simon, 1958; Nelson & Winter, 1982). However, this accomplishment is not necessarily conflict-free, because mindful individuals who enact the routine can vary in their cognition (knowledge asymmetries) and motivation (divergent interests), which can both lead to intraorganizational conflicts (Nelson & Winter, 1982). While prior research has focused mainly on cognition (Gavetti et al., 2007), we will expand upon the more recent discussion regarding motivational conflicts (cf. Cacciatori, 2012; Zbaracki & Bergen, 2010). Considering the potential for conflicts, routines as collective accomplishments require some degree of consensus and collaboration, described as a 'truce', to function effectively (Nelson & Winter, 1982). Against the backdrop of recent processual theorizing of routines as ongoing accomplishments (Feldman et al., 2016; Feldman, 2016), and in line with dynamic approaches to truces (Kaplan, 2015; Zbaracki & Bergen, 2010), we understand a truce to be the temporary settlement among competing interests that enables a routine to proceed.

Scholars examining how intraorganizational conflicts are solved have recognized the central role of artefacts (Cacciatori, 2012; D'Adderio, 2008) in mediating the interactions among routine actors (D'Adderio, 2001, 2003; Kaplan, 2011; Yates & Orlikowski, 2007). On the one hand, artefacts—in particular, standardized software—can facilitate and constrain specific actions, which can effect a truce by both stabilizing existing action patterns (D'Adderio, 2003) and containing conflict latent in routine dynamics (Cacciatori, 2012; Zbaracki & Bergen, 2010). On the other hand, each enactment of a routine provides an opportunity for individuals to use the artefact for their own interests (Howard-Grenville, 2005; Leonardi, 2011; Pentland & Feldman, 2008). Artefacts may thus be mobilized to shape information, negotiate meaning, and recombine information in a way that supports those individual interests (Kaplan, 2011). Whereas small variations in the enactment of a routine may not place truces at risk, large changes can reveal motivational conflicts and break a truce (Zbaracki & Bergen, 2010). This suggests that artefacts can be crucial in mediating and preserving patterns of interaction within the routine as an ongoing accomplishment. However, the underlying mechanisms that explain how a truce is continuously achieved remain unclear. Accordingly, we pose the following research question: how do artefacts influence the ongoing formation of truces in light of the dialectical tension between individual interests and collective consensus in organizational routines?

To address our question, we conducted a single case study of a firm that is a global leader in the production of high-performance macromolecules for material solutions. We focus in particular on a management routine: the bi-weekly leadership team meetings at which actors present and discuss information from their area of responsibility to aid decision making. More precisely, we closely examined a change in the management routine's central artefact, from Microsoft PowerPoint decks to a business intelligence (BI) software that provides automated, near real-time dashboards. Due to this change, a conflict among the heads of the business units arose that limited their ability to accomplish their work, disrupting an existing truce within the management routine. We examine how this disruption was repaired through the creation of a meta-routine that enabled continuous adjustment of the artefact and the recreation of a truce that allowed the original management routine to restabilize.

By shedding light on artefacts' role in the breaking and reforming of truces, our chapter contributes not only to scholarly discussion about the role of artefacts in organizational routines, but also to the discussion on the dynamics of truces in two ways. First, we show that a truce does not necessarily need to be enforced by an authority figure (Kaplan, 2011; Zbaracki & Bergen, 2010), but can also be collectively formed in a meta-routine. This is possible because the creation of a meta-routine in parallel with an original routine splits apart the dialectical tension between individual and collective interests, reinstating the stabilizing effect of the central artefact within the original routine. Second, by assuming a process perspective, we also show that the reforming of a truce is not necessarily a result of a single situation of major change (Zbaracki & Bergen, 2010) but rather an ongoing accomplishment that must be continuously managed, since diverging interests are never fully resolved but are instead persistent.

10.2 Theoretical Foundation

Scholars have portrayed actors as mindful and often reflective when enacting their individual actions (Bucher & Langley, 2016; Dittrich et al., 2016). When enacting their individual actions they carefully consider past thoughts and actions, judge the current situation, and imagine and evaluate future scenarios (Emirbayer & Mische, 1998). In conjunction with individual motivations (Burns, 2000; Lazaric & Raybaut, 2005; Nelson & Winter, 1982), the conclusion formed by actors in this process might differ from one actor to the next and become visible in the form of heterogeneous preferences (Cyert & March, 1963), diverse goals (Feldman & Pentland, 2003; Howard-Grenville, 2005), differing points of view (Zbaracki & Bergen, 2010), divergent perspectives (D'Adderio, 2014; Nelson & Winter, 1982), and vested interests (Milgrom & Roberts, 1988). These differences can be among actors at different hierarchical levels (Nelson & Winter, 1982), across different functional areas within organizations (Zbaracki & Bergen, 2010), or between actors in different positions at the same level (Kaplan, 2015). Scholars have shown that actions are, to a certain extent, inherently novel (Feldman, 2000; Orlikowski, 2000), meaning that, based on this plurality of interests, actors can introduce variation (Howard-Grenville, 2005) or change (Pentland et al., 2011) to their actions, which then shapes their performances in distinct ways.

Despite these individual interests, scholars have also emphasized the interest of the organization as a whole in maintaining smooth functioning (Nelson & Winter, 1982) and, thus, the need for consensus—at least to some degree. In order to address this dialectical tension between diverging individual interests and collective consensus, scholars suggest that organizational routines may serve as a coordinating mechanism (Okhuysen & Bechky, 2009). Routines are commonly defined as 'repetitive, recognizable patterns of interdependent actions, carried out by multiple actors' (Feldman & Pentland, 2003, p. 95). Crucial to this ongoing process of accomplishment is that individual interests must be somehow balanced in some kind of settlement or 'truce' (Nelson & Winter, 1982) that participants largely take for granted, as intraorganizational conflicts (e.g. over roles or jurisdictions) can otherwise become overt (Barley, 1986; Bechky, 2003) and cause routines to collapse (Zbaracki & Bergen, 2010). This would be contrary to the objective of smooth organizational functioning described above (Nelson & Winter, 1982).

In the context of organizational functioning, and considering the dialectical tension between individual and collective interests, scholars have researched the underlying mechanisms of coordination (cf. Jarzabkowski et al., 2012) that help organizations to be flexible but simultaneously efficient (Adler et al., 1999). In light of this, scholars have pointed to the relevance of, for instance, meta-routines for coordinating across routines as well as for creating or changing routines (Adler et al., 1999). In terms of organizational routines, specifically, scholars have additionally identified the central role that routines' interrelated artefacts can play (Bechky, 2003; Cacciatori, 2012; D'Adderio, 2014). However, prior literature has suggested that artefacts play an ambiguous role in organizational routines. Depending on their nature, they can encourage flexibility that might lead to conflict and put truces at risk, but they can also standardize actions and potentially contribute to the forming of truces in routines.

Artefacts have the capacity to propagate information (D'Adderio, 2011) that actors may intentionally use to inform decisions in accordance with their individual interest (Yates & Orlikowski, 2007), for instance, in discussions where actors renegotiate meaning or recombine information (Kaplan, 2011). However, in cases where diverging interests need to be reconciled, this may lead to conflict and damage a truce. However, prior research suggests that the extent to which actors may act out their individual interests depends on how routines are codified in artefacts (Lazaric et al., 2003; Lazaric & Denis, 2001). Artefacts can act as standardizing devices that guide actions, frame understandings of a routine (D'Adderio, 2003; Sonenshein, 2016) and determine who has a voice in accomplishing a task and who does not (Cacciatori, 2008). In this sense, they can also foster coordination and consequently suppress conflicts that can break a truce (Cacciatori, 2012). In other words, whether an artefact contributes to the forming or breaking of a truce depends on the possibilities it provides for individuals to adapt it as they perform their actions. For instance, Sonenshein (2016) showed that actors recognize the incompleteness of artefacts and make use of this incompleteness through personalization. That is, actors combine their idiosyncratic backgrounds with the artefact to introduce creativity while adhering to standards. Similarly, affordance of artefacts (i.e. the properties that define possible actions; Leonardi, 2011) can create space for discussions that allow for combining and recombining diverging information (Kaplan, 2011). Likewise, the extent to which artefacts allow for manipulating the information inscribed in them (e.g. by juxtaposing, reordering, combining, or visualizing) can address individual problem-solving needs; however, on a collective level it can go along with control over information, which may spark conflicts (Cacciatori, 2012).

While artefacts can thus contribute to working out truces, they are likely not a stable resolution, because interests can change over time, which implies that truces are relative in nature (Pentland & Feldman, 2005). Moreover, the terms of a truce may never be totally defined (Nelson & Winter, 1982); and major changes might reveal suppressed conflicts that lead to a breakdown (Zbaracki & Bergen, 2010). Given the constant threat that truces may break down and need to be reformed, it is important to examine the underlying mechanisms through which truces are continually worked out despite divergent interests.

To do so, we follow recent thinking on routines that has argued for a stronger process orientation and considers routines as a 'tangle of action' (Feldman, 2016, p. 40). Following from the conceptualization of routines as consisting of an ostensive aspect (i.e. the abstract pattern of a particular routine) and a performative aspect (i.e. the specific actions that bring the routine to life) (Feldman & Pentland, 2003; Pentland & Feldman, 2005, 2008), this recent thinking makes actions (consisting of 'doings' and 'sayings') more central not only in the ongoing performances ('performing') but also in the ongoing constitution of patterns through actions ('patterning') (Feldman, 2016). Given the recursive relation truces may be formed and broken (Zbaracki & Bergen, 2010), drawing on this process perspective may consequently allow us to more deeply analyse how truces continuously evolve over time and advance our understanding of the role artefacts play in this ongoing accomplishment.

10.3 Method

In 2013, we initially approached Macromolecule Inc. (pseudonym) to study a change of the key artefact used in the management routine of top-level executives from Microsoft PowerPoint decks to a BI software. We approached the study in an open-ended and inductive manner. Our conceptualization in terms of the dynamics of truces and the role of artefacts emerged as we linked insights from the data with existing theory (Vaughan, 1992).

10.3.1 *Research Setting*

Macromolecule Inc. is one of the world's largest suppliers of numerous materials based on macromolecule polymers. It employs approximately 15,000 employees and generated 15 billion in sales in 2015. Macromolecule Inc. is organized into three business units (BUs), each with a homogenous product portfolio. These product families include adhesives and coatings (BU A), high-performance plastics (BU B), and special foams (BU C). The characteristics of the units' business activities differ in three facets: first, the BUs are differently successful. Second, the BUs' main sales markets are subject to varying levels of volatility. Third, these markets are expected to be growing at different rates in the long term. These facets led to conflict and the breaking of a truce (which we outline below), when examining the emergent patterning of the management routine over time.

The management routine is enacted by the leadership committee, consisting of the heads of the three BUs as well as the chief executive officer (CEO), the chief financial officer (CFO), and the chief operational officer (COO).

Collectively, these six executives are responsible for ensuring the organization's productivity, which involves managing the organization as a whole and directing the business units according to Macromolecule Inc.'s overall objectives. In our case, the leadership committee met bi-weekly for what we will term the 'management routine'. The routine began with an opening led by the CEO. Next, the heads of the BUs spoke about their areas of responsibility—which typically involved reporting current performance, forecasting future performance, and presenting operational recommendations. This procedure was repeated for each BU with the objective of coming together and developing a holistic view of the organization. Based on this same level of information, a discussion about company-wide topics affecting all actors present took place. This conversation enabled the committee members to evaluate ensuing consequences, discuss the actions to be taken, and ultimately make relevant decisions. At the time we approached Macromolecule Inc., this routine was centred on a centrally provided PowerPoint template that each BU head completed for his presentation. This template defined which information was depicted in which manner, so that actors had in the PowerPoint presentation essentially no opportunity to selectively mobilize information in favour of their own interests. Accordingly, the PowerPoint template acted as a standardizing device (D'Adderio, 2003) that kept conflicts latent.

The replacement of the PowerPoint template with an in-house-developed BI software stemmed from the aim to improve reporting processes at Macromolecule Inc. The software was designed to eliminate the manual work of filling out PowerPoint templates. It was envisioned that the software would automatically gather near real-time data from subsidiaries and subregions and generate appropriate visualizations such as charts and graphs. In addition, the presentation of information would be more concise, reducing the approximately 200 slides per PowerPoint deck to only a few information-rich dashboards. This would make accessing information easier and more intuitive and thus allow actors without expert knowledge (i.e. managers) to use the information provided according to their individual needs. This software turned out to be crucial in balancing interests, as we will discuss in more detail in Section 10.4.

10.3.2 Data Collection

After an initial phase in July 2013 to familiarize ourselves with the organization, we had the opportunity to closely follow Macromolecule Inc.'s change project and gather data on it up to September 2016. We used the routine as the unit of analysis (Pentland & Feldman, 2005) and focused on the patterning of the routine over time (Feldman, 2016), as well as the interests of different actors and how they evolved. To capture these processes, we conducted interviews, observed actors (including informal observations), and collected internal documents.

We conducted twenty semi-structured interviews (Meuser & Nagel, 2009) to provide a degree of direction for comparisons while allowing interviewees to provide subjective content and interpretations. Interviews lasted from thirty to seventy-four minutes and were recorded and transcribed verbatim. To forestall potential reservations regarding a study about personal motivations, we executed a non-disclosure agreement (Miles et al., 2014) with Macromolecule Inc. and assured all informants that anonymity would be maintained (Gioia et al., 2013). This helped to increase trust and data quality as well as reduce potential informant bias.

We asked informants about their work (i.e. actions they typically take), their perceptions of the artefacts (the initial and the new one), and about ongoing collective interaction. We began our interviews with management accountants because they were the ones who used the initial PowerPoint templates and were later entrusted with other tasks within management accounting. We selected our subsequent informants based on theoretical sampling (taking into account their affiliation with a certain BU) and recommendations of previous informants (Miles et al., 2014). This permitted us to interview actors involved in the management routine and the change and adjustment of the artefact, including the CFO and heads of the BUs as well as people from the business intelligence and software development team. The latter helped us to understand the new BI software not only from a technical perspective but also regarding the change and ongoing adjustment process.

As a second data source, we observed actors during formal interactions. We attended a meeting of the software development team along with various presentations and demonstrations of the artefact. These insights were helpful in gaining a detailed understanding of the artefact's features, how it operated, and how it was ultimately used. We captured our observations in field notes that were then recorded in a digital file folder (Emerson et al., 2011). Based on these notes, we prepared a comprehensive narrative of over fifty pages. Furthermore, the observations provided the opportunity to engage in informal conversations, which allowed us to obtain any necessary additional information or clarify evolving issues. Informal conversations were also documented in field notes.

In addition, we analysed internal company documents. A company database ('wiki') contained detailed explanations of various aspects of the new dashboard artefact, which helped us to better understand its features. Lastly, we had access to a duplicate dashboard artefact for our research purposes. Although the data was no longer near real time, it was sufficient to experiment with the program's functionality and obtain a deeper understanding.

10.3.3 *Data Analysis*

After the first three interviews, we followed the general procedure for process analysis (Langley, 1999) of iteratively analysing our data to improve subsequent data collection (Gioia et al., 2013; Miles et al., 2014). We chose 'thematic coding' (Flick, 2014)—that is, we did not impose codes or topics a priori but, rather, allowed them to emerge from the data. First, we began by identifying all actions and processes related to the management routine that were reported by informants and analysed how they were linked to the management routine. Once trends became visible, we deepened this analysis in a second step. Specifically, we broke the data down at the individual and collective levels as well as by actions, interests, accomplishments, conflicts, and truces. With each additional interview, we cross-checked and adapted the results accordingly. We alternated between discussions in regular case analysis meetings (Miles et al., 2014) and cross-examinations of the gathered data. In a third step, we more closely focused on actions by writing narratives (Langley, 1999) about routine actions that were described by our informants. We identified three concomitant aspects of a conflict that broke the truce and ultimately disturbed routine operations. Moreover, we recognized how routine operations improved after the truce was reformed. In a fourth step, we identified differences in the patterning of the routine over time. Finally, we closely examined the role of the artefact in the patterning of both the routine and the truce. Based on this examination, we identified how artefacts can affect the success with which actors continuously form truces.

10.4 Findings

10.4.1 *An Inadvertent Change*

One of Macromolecule Inc.'s objectives was to decrease managers' perceived information overload due to the approximately 200 slides in the PowerPoint templates. The chief information officer (CIO) and head of the project's development and implementation explained the rationale behind how they aimed to realize the reduction of the scope but still preserve relevant information for all involved parties: 'It is a lot better to develop a hammer than to walk around nailing. Well, I'm better off selling hammers than offering my nailing service.' With this metaphor, he pointed out that the objective was not to develop a specific number of pre-defined solutions, because it would require too much effort to launch and maintain them all, but instead to develop a universal toolbox that would enable users to compile their own personalized solutions. His general assumption was that he could not predict what users would require, especially when looking ahead. Accordingly, he decided to utilize a dashboard technology, which automatically extracts, calculates, and visualizes reporting and forecasting measures.

A dashboard consists of one or more pages containing at least one portlet (see Figure 10.1 for an illustration). A portlet is a component with information organized for a specific purpose. For instance, one might depict three measures in a chart and compare their progress over time. Portlets provide various functions (e.g. in-depth analyses on different levels) to facilitate the monitoring and analysis of historical trends, current performance, and future forecasting. The virtual portlet catalogue offered 178 portlets, which users (e.g. managers and management accountants) could easily select and flexibly arrange according to their preferences. To further increase the added value of the dashboard, there were 127 filters that allowed assumptions and comparisons to be made to show important relationships between variables (e.g. periods, key figures).

These options for personalizing the information provided were perceived as incredibly beneficial to focus and save time, as users needed to look only at parts they found relevant rather than sorting through 200 (partly irrelevant) PowerPoint slides. Furthermore, informants reported that it was helpful for gaining a better understanding about the relationships between the various measures by playfully analysing and simulating information with the portlets. The CIO described the creation of ways to personalize information as essential to the project, as the following quote illustrates:

> In the communication, we strongly addressed options for personalization and self-service [i.e. the possibility for users to analyse information on their own] in comparison with the [simplicity of the usage of an] iPhone, and the fact that you can focus exactly on what you're interested in. This has convinced the people.

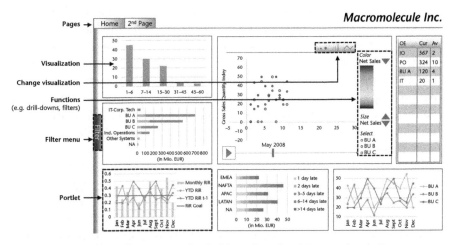

Figure 10.1. Illustration of a dashboard used at Macromolecule Inc.

In conclusion, the dashboard technology allowed individual users to decide not only which information was selected and how it was combined with other information but also how was is modified by choosing various filter options.

After the implementation of this new software, the CFO described how users translated the personalization: 'Now there is really the option to "pick and choose." And, because the [dashboard artefact] is really so diverse and offers so much, there is simply the risk—and not only the risk, but the harsh reality— that everybody is designing their own dashboard.' The risk mentioned in the quote referred to the fact that the heads of the BUs had begun to increasingly utilize the prevailing flexibility and develop different BU-specific dashboards. In meetings, however, this caused the problem of having 'centuries of endless discussions on whether your numbers are right or mine', as the COO put it. The head of BU B stated more precisely, 'Instead they were all special reports aimed at developing a certain image, but which were never consistent with other official reports. This led to endless discussions, battles, and great inefficiency', because 'if you have two clocks, you never know what time it is', as the COO said. These quotes demonstrate the development of a major conflict that disrupted the smooth functioning of the routine, as the Head of BU A noted: 'Well, there were meetings where we had to send the people home because of a discussion regarding the figures. Indeed, this happened multiple times.' Accordingly, decisions had to be postponed; and routine operations were disturbed.

The possibility of disturbance was enabled by the change of the artefact, as one of the management accountants indicated in comparing the new system with the previous PowerPoint template, 'With the new dashboard, it's simply a matter of deleting a portlet and adding another one and you will have a completely different view.' In this context, he also pointed out that the generation of a meaningful visualization in PowerPoint required a comparatively high level of expertise and time to extract data from a warehouse and process it, whereas the dashboard technology allowed individuals to try out different possibilities and create a different visualization with a few simple clicks. In addition, independent of the technological possibilities, with the new artefact, actors could have chosen to generate the same or similar information as previously depicted in PowerPoint. However, as outlined previously, users were even encouraged to draw on only the information that they wanted to consider. Consequently, users started to make use of the possibilities to personalize information.

These possibilities resulted in dashboards that were set up in such a way that the depicted information supported the respective BU heads' arguments and interests, promulgating a certain impression of the BU. In this way, the new artefact made conflicting interests overt that had been latent during the time in which information was depicted in PowerPoint. One of the corporate management accountants pointed to these conflicting interests by stating:

Well, of course, I do not want to accuse my colleagues of anything, but of course everybody who has calculated a business case or something similar once in his life, or tackled topics regarding financial assessments, has a relatively good impression that small drivers or re-evaluations or the smallest changes in input factors... can have effects! Of course, there are always interests that this person is trying to achieve.

While the management accountant was rather cautious in his description, the Head of BU A describes the issue much more clearly: 'Well, we are very good at polishing numbers.' In conclusion, by being so tailored to the BUs' perspectives, the dashboards reduced information overload for the BU heads but also inadvertently enabled the development of stories that they could craft around their interests, thus resulting in ineffective discussions regarding the validity of information. From a theoretical perspective, the artefact's role was no longer that of a standardizing device; instead, it was used to personalize information, which subsequently revealed a conflict in the management routine among the heads of the BUs.

10.4.2 *Breaking the Truce: the Conflict*

As already outlined, instead of discussing issues and subsequently making decisions during management routine meetings, people were sent back to change measures following debates challenging their validity and definition. This general conflict concerned three aspects of the management routine: (1) the basis of comparison for measuring performance, (2) assumptions underlying forecasts, and (3) the consideration of additional qualitative information when evaluating the overall situation of the BU.

Generally, the management routine was intended to proceed according to the following pattern. After the CEO's opening statements, the meeting was structured into two main parts (see Figure 10.2). The first part involved the individual presentations of the three BU heads. Each of these BU presentations consisted of a report about the past performance, a performance forecast, and an evaluation of the overall situation of the BU. Although these were individual presentations for each BU, the objective of the routine and the requirement for smooth routine operations was to bring the information about all BUs together to develop an overall perspective, because the leadership committee was responsible for Macromolecule Inc. as a whole. For this purpose, actors developed and discussed in the second part potential scenarios of how Macromolecule Inc. could develop in the future. These scenarios were subsequently evaluated and decisions concerning actions that had to be taken were made.

However, following the implementation of the dashboard, in contrast to this pattern, the management routine was reported to be enacted as illustrated in Figure 10.2. Our informants recounted in interviews that it was very

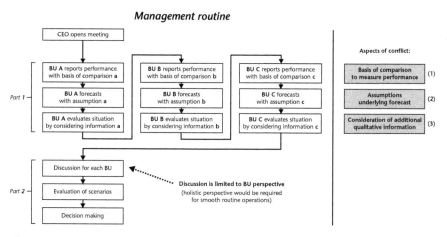

Figure 10.2. Action pattern that shows the conflict during the management routine

challenging to bring the BU presentations presented in the first part together in the second part of the meetings. The reason for this was that although they reported on performance, presented a forecast, and evaluated the situation, these actions differed in the three previously mentioned aspects that will be subsequently outlined in detail. Consequently, actors were limited in their discussion in the second part, because it was almost impossible to develop a view across BUs or holistically for Macromolecule Inc. This caused disturbances in the development and evaluation of potential scenarios and, ultimately, delays in decision making.

The first aspect of conflict was the *basis of comparison for measuring performance*, which became evident in the first step of the BU presentations, where BU heads presented the performance of their BUs. At Macromolecule Inc. performance was typically measured in terms of total revenue. However, this indicator can still be viewed from multiple perspectives. For instance, in comparison to the previous month, the business may appear to be doing much better than if compared to the same month of the previous year or the forecasted value. The head of management accounting at BU C illustrated this with an example: 'Someone is saying the month is going well, and he compares to the previous month. Then the second is saying we are below expectations. And finally, the third is saying that he is on track.' In other words, being unable to assess 'true' comparative performance between BUs caused a problem. The head of BU A drew an analogy to sports: 'If you do not have a proper measuring instrument that lets you know who was running fastest, how would you determine the winner?' Thus, due to the undefined basis of comparison, the leadership committee was neither able to compare the performance of the three BUs, assess the development of a single BU, nor develop a holistic view of the organization. Informants argued that divergent interests, which were reflected in the preference for different bases of comparison, could derive from the different volatility of the BUs' sales markets. While it is easier for less volatile businesses to perform as expected (i.e. as forecasted), this is much more difficult for a volatile business. Thus, BUs with volatile businesses argued that good performance meant sticking with a comparison of the key figures to the previous year.

The second aspect of conflict was the definition of *assumptions underlying forecasts*. Based on the assessment of the BUs' respective performance, BU heads had an interest in calculating forecasts for their respective BUs in a way that supported their opinion. Assumptions play a crucial part in analytics, because they allow for modelling under uncertainty. Results of such modelling depend heavily on these assumptions and are therefore prone to manipulation. Consequently, BU heads used these assumptions to create a specific impression of their BU. For instance, due to the different industries in which Macromolecule Inc.'s BUs were operating, the importance of petrochemicals as input materials varied greatly between the BUs. The COO illustrated how the divergent interests became visible with the help of assumptions regarding oil prices:

> The oil price is in freefall and then you have to forecast for the next year. Which price do you predict? $100, $95 or $80? You can have a hundred thousand opinions for that! If somebody has enough room, then they will set the price high so that the results are not going through the roof. Conversely, if the person is guessing that it will be challenging to achieve the targets, then they will set it lower.

The third aspect of conflict was the *consideration of additional qualitative information* to evaluate the overall situation of the BU. The focal dispute was whether and to what extent qualitative information should be included in addition to the quantitative analysis. Whether actors preferred qualitative information depended on if it allowed them to present a BU more favourably. In contrast to the previous PowerPoint decks, the BI system contained solely quantitative analyses and did not consider complementary, qualitative information. In this context, the head of global product management at BU B reasoned in an interview: 'The problem is, from my point of view, that the dashboard consists only of numbers, thus it cannot give the complete picture.' For instance, when BU heads talked about investment cycles of seven to eight years, some BU heads were satisfied with using only quantitative analyses while others demanded additional qualitative information. This was because in the event that a BU's businesses were doing well and clearly showed a positive expected growth rate, the BU head's interest was to underpin this expected positive development with quantitative analyses. However, in cases where quantitative analyses did not suggest a good performance, BU heads had an interest in using additional qualitative information to enhance how their BU was represented. For instance, a BU head stated that, in one case, it was argued that a weak current performance in isolation would not fully reflect the business due to heavy investments—that is, he argued that the business was not weak, in general, but rather was currently at a low point but would improve in the future due to the heavy investments that had been undertaken.

The divergent interests of the actors of the management routine thus became manifest in terms of these three specific aspects. In the end, this revealed a more fundamental conflict concerning the precise selection of performance measures from all the measures available in the artefact. This conflict inadvertently became overt due to the change of the artefact used in the management routine, where Macromolecule Inc. did not consider the previous artefact's role as a standardizing device that contributed to the balancing of interests and enabling of collective consensus. Instead, it became difficult for managers to bring the views of individual BUs together, as the head of corporate management accounting described: 'There are multiple ways to talk about the status. One person is talking about volume development in a certain region and somebody else about how the costs are developing at headquarters. But ultimately, I cannot bring it [i.e. volume and cost development in different regions and functions] together.' The reason for this was the new artefact's capacity to allow for the personalization of information. Our analysis showed that the discussion was limited to BU views. This meant that it was almost impossible to develop a holistic perspective of Macromolecule Inc. although this was the original rationale for setting up the routine. Thus, we can conclude that the change disturbed smooth routine functioning; the truce was broken.

10.4.3 *Reforming the Truce: the Artefact as Object in a Meta-Routine*

After the conflict became overt, the head of strategy at BU C commented, 'We do not want a situation where everybody is saying "well, now we are looking from the north, but I would also like to look from the northwest". Honestly, it does not make any sense.' Consequently, the truce had to be reformed. However, neither the CEO nor the CFO wanted to unilaterally dictate a specific solution to the conflict. Thus, a so-called Single Point of Contact (SPoC) committee, in which 'developers, as well as users, look together in one committee at new dashboards, portlets, etc.', as one corporate management accountant explained, was entrusted with adjusting the artefact to again enable users to enact the management routine effectively. Therefore, the SPoC committee had to find a solution for the three controversial aspects that constituted the conflict in the management routine. The committee was led by the head of business intelligence and consisted of managers and management accountants from different BUs as well as people from the business intelligence department.

In the beginning, the committee met once per week and then reduced the meeting frequency over time while they were adjusting the artefact. Based on this, we theorize that the enacted process of continuously changing the artefact by adjusting the embedded methodologies is itself a routine intended to change the management routine and (re)form the truce. In that sense, this accounting routine can be considered a meta-routine (cf. Adler et al., 1999). We therefore now examine the patterning of this accounting meta-routine to understand how Macromolecule Inc. managed to reform the truce for the operation of the management routine over time, despite conflicting interests and the role the artefact played therein (see Figure 10.3 for an illustration).

Based on our analysis, the meta-routine began when any manager, management accountant, or other person (e.g. people of the business intelligence department) filled in a form in a software (similar to an issue tracking system) to submit a request for changes to the BI system. These changes could concern

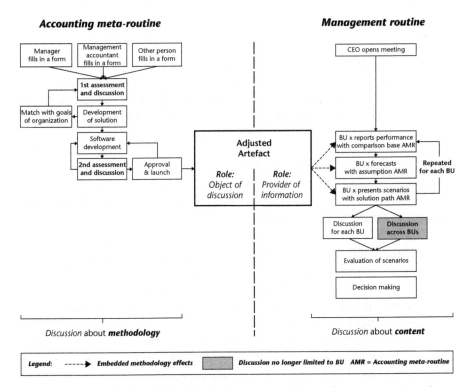

Figure 10.3. Symbiotic relationship between accounting and management routines

adjustments of existing portlets (e.g. changes in visualizations or additional filters) as well as the development of new portlets. Nevertheless, requests had to fulfil pre-defined requirements to ensure that they not only provided relevant information for a sufficient number of users but also could be translated eventually into a positive return on investment for Macromolecule Inc. The chief procurement officer (CPO) explained: 'It was not a free-for-all, you know, and that everybody can do whatever they want to do...You had to come up with a justification. What is the business case? What is the effort? What is the value? Why do you have to do it?' The requests that fulfilled the above-mentioned requirements, proceeded then to two rounds of assessment and discussion (see Figure 10.3). In the first assessment and discussion round, the requests were examined in detail from multiple angles. The essential part of this discussion was to exchange information in order to reconcile opinions and to provide a basis for the next actions. The head of a BU management accounting department and participant of the SPoC committee explained,

> Then, we think of a precise solution [i.e. how a requested portlet should look like regarding functionality, scope, authorization to address the demands of its prospective users] and define in detail what we want [i.e. for a BU and Macromolecule Inc. as a whole]. Afterwards, a beta version of [a requested] portlet will be programmed.

Informants reported that, if it was unclear whether the developed solution resonated with the objectives of the organization, the SPoC committee reviewed it again before the programming of the beta version was commissioned. In this way, a general conformity with a holistic perspective was ensured. Based on the beta version developed, the SPoC committee initiated the second round of assessment and discussion. The head of a BU management accounting department stated that the aim was to discuss questions like, Who needs what? Which layout? For who else could it be useful? Are there preferences in one or the other area? Subsequently, if for instance a portlet was approved, it was set as active in the system and users were informed. If it was not approved, a detailed outline of issues that needed to be addressed was passed on to the development team.

Within the outlined pattern of action of the accounting meta-routine, we now examine the two assessment and discussion rounds in more detail, because it is through these that consensus was reached regarding the adjustment of the artefact and, in particular, regarding the three aspects of controversy in the management routine. In other words, these assessment and discussion rounds were crucial for the reforming of a truce in the management routine. Whereas the three controversial aspects led to conflict in the management routine, our informants did not report similar motivational conflicts in the meta-routine, although participants were also working in the respective BUs. A corporate management accountant elaborated: 'It is very, very useful that everybody who is in the [SPoC] meetings, and this shouldn't sound disrespectful, has hardly any interest in the measures. We do not follow political interests with these measures.' This raises the question why and how, in the meta-routine, it was possible to reach consensus that was not achieved in the management routine. The CPO points to the different roles the artefact played in the particular routines:

> I think it means that there is less argumentation, less positioning around 'this measure is supposed to be like this' or 'have you included this or not?' Those basic principles may still be discussed at times, but then it is based on a general discussion. Is this measure representative of what we are trying to see, knowing how it is coming out? It is not questioning the result. It is more questioning the methodology. And I think that is a very productive discussion to have as an organization. Saying are we really measuring the right thing holistically and then doing it because of the real value of that measure rather than because you do not like the number coming up.

The CPO indicates that, while the artefact served in the management routine as a provider of information that could be mobilized in accordance with individual interests, in the meta-routine it instead became the object of a more abstract discussion regarding methodology. In particular, the artefact was no longer a means to depict a specific image of a BU according to its own interests. Instead, the discussion centred on how it should be improved to solve conflict in the best possible manner for the organization. From a process perspective, this organizational setup also helped by mitigating future conflicts. We therefore theorize that an artefact can have the capacity to depersonalize a discussion. This can be an important underlying mechanism in aligning divergent interests and reaching consensus.

Concerning the management routine, we identified three changes that addressed the divergent interests and resolved the outlined controversial aspects of the conflict. First, dashboards and portlets to be used in the management routine were standardized. In particular, it was determined which measures should be represented with which portlet and which scales and filters were allowed to be presented and compared with each other. In this way, the controversy regarding the basis of comparisons could be solved and performance compared and holistically measured in the management routine. Second, a sharing and subscription function was implemented, which allowed users to distribute information among the actors of the routine. Because of this, actors drew upon the same assumptions for their forecasts, which had previously not been possible in the absence of a centrally determined source. In this way, the second controversy could be solved; and the management routine benefited from standardized assumptions for their forecasts. Third, a new type of portlet was developed, namely the annotation portlet, to address concerns that measures without complementary qualitative information provide only a partial picture of the reality (i.e. the third controversial aspect). The annotation portlet allowed users to provide information such as centrally provided annotations. Based on these three changes, the controversial aspects of the conflict could be solved and a truce in the management routine reformed.

Although these three changes were implemented, informants stated that it did not eliminate interests; instead, diverging interests persisted. One of the BU heads described the threat of persistent divergence as follows:

> Let's stop fooling ourselves. In a board room, there are people with an ego. It's the truth. If you give this ego room for interpretation and allow insecurity, then it is—I think—counterproductive. From the moment, you work on a highly professional basis and the figures are part of it, and there is transparency, egos are still flourishing there, but concentrate on the content and more about who has the better action or a better quality of argumentation . . . Decisions are made by people who are not always in agreement. Hopefully not—otherwise it wouldn't be fun.

Interestingly, informants reported that, due to the symbiosis of the two routines and the way in which the artefact moved across routines by separating the discussions, Macromolecule Inc. managed to reform not only a truce concerning the specific conflict regarding the three aspects outlined above but also other and even future conflicts. In other words, the symbiotic arrangement of routines and the artefact's role in each enabled the organization to manage the dialectical tension between individual interests (most obvious in the management routine) and collective consensus (most obvious in the accounting routine). We therefore theorize that the double role of the artefact as an object of discussion (in the accounting meta-routine) and as a provider of information (in the original management routine) contributed to the continuous reforming of truces, which is necessary to ensure smooth functioning despite persistent diverging interests.

10.5 Discussion and Conclusion

The aim of this chapter was to investigate the role that artefacts can play within the dialectical tension between actors' interests and the need for collective consensus in organizational routines. The case study shows how the implementation of a new artefact disturbs how actors commonly balance their interests and reveals latent conflict that leads to unproductive routine operations. Once noticed, actors established a meta-routine that could continuously adjust the artefact to enable truces to be reformed and restabilize smooth routine operations. Based on this case, we contribute to scholarly literature on the role of artefacts and the dynamics of truces in organizational routines.

First, we shed light on the role of artefacts. Scholars have shown how artefacts can be used to mobilize information in order to promote individual interests (Yates & Orlikowski, 2007) by recombining information and renegotiating meaning (Kaplan, 2011), which can threaten collective consensus. At the same time, artefacts can act as standardizing devices that guide (D'Adderio, 2003) and/or depersonalize (Sonenshein, 2016) actors' actions and can thus suppress conflicts (Cacciatori, 2012; D'Adderio, 2003). In our case, the new artefact contributed to the breaking of a truce by allowing for personalized content consistent with actors' individual interests. The truce was subsequently reformed by establishing an accounting meta-routine to separate discussions about the methodology (i.e. how measures are generated) from discussions in the management routine about the content (i.e. the measures for decision making) that the artefact provided. Building on this symbiotic relationship, we add to the literature by showing that artefacts can play a key role in the ongoing accomplishment of (re)forming truces by playing different roles in the routines: on the one hand as an object of the discussion, and on the other hand as provider of information. Thus, artefacts are essential for the breaking and (re)forming of a truce as the methodology embedded in them contributes to the patterning of the management routine by determining in what way content can be personalized and by depersonalizing methodology discussions. This also shows how personalizing and depersonalizing mechanisms can not only contribute to cognitive conflicts (Sonenshein, 2016) but also to motivational conflicts.

Second, we contribute to the discussion of the dynamics of truces in relation to routines. Prior scholars argued that the threat of conflict that may disturb the smooth functioning of a routine (Nelson & Winter, 1982) is rather persistent and provisional (Zbaracki & Bergen, 2010). This is because truces are relative in nature as interests (Pentland & Feldman, 2005) and circumstances may change (Zbaracki & Bergen, 2010) and the terms of truce may be challenging to define (Nelson & Winter, 1982). Similarly, scholars have studied the dynamics of breaking and (re)forming truces (Zbaracki & Bergen, 2010). Building on these dynamics, the case shows that the initial intention to increase decision-making capability by personalizing artefacts results in the breaking of a truce, while coordination through establishing a meta-routine and separating discussions of the nature of the artefact from its use in decision making leads to the reformation of the truce. With regards to the dialectical tension between individual interests and collective consensus, this implies that coordination of individuals needs to be balanced with individual decision-making capability and that separating the personalization and coordinating effects of an artefact can be a constructive way of reforming truces over time.

In addition, scholars have shown that the reformation of truces can be enforced by formal authority (Kaplan, 2015; Zbaracki & Bergen, 2010). Extending prior literature, we found in our case that conflicts due to diverging interests were never fully resolved and not necessarily limited to a specific situation—rather, they varied dynamically between being rather latent to rather overt. In addition, and in contrast to prior research, truce reformation was in our case not enforced by an authority figure. Instead, a meta-routine (cf. Adler et al., 1999) was established, in which the general rules for interacting in the management routine (i.e. the methodology as basis for discussions) were (re)defined and embedded in the artefact. In other words, the terms of truce for the management routine are constantly worked out in the meta-routine. Over time, this led in our case to a process in which conflicts were increasingly managed. However, this process could also arguably lead to the opposite if the methodology is changed in a way that activates other conflicts in the management routine. Thus, we contribute to the literature by illustrating that managing the dialectical tension between individual interests and collective consensus in organizational routines and, in so doing, (re)forming truces, can also be, firstly, a collective and, secondly, an ongoing accomplishment. As such, it is an arrangement that enables the (re)forming of truces on a continuous basis in multiple situations rather than in a one-time single initiative.

This study has two limitations that suggest opportunities for further research. First, despite the confidentiality agreement, we could not observe specific performances of the routines. To understand the patterning of the routine, we conducted several interviews with the participating managers and, additionally, with management accountants because they were operationally involved in information preparation. Thus, future research could observe actual performances over time to more deeply analyse how variations in the actions affect the dynamics of truces. Second, the artefact appeared to play a key role in reforming truces by moving between the management and accounting meta-routine. However, it is conceivable that the embedded methodology not only sequentially affected the management routine but, also, that the management routine affected the meta-routine. In addition, although the artefact played a key role, there might have been close relations between actors across routines and the nature of these interrelations might play a role in determining whether the two routines can play their symbiotic role in assuring the dynamic reformation of truces. Consequently, we encourage scholars to further examine the influence of interrelations between routines and meta-routines.

Whereas this study relied mainly on semi-structured interviews, our access to the duplicate dashboard indicated that it could, itself, also be a fruitful data source for future research. This is because meta-data extracted from a log file—data that is used to process actions of the dashboard—could be used to precisely measure and compare numerous patterns of actions and analyse deviations. Combined with qualitative data, it could generate a more complete and comprehensive understanding of the actual process of using/personalizing/depersonalizing artefacts and the dynamics of truces.

Acknowledgements

We would like to sincerely thank the Hanns Seidel Foundation, which supported this research through a scholarship to the first author. Furthermore, we would like to thank the participants of the pre-symposium workshops of the eighth International Symposium on Process Organization Studies as well as the participants of the EGOS pre-colloquium workshops (2016) for their valuable comments on earlier versions of this chapter.

References

Adler, P.S., Goldoftas, B., & Levine, D.I. 1999. Flexibility versus efficiency? A case study of model changeovers in the Toyota production system. *Organization Science*, 10(1): 43–68.

Barley, S.R. 1986. Technology as an occasion for structuring: Evidence from observations of CT scanners and the social order of radiology departments. *Administrative Science Quarterly*, 31(1): 78–108.

Bechky, B.A. 2003. Object lessons: Workplace artefacts as representations of occupational jurisdiction. *American Journal of Sociology*, 109(3): 720–52.

Becker, M.C. 2004. Organizational routines: A review of the literature. *Industrial and Corporate Change*, 13(4): 643–77.

Bucher, S. & Langley, A. 2016. The interplay of reflective and experimental spaces in interrupting and reorienting routine dynamics. *Organization Science*, 27(3): 594–613.

Burns, J. 2000. The dynamics of accounting change: Inter-play between new practices, routines, institutions, power and politics. *Accounting, Auditing and Accountability Journal*, 13(5): 566–96.

Cacciatori, E. 2008. Memory objects in project environments: Storing, retrieving and adapting learning in project-based firms. *Research Policy*, 37(9): 1591–601.

Cacciatori, E. 2012. Resolving conflict in problem-solving: Systems of artefacts in the development of new routines. *Journal of Management Studies*, 49(8): 1559–85.

Cyert, R.M. & March, J.G. 1963. *A Behavioral Theory of the Firm*, Volume 2. Hoboken, NJ: Blackwell.

D'Adderio, L. 2001. Crafting the virtual prototype: How firms integrate knowledge and capabilities across organisational boundaries. *Research Policy*, 30(9): 1409–24.

D'Adderio, L. 2003. Configuring software, reconfiguring memories: The influence of integrated systems on the reproduction of knowledge and routines. *Industrial and Corporate Change*, 12(2): 321–50.

D'Adderio, L. 2008. The performativity of routines: Theorising the influence of artefacts and distributed agencies on routines dynamics. *Research Policy*, 37(5): 769–89.

D'Adderio, L. 2011. Artefacts at the centre of routines: Performing the material turn in routines theory. *Journal of Institutional Economics*, 7(2): 197–230.

D'Adderio, L. 2014. The replication dilemma unravelled: How organizations enact multiple goals in routines transfer. *Organization Science*: 1–26.

Dittrich, K., Guérard, S., & Seidl, D. 2016. Talking about routines: The role of reflective talk in routine change. *Organization Science*, 27(3): 678–97.

Emerson, R.M., Fretz, R.I., & Shaw, L.L. 2011. *Writing Ethnographic Fieldnotes*. Chicago, IL: University of Chicago Press.

Emirbayer, M. & Mische, A. 1998. What is agency? *American Journal of Sociology*, 103(4): 962–1023.

Feldman, M.S. 2000. Organizational routines as a source of continuous change. *Organization Science*, 11(6): 611–29.

Feldman, M.S. 2016. Routines as process: Past, present and future. In J.A. Howard-Grenville, C. Rerup, & A. Langley (eds), *Perspectives on Process Organization Studies: Organizational Routines. How They Are Created, Maintained, and Changed*. Oxford: Oxford University Press.

Feldman, M.S. & Pentland, B.T. 2003. Reconceptualizing organizational routines as a source of flexibility and change. *Administrative Science Quarterly*, 48(1): 94–118.

Feldman, M.S., Pentland, B.T., D'Adderio, L., & Lazaric, N. 2016. Beyond routines as things: Introduction to the special issue on routine dynamics. *Organization Science*, 27(3): 505–13.

Flick, U. 2014. *An Introduction to Qualitative Research*, 5th edition. Los Angeles, CA: Sage.

Gavetti, G., Levinthal, D.A., & Ocasio, W. 2007. Neo-Carnegie: The Carnegie School's past, present, and reconstructing for the future. *Organization Science*, 18(3): 523–36.

Gioia, D.A., Corley, K.G., & Hamilton, A.L. 2013. Seeking qualitative rigor in inductive research: Notes on the Gioia methodology. *Organizational Research Methods*, 16(1): 15–31.

Howard-Grenville, J.A. 2005. The persistence of flexible organizational routines: The role of agency and organizational context. *Organization Science*, 16(6): 618–36.

Jarzabkowski, P.A., Lê, J.K., & Feldman, M.S. 2012. Toward a theory of coordinating: Creating coordinating mechanisms in practice. *Organization Science*, 23(4): 907–27.

Kaplan, S. 2011. Strategy and PowerPoint: An inquiry into the epistemic culture and machinery of strategy making. *Organization Science*, 22(2): 320–46.

Kaplan, S. 2015. Truce breaking and remaking: The CEO's role in changing organizational routines. In G. Gavetti & W. Ocasio (eds), *Advances in Strategic Management: Volume 32. Cognition and Strategy* (pp. 1–45). Bingley: Emerald.

Langley, A. 1999. Strategies for theorizing from process data. *Academy of Management Review*, 24(4): 691–710.

Lazaric, N. & Denis, B. 2001. How and why routines change: Some lessons from the articulation of knowledge with ISO 9002 implementation in the food industry. *Economies et Societes*, 35: 585–612.

Lazaric, N. & Raybaut, A. 2005. Knowledge, hierarchy and the selection of routines: An interpretative model with group interactions. *Journal of Evolutionary Economics*, 15(4): 393–421.

Lazaric, N., Mangolte, P.-A., & Massué, M.-L. 2003. Articulation and codification of collective know-how in the steel industry: Evidence from blast furnace control in France. *Research Policy*, 32(10): 1829–47.

Leonardi, P.M. 2011. When flexible routines meet flexible technologies: Affordance, constraint, and the imbrication of human and material agencies. *MIS Quarterly*, 35(1): 147–68.

March, J.G. & Simon, H.A. 1958. *Organizations*. New York: Wiley.

Meuser, M. & Nagel, U. 2009. The expert interview and changes in knowledge production. In A. Bogner, B. Littig, & W. Menz (eds), *Interviewing Experts* (pp. 17–42). London: Palgrave Macmillan.

Miles, M.B., Huberman, A.M., & Saldaña, J. 2014. *Qualitative Data Analysis: A Methods Sourcebook*, 3rd edition. London: Sage.

Milgrom, P. & Roberts, J. 1988. An economic approach to influence activities in organizations. *American Journal of Sociology*, 94: 154–79.

Nelson, R.R. & Winter, S.G. 1982. *An Evolutionary Theory of Economic Change*, 4th edition. Cambridge, MA: Belknap Press.

Okhuysen, G.A. & Bechky, B.A. 2009. Coordination in organizations: An integrative perspective. *Academy of Management Annals*, 3(1): 463–502.

Orlikowski, W.J. 2000. Using technology and constituting structures: A practice lens for studying technology in organizations. *Organization Science*, 11(4): 404–28.

Parmigiani, A. & Howard-Grenville, J.A. 2011. Routines revisited: Exploring the capabilities and practice perspectives. *Academy of Management Annals*, 5(1): 413–53.

Pentland, B.T. & Feldman, M.S. 2005. Organizational routines as a unit of analysis. *Industrial and Corporate Change*, 14(5): 793–815.

Pentland, B.T. & Feldman, M.S. 2008. Designing routines: On the folly of designing artefacts, while hoping for patterns of action. *Information and Organization*, 18(4): 235–50.

Pentland, B.T., Haerem, T., & Hillison, D. 2011. The (n)ever-changing world: Stability and change in organizational routines. *Organization Science*, 22(6): 1369–83.

Sonenshein, S. 2016. Routines and creativity: From dualism to duality. *Organization Science*, 27(3): 739–58.

Vaughan, D. 1992. Theory elaborating: The heuristics of case analysis. In C.C. Ragin & H.S. Becker (eds), *What Is a Case? Exploring the Foundations of Social Inquiry* (pp. 173–202). Cambridge: Cambridge University Press.

Yates, J. & Orlikowski, W. 2007. The PowerPoint presentation and its corollaries: How genres shape communicative action in organizations. In M. Zachry & C. Thralls (eds), *Communicative Practices in Workplaces and the Professions: Cultural Perspectives on the Regulation of Discourse and Organizations* (pp. 67–92). Amityville, NY: Baywood Publishing.

Zbaracki, M.J. & Bergen, M. 2010. When truces collapse: A longitudinal study of price-adjustment routines. *Organization Science*, 21(5): 955–72.

Index